To Howard Dean,

A true popular and

progressive leader

Luca Menzies

RECLAIMING GOTHAM

Also by Juan González

*News for All the People: The Epic Story of Race and the American
Media* (with Joseph Torres)

*Fallout: The Environmental Consequences of the
World Trade Center Collapse*

Harvest of Empire: A History of Latinos in America

Roll Down Your Window: Stories of a Forgotten America

RECLAIMING
GOTHAM

BILL DE BLASIO and THE MOVEMENT TO END AMERICA'S TALE OF TWO CITIES

Juan González

THE NEW PRESS

25 YEARS

NEW YORK
LONDON

Requests for permission to reproduce selections from this book should be mailed to: Permissions Department, The New Press, 120 Wall Street, 31st floor, New York, NY 10005.

Published in the United States by The New Press, New York, 2017
Distributed by Perseus Distribution

ISBN 978-1-62097-209-0 (hc)
ISBN 978-1-62097-286-1 (e-book)
CIP data is available

The New Press publishes books that promote and enrich public discussion and understanding of the issues vital to our democracy and to a more equitable world. These books are made possible by the enthusiasm of our readers; the support of a committed group of donors, large and small; the collaboration of our many partners in the independent media and the not-for-profit sector; booksellers, who often hand-sell New Press books; librarians; and above all by our authors.

www.thenewpress.com

Book design and composition by Bookbright Media
This book was set in Bembo and Gotham

Printed in the United States of America

10 9 8 7 6 5 4 3 2 1

Contents

For Lilia

RECLAIMING GOTHAM

Introduction

*It is easy to blame the decay of cities on traffic . . . or immi-
grants . . . or the whimsies of the middle class. The decay of
cities goes deeper and is more complicated. It goes right down
to what we think we want, and to our ignorance about how
cities work.*

—Jane Jacobs[1]

A bone-chilling cold descended over Lower Manhattan that New
Year's morning of 2014, engulfing the thousands of people who
sat bundled up for hours in the open air to witness the inauguration of a new leadership at city hall. Such swearing-in rituals
take place routinely in towns and cities across America, and they
typically draw attention only from the local press, but this was no
mere changing of the guard in some run-of-the-mill town, as the
throng of cameras and reporters assembled since early that morning to record the event made clear. Many in attendance sensed the
start of a new era. That feeling intensified when the new mayor-
elect suddenly emerged from the bowels of a nearby subway station, his wife and teenage children at his side—the whole family,
we later learned, had opted to hop on a train to the ceremony
from their home across the river in Brooklyn, the way millions
of ordinary New Yorkers have commuted to work each day for
more than a century—and, having arrived at the biggest event

of their lives in such a deliberately modest fashion, strode confidently into City Hall Plaza to the cheers of the crowd.

But the best indicator of that day's importance was the presence among the dignitaries on stage of both a former president and a future presidential candidate. Bill and Hillary Clinton sat patiently in the front row for hours, listening to a raft of warm-up speeches and inaugural addresses by other newly elected city officials, some eloquent and inspiring, a few peppered by tasteless parting jabs at the outgoing mayor, billionaire Michael Bloomberg, who, unaccustomed to such public rebuke, sat seething stoically near the Clintons. As the ceremony moved to its climactic end, Bill Clinton, wearing a charcoal top coat and black-and-white checkered scarf, his mane of wavy white hair rustling in the icy wind, rose to speak in praise of the new mayor and his biracial family, while also thanking Bloomberg for his years of service. The former president then administered the oath of office to a beaming Bill de Blasio, the 109th mayor of New York City, who at 6 feet 5 inches towered that day over every celebrant onstage.

Yes, the legendary Gotham itself—our nation's biggest and most important metropolis and the financial center of the world, an urban colossus whose population and gross annual product dwarf those of many nations, whose local government administered in 2013 an astonishing budget of nearly $70 billion, employed close to 300,000 people, and educated more than 1 million school-children, a city whose urban planners and politicians have shaped for nearly two centuries how government envisions the role of our cities, this quintessential and chaotic metropolis of modern capitalism—was about to come under new management.

And not just *any* management.

De Blasio, a little-known fifty-two-year-old politician, had stunned the financial and social elite of Manhattan two months earlier by capturing the mayoralty. Most experts had initially given him no chance of victory. Sure, the onetime city council-man from Park Slope, a genteel Brooklyn neighborhood of white professionals living in meticulously renovated brownstones, had managed in 2009 to win election to the largely ceremonial city-wide post of public advocate, but in the Democratic mayoral primary race of 2013 he was facing four better-known and better-financed contenders—Council Speaker Christine Quinn, the sitting city comptroller John Liu, and two well-liked politicians who had made strong runs for mayor previously, former comptroller William Thompson and former Brooklyn congressman Anthony Weiner. Despite those odds, de Blasio suddenly zoomed up that summer in the public opinion polls and narrowly prevailed in the September Democratic primary. He then amassed a landslide vote in November against a weak Republican opponent, Joseph Lhota, thus returning New York City to Democratic rule for the first time in twenty years.

De Blasio achieved that feat by vowing to end New York's "Tale of Two Cities," by calling income inequality the "moral issue of our time" and declaring the fight against it the central plank of his campaign, and by promising a raft of ambitious reforms to improve the daily lives of working-class New Yorkers. Among his promises: universal pre-kindergarten classes, expansion of paid sick leave for low-wage workers, an overhaul of the notorious stop-and-frisk policies of the city's police department aimed at black and Latino neighborhoods, and a massive plan to build or preserve 200,000 units of affordable housing. Raw data would later confirm just how shockingly wide the city's income gap had become. While in 2002 the top 1 percent of New York City residents had taken in 27 percent of all income, by 2012 that share had nearly doubled to 45 percent—a spiraling divide far greater than in the rest of the nation, where the 1 percent's share of income rose from 17 to 23 percent over the same period.[2] And in Manhattan, the wealthiest of the city's five boroughs, nearly 5 percent of households had median incomes of $864,394 in 2014, even though 21 percent of all households in the city, or 1.7 million people, earned less than the federal poverty level of

$23,550 for a family of four.[3] By then, wealth inequality had become such a paramount public concern that a Pew Center poll reported 32 percent of Europeans and 27 percent of Americans considered it "the greatest threat to the world."[4]

De Blasio's message struck a chord among ordinary residents still struggling to recover from the Wall Street meltdown of 2008 and the Great Recession that followed. Even before announcing his run, while still serving as the city's public advocate, he had dared to endorse and speak at a rally of the hundreds of young Occupy Wall Street activists who in September 2011 camped out in Lower Manhattan's Zuccotti Park only to be brutally evicted weeks later when Bloomberg ordered the police department to clear their encampment. By then, the simple slogan of those protesters, "We are the 99 percent!" had inspired similar camp-ins at town squares across the country and had transformed almost overnight the national conversation over income inequality. De Blasio and his advisers were quick to note that change in the public's mood. They soon embraced aspects of the Occupy message into their campaign pronouncements, his candidacy becoming in some ways an extension into mainstream politics of the issues raised by the young activists.

Many older New Yorkers were already deeply frustrated and dissatisfied as well after twenty years of conservative business-friendly administrations, first under crime buster Rudy Giuliani (1993 to 2000), and then under media mogul Bloomberg (2001 to 2013). Both Giuliani and Bloomberg disdained the era of New Deal liberalism that New York's local government had pioneered from the days of the legendary Fiorello La Guardia. That era of massive social spending for the city's working masses—best exemplified by free tuition at the City University of New York—ended abruptly during the city's near economic collapse and bankruptcy in the 1970s, though its dismantling only commenced in earnest during the reign of another larger-than-life occupant of city hall, Ed Koch, the mayor from 1978 to 1989.

During the Giuliani and Bloomberg eras, crime rates plummeted, the local economy rebounded, the famed Times Square Theater District was transformed from a seedy, menacing locale for peep shows and petty hustlers into a thriving Disney-style tourist mecca. Real estate developers feverishly refashioned huge swaths of rundown inner-city neighborhoods, erecting new luxury housing that aimed to attract younger, wealthier, and whiter residents but that inexorably displaced older, poorer, and darker ones. The Bloomberg years, in particular, accelerated those changes. Bloomberg launched laudable public health initiatives against smoking and soft drinks, created an amazing system of bicycle lanes, and lured thousands of young technology entrepreneurs and workers to relocate to the city. Yet he also turned New York into a place where bankers, developers, and the wealthy were openly accorded special treatment and lavish subsidies by government, even as the vast majority of longtime city residents in the outer boroughs had trouble, especially after the Great Recession, in finding living-wage jobs, affordable dwellings, decent public schools, or even city parks they could use. Toward the end of his second term, Mayor Bloomberg even alienated many of his supporters when he overturned the will of the people, expressed through two previous referenda, to uphold municipal term limits. He successfully maneuvered, instead, with the backing of the financial community and most of the city's major media companies, to get the city council in 2008 to eliminate those limits so he could seek a third term as mayor.

The municipal election of 2013, however, did not simply elevate de Blasio to office. Voters chose an even more radical African American woman, Letitia James, to replace him as public advocate; they rallied behind the liberal Manhattan borough president Scott Stringer as their new comptroller, and they propelled nearly twenty candidates into the city council who had been backed by a small yet influential left-oriented third party, the Working Families Party. At its first session, the reconstituted council then tapped as its speaker—the second most powerful post in local government—Melissa Mark-Viverito, a young Puerto Rico–born former labor union staff member who had co-founded the council's Progressive Caucus.

The result was the most left-leaning government in the history of America's greatest city. Not even during La Guardia's heyday had so many candidates with progressive leanings ascended to key posts in city hall. And all were swept into office not by the tired old Democratic political machine of prior eras, but by resurgent popular movements of affordable housing and climate change activists, by parents advocating to improve their public schools, by organizations of immigrant and low-wage workers, by unions of hospital and city workers, and by black and Latino groups battling police abuse.

This new opposition movement had suddenly reclaimed Gotham in the name of its people.

Why and how did this happen? Would it prove to be just a curious digression in the convoluted history of New York City politics, a transitory attempt, as some claimed, to resurrect past liberal policies, only cloaked this time in slick new "progressive" packaging? Or was it something more?

The victory of the de Blasio coalition, I argue, represented the maturing of a new grassroots urban political revolt in America. It was an early indicator of what two years later would come to be known as the Bernie Sanders phenomenon: huge swarms of voters rallying behind a crusade against income inequality and roundly rejecting a conservative free-market worldview that has dominated American urban policy for the past fifty years. No longer could the growing chasm between the ultra-rich and the rest of the country be ignored. By 2012 the nation's wealth inequality was nearly as high as in 1929 before the Great Depression, and it was three times greater than it had been in the 1970s.[5]

Leaders of the new movement share a starkly different vision of how cities should be governed in the twenty-first century; how our streets, parks, schools, and public safety services should be utilized; how our zoning, land use, and local tax policies fashioned; how we define the nature of the "public interest" at a time when cities have become more unequal economically yet more racially and ethnically diverse than ever. These are crucial issues for modern civilization, given that more than half of Earth's 7 billion people now reside in cities. Over the next twenty years, another 3 billion are expected to leave the countryside, at which point 70 percent of humanity will be urbanized.[6]

The modern city, after all, has always held the promise of an easier and more enjoyable life, of greater economic opportunity and a more diverse social and cultural exchange, of a more democratic environment. Nonetheless, conservative politicians too often regard that promise as a threat. As the Center for Popular Democracy, a national coalition of advocates that has helped spur this new urban reform movement, noted recently, "The American Right . . . basically hates cities. Its politicians always run against cities, demonize their residents, deny them resources once in office, and dilute their vote through the cracking and packing techniques of gerrymandering election districts."[7]

This is especially true of the current U.S. president. "Our inner cities are a disaster," Donald Trump declared in a campaign debate in 2016. "You get shot walking to the store. They have no education. They have no jobs." Trump deliberately courted white conservative voters in rural counties and small-town America during his presidential campaign, asserts writer Will Wilkinson, "by tracing their economic decline and their fading cultural cachet to the same cause: traitorous 'coastal elites' who sold their jobs to the Chinese while allowing America's cities to become dystopian Babels, rife with dark-skinned danger—Mexican rapists, Muslim terrorists, 'inner cities' plagued by black violence." He did so despite the fact, as Wilkinson notes, that "the American metropolis is more peaceful and prosperous than it has been in decades," and even though FBI crime data show that so-called sanctuary cities that welcome immigrants "have lower crime rates than comparable non-sanctuary cities."[8]

Little wonder that the vision espoused by these new urban progressive leaders depends less on centralized policies dictated from Washington, where Congress and the White House seemed for years paralyzed by partisan gridlock and now are in the grip of blatantly anti-urban forces; less on what local bankers, real estate developers, and other commercial interests want; less on privatizing public space or on siphoning off tax revenues for sports stadiums, civic centers, and market-rate housing, those grandiose projects often spearheaded by semipublic authorities that cede minimal authority to local elected officials. Instead, the rebels pursue economic growth through a far different model, one that aims to address the most pressing needs of a city's increasingly diverse working masses. They pursue living-wage, paid sick- and family-leave laws, subsidies for affordable housing, community oversight of policing practices, and minimal requirements for city contractors to employ local residents and purchase from local businesses. They regard development that is environmentally sustainable as essential to the future of their cities. They demand maximum control over local decisions and budgets but also are willing to be held accountable by neighborhood activists through what one of the movement's leading theorists, New York City councilman Brad Lander, has dubbed an "inside-outside" strategy.

Vermont senator Bernie Sanders pursued the same kind of "inside-outside" strategy at the national level in his 2016 run for the presidency. Most political experts at first dismissed Sanders as a quixotic fringe candidate, yet the fervent army of young people he drew to his campaign, and the 12 million votes he amassed in support of his "political revolution" against wealth inequality, wound up pushing Hillary Clinton and the traditional Democratic Party machinery to adopt many of his movement's proposals to narrow wealth inequality. And once Sanders conceded defeat, he immediately urged his followers to turn their energies to their own local cities and towns, to run for election themselves to seats on school boards, city councils, and state legislatures. A lasting political revolution, Sanders insisted, must be built from the ground up, neighborhood by neighborhood, for it is at the local level that all the exciting innovation in government policy is occurring today. Such a revolution, it should be noted, has little in common with the populist upsurge of white upper-strata workers, Christian evangelicals, and small-business owners that billionaire real estate developer Donald Trump rode to victory during his presidential run. The true nature of the Trump revolution as a hostile takeover of government by the right-wing sector of the country's ruling circle became apparent once the new president started to fill the top ranks of his administration with a coterie of fellow billionaires from banking, private equity, energy, real estate, and fast-food industries, all of them in favor of slashing government regulations that hamper business profits.[9]

The new generation of urban leaders you will meet in the pages of this book now view themselves as part of a broader worldwide movement of left-oriented city officials who, for the most part, rose to office in the aftermath of the Great Recession. Their foreign counterparts include people like Sadiq Khan, London's first Muslim mayor; Anne Hidalgo, the socialist mayor of Paris and a leading European figure on climate change; Ada Colau, who led a movement of resistance to home foreclosures in Spain to become mayor of Barcelona in 2015; and Carmen Yulín Cruz, the charismatic mayor of San Juan, Puerto Rico.

Like their international brethren our nation's urban rebel leaders were products of grassroots protest movements that sought over the past two decades to tackle issues such as climate change, income and gender inequality, affordable housing, police brutality and racial profiling, workplace and immigrant rights, or the saving of public education. The rank-and-file members of these movements, in turn, supplied the volunteer workers these novice politicians relied upon to win their first elections.

Social movements, of course, come and go periodically, surging at moments when large groups of people refuse to accept their existing conditions and demand change from the established order. But as those movements mature they typically splinter; one section remains outside the system, its leaders preferring the role of constant dissidents and agitators; another "reform" section chooses to elect leaders to office who then pursue pragmatic compromises with the old establishment, rewriting laws and policies in hopes of achieving at least a portion of the movement's original goals. More often than not, however, those reform leaders end up co-opted by the trappings of power and estranged from their original followers. But something different has happened with the current progressive wave; its elected officials are consciously attempting to remain connected to their base of supporters in the way they govern.

To fully understand this new and growing urban revolt, this book chronicles three distinct yet intertwined sagas. The main story is that of the de Blasio coalition itself: how it came together to achieve its historic come-from-behind election victory, the actual policies it has implemented so far, the impact of those policies on the people of New York City, and the prospects for the coalition to continue in power. In the process, I recount some of the pivotal neighborhood battles of the Bloomberg era against the privatizing of public resources. While many of those battles did not completely halt that privatization, they did slow its momentum, and they ended up producing a network of seasoned local activists who later formed the basis of de Blasio's volunteer army.

The second and much broader story traces the impact of more than forty years of neoliberal policies on New York and other great American cities. It traces how Democrats and Republicans at both the federal and local levels directly fostered the Tale of Two Cities—rich and poor, white and nonwhite—that exists today from coast to coast. They did so by repeatedly joining with the real estate and banking industries to redesign our cities through policies that were consciously or effectively discriminatory toward racial minorities and the poor and that have made it increasingly difficult for those groups to continue residing in cities.

The third story documents how and why the political events in New York City in 2013 formed part of a broader progressive revolt that has now taken hold in scores of cities nationwide. Even today, more than fifteen years after the new movement was born, most experts in urban policy and most journalists who cover the nation's city halls are barely aware of its existence. I trace here its origin and evolution from scattered insurgencies in a few municipal elections by grassroots leaders, many of whom did not even know each other at first, into what is now a cohesive network of mayors and city council members who regularly support each other, who exchange information on model laws and reforms, and who develop common strategies to transform American cities to meet the needs of their working-class majorities.

Each of these three sagas can be better understood only by getting to know the flesh-and-blood figures that played key roles in their unfolding, for when all is said and done, governments with all their laws and policies, along with social movements, are all products of human activity, and they are constantly changed through human conflict. Each of the stories presented here is replete with extraordinary characters. They include the famous and little known, the heroic and the disgraceful, the idealists, pragmatists, and opportunists, the grand visionaries and the gutter-style connivers, all of whom sought to make real their own image of the great American city.

Our main story, the de Blasio phenomenon, is a fascinating political tale of a ramshackle alliance of activists who brilliantly figured out how to win control of our greatest city, then had to tackle how to run things. It begins with the future mayor's early years as the child of middle-class, politically liberal parents who became targets of the McCarthy-era witch hunts, his father eventually descending into alcoholism that destroyed his marriage and ended in a tragic suicide. Their son Bill would become a leftist radical, then a Brooklyn community organizer, then a political aide to Hillary Clinton in her run for the U.S. Senate, and eventually a leader of the city council's progressive wing. The story retraces key aspects of his nearly flawless nine-month campaign for mayor, one that drew unexpected energy from his family—both through the very public role played by his wife, Chirlane, and their biracial children, Dante and Chiara, and through the pivotal behind-the-scenes role of de Blasio's older cousin, long-time national labor union leader John Wilhelm. It sketches as well the personal journeys of those who would become the new mayor's key allies in government, Public Advocate Letitia James and Council Speaker Melissa Mark-Viverito, exploring how each arrived at her own vision of governing New York, and how both helped de Blasio produce the most united administration in the city's modern history. It examines as well the actual record of the de Blasio administration's first three years, both its successes and its failures. Many expected the untested new mayor to tamp down his rhetoric and dial back his promises once he got into office. But he promptly dispelled such notions. Together with his allies in city council, de Blasio rolled out a dizzying set of reforms aimed at lifting the economic and social conditions of the city's working-class residents while also reversing key policies that Giuliani and Bloomberg had implemented. They included a new universal pre-kindergarten program that eventually serviced some seventy thousand children, paid sick leave for all workers, a virtual freeze to rent hikes for tenants in rent-regulated private buildings, a major reform of the police department's stop-and-frisk policies that had disproportionately targeted African American and Latino residents, and a new municipal ID system that would eventually be utilized by more than 1 million residents, many of them undocumented.

So quickly did those reforms take place that most observers have failed to comprehend their cumulative effect on the city's wealth inequality. This book catalogs and quantifies for the first time the real financial impact of de Blasio's initiatives on ordinary city residents, and what it finds is nothing less than staggering. Between mid-2014 and mid-2017, New Yorkers benefited to the tune of at least $21 billion—either in direct cash payments, or in the value of new city services they had not previously enjoyed, or in money de Blasio's programs saved them from having to spend. That, of course, is an *estimated* $21 billion, for when dealing with such huge sums of money, one can only make a ballpark estimate, but it is most surely a conservative estimate.

The universal pre-kindergarten program, for example, did not merely add an entire year to the school experience of every child; it also saved parents who utilized the program a full year of child-care costs, which in New York City run an average of $12,500 for a four-year-old child in a private program. Thus, by the third year of the universal pre-K program, New York families had saved $1.4 billion in childcare expenses, according to calculations by the city's Office of Management and Budget. So, too, with the new law mandating five days of paid sick leave for all work-ers. More than 500,000 city residents gained coverage under the expanded version of the paid sick leave law that de Blasio signed in March of 2014. By mid-2017, those workers had received near-ly $500 million in benefits from their employers—none of which had been previously available to them.[10]

The biggest single direct infusion of money, however, came from new labor contracts the city reached in swift and amicable negotiations with its own employees. Those contracts resulted by the middle of 2017 in more than $15 billion in wage hikes, back pay, and benefits for some 300,000 workers. Much of that money, needless to say, was then spent by those workers in the municipal economy, thus sparking what growth machine advocates love to describe as a "multiplier effect."

I delineate in chapter 8 a half dozen other reforms that also resulted in huge expenditures, including one of the largest unreported wealth transfers from landlords to a city's working class in modern U.S. history—three years of a near-total freeze on rents for regulated apartments that occurred under de Blasio. Ever since World War II, prices for a large portion of New York City's private rental apartments have been determined by the rent guidelines board, an obscure agency whose members are appointed by the mayor. New York rent regulations are in place to prevent price gouging by landlords because of a perennial acute scarcity of available rental units—vacancy rates were less than 3 percent in 2014. There are more than 1 million of these regulated apartments in New York City, including units in public housing projects, and for the bulk of them, about 841,000 units that are privately owned and that receive no government subsidies, the rent board determines each year how much landlords can increase the rent. Public meetings of the board are always raucous affairs pitting tenants against landlords. Over the past two decades, the board has granted average annual increases of 3.2 percent, so that property owners had grown accustomed to the steady increase in their revenues. Under de Blasio, however, the board authorized astoundingly low hikes of just 1 percent, 0 percent, and 0 percent. That change in policy alone represented an estimated dollar savings to tenants of more $2.1 billion over the first three years of the new administration. The combination of those historically low rent increases, along with universal pre-K, paid sick leave, and other de Blasio reforms, thus amounted to an unprecedented multibillion-dollar improvement in the economic life of the city's working-class and poor majority.[11]

The book also examines the deep enmity such policies provoked in the city's elite and the almost nonstop anti–de Blasio commercials that filled the airwaves from police unions, billionaire hedge fund supporters of charter schools, and the landlord lobby; it catalogs the missteps and blunders by de Blasio and his administration that led to bitter conflicts with low-income housing advocates who had initially backed him; and it looks at the handful of scandalous incidents that led toward the end of his first term to multiple corruption investigations by a federal prosecutor—probes that threatened to endanger the first-term mayor's hopes of reelection.

But de Blasio is only the most prominent example of the new progressive leaders who are directly challenging the "growth machine" model that has dominated urban America since the 1920s. As the second major story of this book documents, most big-city politicians and urban planners have long sought to refashion our cities to serve economic elites, whether free-market conservatives of the early twentieth century, the liberal Democrats of mid-century, or neoliberals who began to champion the privatization of government during the 1970s. The classical conservatives sought initially to remove the poor from the areas they formerly inhabited around downtown business districts, pushing them to the city's outskirts and fostering in their place large commercial developments. A long line of scholars has documented how the federal government and local politicians razed entire inner-city minority neighborhoods during the 1950s and 1960s while deliberately creating segregated white, affluent suburban rings that were subsidized by federal tax breaks and mortgages from the Federal Housing Administration and the Veterans Administration. Proponents of these massive urban renewal programs proclaimed more commercial development as the economic engine to restore declining tax bases. But sacrificed in all of this development was the use of public space for the benefit of city residents. As sociologists John Logan and Harvey Molotch have noted, "the most durable feature in U.S. urban policy is the manipulation of government resources to serve the exchange interests of local elites, sometimes at the expense of one another and often at the expense of local citizens."[12]

By 1968, President Johnson's National Commission on Urban Problems noted in an exhaustive report that "[O]ver the last decades, Government action through urban renewal, highway

programs, demolitions on public housing sites, code enforcement, and other programs has destroyed more housing for the
poor than government at all levels has created." The commission's tabulation of such demolition on a city-by-city basis was
startling. For all seventy-four cities it studied, government demolitions had eliminated 397,287 private units for the poor, while
only 357,291 public housing units had been constructed in their
place by 1967—a net loss nationwide of more than 40,000 units.
And this occurred even in the midst of Johnson's War on Poverty,
an effort that witnessed the largest number of public housing units
constructed by the government.[13]

Historian Robert Caro subsequently exposed the tragic under-
side of how master builder Robert Moses had rebuilt huge portions of Gotham over forty years by relentless bulldozing of its
inner city. Caro's epic biography of Moses, *The Power Broker*,
depicted the human toll of those Moses mega-projects and how
urban planners inspired by him pursued the same wrecking-
ball approach on a national scale throughout the mid-twentieth
century.

"To build his highways," Caro noted, "Moses threw out of
their homes 250,000 persons. . . . He cut the hearts of a score of
neighborhoods, communities the size of small cities themselves,
communities that had been lively, friendly places to live, the vital
parts of the city that made New York a home to its people."

The demolition of inner-city neighborhoods, with the poor
herded into teeming, largely segregated high-rise housing projects in adjacent neighborhoods, only deepened racial tensions and
helped fuel the riots and civil disorders that erupted across the
country in the 1960s. So beginning with the Nixon administration, Washington responded by turning away from direct construction of public housing. Lawmakers gradually opted instead
for housing vouchers subsidized by the government that the poor
could use to rent private housing—a program popularly known
as Section 8 certificates. Another clear aim of the new rent cer-

tificate program was to sharply reduce the concentration of black and Latino low-income residents in our inner cities, especially when combined with other initiatives such as the building of small "scattered-site" public housing units in the suburbs, and later with the selling off or demolition of high-rise public housing projects.

By the 1970s, neoliberalism supplanted the old conservative strategies. No longer could government simply bulldoze entire communities with what civil rights leaders dubbed "Negro" or "Hispanic" removal. It became clear, as well, that our cities, which remained the nexus of the American economy, had to be rebuilt, and that upper- and middle-class whites must be lured back to inhabit them, with the poor relocated to faraway suburban rings, as had already occurred in Europe's cities after World War II. Congress spelled out that goal in the 1974 Community Redevelopment Act, when it called for "spatial deconcentration of housing opportunities for persons of lower income and the revitalization of deteriorating or deteriorated neighborhoods."

Admittedly, there is still considerable debate among urban scholars on the meaning of neoliberalism, or whether it is even appropriate in describing local city policies.[14] Here, I use the term not as a theoretical abstraction, but to outline a specific political-economic project by which capital seeks greater profit through privatizing government services, appropriating major portions of the public commons, and curtailing democratic accountability by public officials to the mass of voters—all in the name of more efficient governance.

The third story of this book chronicles the origin and evolution of this new urban resistance movement, of which New York City and the de Blasio coalition are only the most visible example. Decades of steady displacement of low-income residents from our major cities, along with the constant push to privatize the public commons, eventually gave rise to a sustained public revolt against the neoliberal version of the growth machine. That revolt has been quietly gathering steam for some time. It began more than fifteen years ago in a few scattered cities and towns, places such as Richmond, California; Seattle, Washington; and Philadelphia, Pennsylvania. In most cases, a local advocacy group formed around a particular issue, challenged the anti-neighborhood policies of the city's established leaders, then backed one of its own for election to a municipal post and somehow pulled off a surprise victory.

At first, each victory appeared to be an isolated occurrence, a rare and unexpected achievement for progressives. Many thought it due to the particular circumstances of that town, or to the qualities of the individual upstart challenger, or to the weaknesses of the candidates he or she vanquished. It is only human nature, after all, to fix our gaze on what is immediately in front of us, but in doing so we often fail to grasp the powerful forces operating in the background—or, as the old saying goes, we miss the forest for the trees. In the case of this new movement, it would take several years for even its key participants to realize they were part of something bigger.

In many of those cities, the neighborhood groups drew support, sometimes guidance, and even members from local chapters of a national organization that has since ceased to exist. That group was the Association of Community Organizations for Reform Now (ACORN), the militant direct-action group that was founded in Arkansas in the 1970s by a former student radical named Wade Rathke. ACORN would eventually spawn scores of local and state chapters and boast a membership of more than 400,000, most of them African American and Latino. With its emphasis on combining massive voter registration drives with constant protests against banks and insurance companies and for affordable housing programs, the group became a potent new force in urban America. Two of ACORN's key national leaders, the brothers Jon and Steve Kest, became more than a decade ago especially close friends of and political advisers to de Blasio. Even after ACORN and its various subsidiaries collapsed in 2010 following revelations of financial improprieties by Rathke, highly publicized attacks from Republican Party operatives who accused the group of voter registration fraud and misuse of federal grants, and a congressional cut-off of its government-funded projects, Jon Kest and several other former ACORN officials continued to play instrumental roles in shaping de Blasio's rise and his message. Likewise, in dozens of other cities, community organizers who originally passed through ACORN can be found active today in several advocacy groups that were offshoots of the original organization, and which continue to help elect progressive leaders to office.

Five years ago, some of the original pioneers of the urban revolt, among them Nick Licata, the longtime unorthodox city councilman from Seattle; W. Wilson Goode Jr., the former city councilman from Philadelphia; and John Avalos, a member of the San Francisco board of supervisors, joined with a small group of other like-minded municipal leaders around the country to launch a new national organization to advocate for cities. They called it Local Progress, and in just a short time it has grown to more than five hundred members. Unlike the more established urban associations, the U.S. Conference of Mayors and the National League of Cities, the new group openly calls for economic justice, immigrant rights, racial equality, and immediate action toward environmental sustainability, and while it promotes the lobbying of state and federal governments for greater assistance to cities, it also advocates grassroots organizing and citizen protest as a necessary tool for achieving justice.

Wherever Local Progress members hold office they have worked closely with community and labor advocates seeking to raise the national minimum wage to $15 an hour, a campaign that was initially dismissed by political experts as an impossible dream. That campaign was launched in November 2012 with a series of isolated protests around Thanksgiving, first by employees walking off the job at a handful of Walmart stores, and then by some two hundred fast-food workers in Midtown Manhattan who held a one-day strike on November 29 at a few McDonald's and Burger King franchise stores.

The following year, however, the tiny Washington jurisdiction of SeaTac became the first to adopt a $15-an-hour rate. The cities of Seattle and San Francisco soon followed suit. By 2015, fourteen states and cities had adopted some form or other of staggered increases to reach $15 for portions or all of their workers, thus raising wages for more than 1 million people. That year, two dozen major private employers announced voluntary plans to lift their hourly wages to $15. The Fight for $15, as advocates dubbed it, was soon so formidable a national movement that Democratic Party leaders found themselves forced to incorporate the goal into the party's 2016 presidential platform.[15]

Once sworn in as mayor, de Blasio backed up his verbal support of that campaign with action. He not only pressured Governor Andrew Cuomo and lawmakers in Albany to pass a higher state minimum wage, he issued an executive order in January 2016 that all municipal workers and all employees of firms that contract with the city would have their pay increased to at least $15 an hour by 2018—an action that directly affected some fifty thousand low-wage workers.[16]

The year of de Blasio's election, in fact, became a breakthrough year for the new urban revolt. That May, Chokwe Lumumba, a longtime black civil rights lawyer associated with the radical Republic of New Africa, startled the political elite of the South when he won election as mayor of Mississippi's state capital, Jackson. Then in November, the same month as New York's change of government, Bill Peduto, a member of the Pittsburgh city council and longtime dissident against the city's Democratic establishment, won election as mayor, as did several allies of Peduto who captured city council seats and formed a progressive majority on that body. All were helped by their close ties to a new alliance of labor, religious, neighborhood, and environmental groups called

Pittsburgh United. Likewise, Betsy Hodges, a longtime nonprofit executive and two-term member of the Minneapolis city council who had opposed public subsidies for a new Minnesota Vikings stadium, emerged from a crowded field of thirty-four candidates to capture the mayoralty, even though most of the city's labor unions backed other candidates. Like de Blasio and Peduto in Pittsburgh, Hodges was aided by her close ties to a five-year-old alliance of grassroots organizations, Minnesotans for a Fair Economy. Out west, where only San Francisco and Berkeley had previously been known as liberal enclaves, a longtime Washington state senator, Ed Murray, won election as Seattle's mayor, while a radical software engineer named Kshama Sawant became the first socialist elected to the Seattle city council since 1916. Sawant's main campaign pledge was to raise the city's minimum wage to $15 an hour, a promise that Murray also backed. Sawant then joined a small progressive bloc in the council that had been quietly racking up significant reforms for some time.[17]

More victories followed in 2014. The biggest came in New Jersey in May, when Ras Baraka, the son of the famed black poet and revolutionary Amiri Baraka, rode the wave of a strong parent movement demanding return of local control to public schools to become the surprise winner of the mayoral race in Newark, that state's largest city. In the months that followed, progressive insurgents won city council races in Tempe, Arizona; Austin, Texas; and a half dozen other cities. Then in 2015, voters elevated another group of left-oriented newcomers to office in Denver, Seattle, Philadelphia, and other cities, while a progressive challenger nearly pulled off an upset in the race for mayor of Chicago. Cook County commissioner Jesús "Chuy" García forced incumbent Rahm Emanuel, a centrist Democrat who had been expected to coast to victory, into a run-off election before finally succumbing to him.

All of these upsurges reflect not only the deep polarization between rich and poor in urban America, but also a vast demographic transformation. Despite all the displacement of the poor from central city neighborhoods the past few decades, urban America keeps growing increasingly black, Hispanic, and Asian. And the elected officials of those cities mirror that population change. In 2015, for instance, voters elected Korean-American lawyer Helen Gym as the first Asian American woman in the Philadelphia city council. That same year, the city of Austin chose city council members under a new system of districts rather than at-large seats; that change propelled three young Latinos into the council, including Gregorio Casar, a twenty-six-year-old community organizer who only ten years before had participated in the great immigration marches of 2006.

So who am I to piece together such a sprawling story? What particular skill or perspective can I offer the reader in making sense of this crucial issue of how our cities can better serve all their people? Well, for half a century now I have had a front-row seat to our country's urban conflicts, the past forty years as a journalist covering day-to-day events in scores of inner-city neighborhoods as well as in the halls of municipal government, and for ten years before that as a community and labor organizer. Throughout that time, I have struggled to unravel the mystery of why these astonishing centers of our civilization, these producers of such vibrant social life and phenomenal wealth, remain so deeply divided by race, by disparities of income, and by conflicts over dwindling public revenues.

One day in 1983, when I was a young reporter at the *Philadelphia Daily News*, my city editor, Mary Jo Meisner, suddenly informed me that she was promoting me to the paper's city hall bureau—a plum assignment at any news organization. The paper boasted four reporters in the bureau at the time—two to cover the mayor's office, one to cover city council, and the crew's chief.

"We want you to become the fifth," Meisner said, "but we're not sure yet what you should cover."

"How about giving me all the agencies that have to do with land?" I asked.

"Which ones do you mean?" Meisner said, a puzzled look on her face.

I blurted out a few: "The Planning Commission, the Redevelopment Authority, the Landmarks Commission, the Buildings Department, the Zoning Board, the Public Housing Authority, the Housing Development Corp., the Office of Property Assessments."

"Why would you want all of those?" she asked.

I'd just finished reading Caro's mammoth *Power Broker* a few weeks earlier and my mind was still trying to digest one of the book's underlying themes, government's huge role as a land management enterprise, so I offered my editor a quick and primitive rationale: "Land in any city is finite and valuable, so what government does with the land determines a city's future." By tracking land policy, I argued, we were bound to unearth terrific hidden stories. In the decades that followed, I ended up stumbling over far more nuggets of news than I could ever have imagined.

Thus my effort to piece together the rise of the de Blasio coalition and the new urban progressive moment is based on decades spent in the streets and alleys of America's cities, reporting how leaders make and implement day-to-day policy and how their decisions affect ordinary people. During that time, I was fortunate to cover up close the administrations of mayors Bill Green and W. Wilson Goode Sr. in Philadelphia, of Ed Koch, David Dinkins, Rudy Giuliani, Michael Bloomberg, and now de Blasio in New York, to witness many of the events that form the backdrop of my main story, so that several vignettes chronicled here or individuals I cite originally appeared in articles or columns of mine in New York's *Daily News*. In preparing this account, I talked with many of the key figures in de Blasio's inner circle and among his grassroots supporters who provided me crucial insight into how his campaign evolved and how he has governed. At the same time, I interviewed dozens of other progressive council members, mayors, and neighborhood activists around the country, gathering details of how the new movement has fared in other cities. Their experiences, along with my forays into a good deal of academic literature on urban policy, aided me in framing those sections of the book that explore the broader issue of the role Washington politicians and the real estate and banking industries have played in shaping our modern cities.

This is mainly a journalistic account. It is the story of leaders who rebel against accepted wisdom, of the rise of new social movements and how they force change in the old order, of how and why our cities became so divided between rich and poor over the past fifty years, why so much urban public space and public resources have been appropriated to serve the elite, and of what can be done by ordinary residents to reclaim their cities.

It is especially timely given that many of those progressive municipal leaders who were first elected to office in the breakthrough year of 2013 face reelection campaigns in 2017. Local elites opposed to them will undoubtedly contest their return to power even more fiercely than they did their initial election. Moreover, Donald Trump's stunning presidential victory, along with the continued Republican dominance of Congress and most state legislatures, has now left the big cities as the nation's last surviving centers of progressive governance. Within the first few weeks of the Trump presidency, for instance, urban mayors banded together and vowed to challenge efforts by the Trump White House to cut off federal aid to sanctuary cities. More such confrontations and direct collisions seem likely in the future.

In the case of de Blasio, the most influential of the progressive mayors, his original coalition, despite an extraordinary record of accomplishment, has been weakened and frayed by some policy decisions that alienated key groups of supporters, by incidents of inept governance, and by the stench of old-style pay-to-play corruption. Nonetheless, decades of a widening gulf between the nation's super-rich and the vast majority has now unleashed a new urban movement that will not be easily contained. The fight to reclaim Gotham in the twenty-first century has only just begun.

1

Family Ghosts: The Making of Bill de Blasio

Wherefore art thou Romeo?
   Deny thy father and refuse thy name.

—*Romeo and Juliet*, Act II, scene 2

In the spring of 1999, the New York City Central Labor Council, the city's main federation of trade unions, held its annual luncheon in the grand ballroom of the famed Waldorf-Astoria hotel on Park Avenue. With some three hundred affiliated locals in both the public and private sector that nowadays claim more than 1.3 million members, the CLC has long been the official voice of labor in the biggest union town in the nation. It is the forum where the leaders of firefighters and plumbers, operating engineers, teachers, school crossing guards, and subway conductors, truck drivers, construction laborers, nurses, janitors, banquet waiters, and hotel maids—that mass of humanity without which the city could not function—meet every month to coordinate their efforts at securing better labor contracts, where they plan how to deal with the city's employer class and how they can affect public policy toward labor, and woe to the politician, Democrat or Republican, who incurs the united wrath of the CLC unions, for that politician will not survive in office for very long.

On this particular day, the council had invited a top labor leader from Washington, D.C., John Wilhelm, to be the luncheon keynote speaker. At the time, Wilhelm was president of HERE, the national union of hotel and restaurant workers, which, despite decades of decline in union membership nationwide, had been growing rapidly under Wilhelm's leadership, thanks to its success in organizing mostly immigrant workers in the hotel and gaming industries of Nevada and California. In contrast, the AFL-CIO, the nation's main labor body, was watching helplessly as its affiliated unions hemorrhaged members and was devoting little attention to recruiting low-wage workers, instead looking suspiciously at new immigrants, especially those who were undocumented, as threats to the living standards of organized labor.

A stocky man, blue-eyed and snub-nosed, Wilhelm is soft-spoken and self-effacing in private and was then a rarity among the country's union presidents, an intellectual who had graduated magna cum laude from Yale University in 1967 with a history degree, before going straight to work for the union of service and maintenance workers at that Ivy League bastion. As an acknowledged rising star of labor, he intended to use the platform of the Central Labor Council that day to shake up the AFL's old-guard leaders, all of them seated at the head table in tuxedos and black ties. He proceeded to deliver a fiery speech on why immigrant workers represented the future of the nation's labor movement. As he was leaving the ballroom, Wilhelm recalled later, "This tall, good-looking young man walks up to me and sticks out his hand, and says, 'Hi, my name is Bill de Blasio. I'm your first cousin.' I said, 'Well, I'm very happy to meet you, but how are you my first cousin?' He explained that his father, who as you probably know left his family when he was little, and my father, who left our family when I was nine years old, were brothers."[1]

Wilhelm suddenly realized the young man standing before him was the son of his father Donald's younger brother, Warren. In fact, John's middle name is Warren, after his uncle. But since both brothers had left their wives when their children were young, there hadn't been much contact over the years between the two families.

"I think I met you when you were four years old or something," Wilhelm recalls telling the tall young man that day. "'But why is your name de Blasio? Why isn't your name Wilhelm?' So he explained to me that when he was in high school, he had been assigned to read the autobiography of Malcolm X and it had gotten him thinking about names, and what do names mean, and as a result of that, because his father had left the family, he took his mother's maiden name, de Blasio. I thought, wow, that's interesting. So we agreed to have a cup of coffee later or something."

That chance encounter in 1999 with his long lost cousin rekindled a family tie that later would prove invaluable when de Blasio began contemplating a run for political office. It suggests as well that de Blasio's choice to begin using his mother's name on some high school records—and eventually to change his legal name to Bill de Blasio—did not stem simply from an impulse to define himself more by his mother and her Italian roots, or to distance himself from a father who had left so much pain in his wake. That name change was a political choice as well.[2]

By the time their last child was born, on the afternoon of May 8, 1961, at Doctor's Hospital on Manhattan's fashionable Upper East Side, Warren and Maria Wilhelm, middle-class professionals from Norwalk, Connecticut, had already withstood their share of joy and heartbreak, of praise and persecution for their beliefs. The hospital, which has since been razed, was known for specializing in the pregnancies of older women. It sat on East End Avenue, just across the street from Gracie Mansion, the residence of New York City's mayors since 1942. Maria Wilhelm, like her husband, was forty-three, and their older children, Steve and Donald, were thirteen and eight. They named the new baby Warren Wilhelm Jr., though they soon took to calling him Bill, and, in an ironic coincidence, the child would end up half a century later moving into nearby Gracie Mansion as New York's 109th mayor—only by then the world would know him as Bill de Blasio.

The transformation of Warren Wilhelm Jr., child of affluence, into Bill de Blasio, standard-bearer against urban inequality, did not come about through a simple petition for a legal name change. Nor was it some clumsy, midlife maneuver of a budding politician intent on crafting a persona more palatable to voters, as some de Blasio critics have inferred. Rather, as with several of the current wave of new progressive leaders in the country, his political evolution has deep roots in his own upbringing. For de Blasio, it was the culmination of personal and political conflicts that raged for decades within his paternal and maternal families. How the youngest son of Warren Wilhelm Sr. and Maria de Blasio Wilhelm chose to resolve those conflicts—in part by adopting his mother's last name and rejecting that of his father—helped determine his views toward family, toward privilege and poverty, and toward the role of government.

In short, the young de Blasio, like many of us, was stamped by both the bliss and the anguish of his childhood, pursued by parental and family ghosts that shaped who he is today. That long journey, however, remained largely hidden from his official biography until only recently. In June 2013, as the mayoral primary was heating up, candidate de Blasio revealed in his first campaign commercial his father's long battle with alcoholism and how it led to a breakup of their family during his childhood. But even then he did not mention that his father had eventually committed suicide. Not until September 2013, when the *New York Post* was preparing a front-page story about his father's death, did de Blasio acknowledge the full story. "I have a real respect, and a real anger and sadness at the same time," he said when a reporter asked about his father's demons. "I don't think I've ever been able to do the math on exactly what it all means."[3]

A Family of Intellectuals

His parents' early years offered little sign of the problems ahead. Both Warren Wilhelm and Maria de Blasio were raised in relative comfort. Both attended elite New England colleges and excelled at their studies—he at Yale and she at Smith College. The Wilhelm family, in particular, produced several notable public intellectuals. Warren, who was born in 1917 in New York City, was the son of Donald George Wilhelm, a Harvard graduate and prolific author who boasted of friendships with both Herbert Hoover and Franklin D. Roosevelt, and even co-wrote a *Saturday Evening Post* article with FDR. Donald Wilhelm's youngest son, Warren, attended a Connecticut boarding school, then enrolled at Yale, graduating Phi Beta Kappa with a degree in economics in 1939. He immediately landed a job as a business reporter at *Time* magazine. Warren's older brother, Donald Jr., had obtained his bachelor's degree at Yale a year before his brother, then went on to Harvard for graduate study before embarking on a cloak-and-dagger personal odyssey as an international economist, a longtime adviser of the shah of Iran, and, most likely, a CIA agent. Their younger sister, Jean Wilhelm, graduated from Smith College and went on to an illustrious career as a theater designer and director, and later worked as a theater professor at Goucher College in Maryland.[4]

At Yale, Warren Wilhelm joined Dwight Hall, the student-run organization dedicated to public service and social action. There he played a leading role in a student campaign that sought higher wages for Yale's maids and campus police. Years later, FBI agents seeking to confirm allegations that Warren was a member of the Communist Party questioned his former classmates about his activities at Yale. One classmate, according to records of the probe, rejected those claims: "WILHELM was definitely pro-labor and an ardent New Dealer. He stated that he recalls that

WILHELM was active with him in a fight against the Communists at Yale, relating that WILHELM pulled his Dwight Hall
group out of the American Student Union, which was completely
Communist dominated."[5]

Soon after arriving at *Time*, Wilhelm, a strapping six feet five
inches tall with a broad forehead, met and fell in love with a
young research assistant, Maria Angela de Blasio, one of the few
women on the magazine's staff. The daughter of immigrants from
southern Italy who established a dress shop in New York City,
she, too, was unusually tall. She was also well-read and extremely
outspoken, having obtained both bachelor of arts and master's
degrees in English from Smith, and having graduated magna cum
laude. Fiercely proud of her ethnic heritage, she was one of only
two Italian American students in her class at Smith. An adminis-
trator there once described de Blasio as "a very intelligent, capable
and aggressive individual, extremely well qualified to handle a
position of responsibility" and "an individualist with a mind of
her own."[6]

From War Hero to Suspected Subversive

Wilhelm and Maria's courtship was cut short by the outbreak
of World War II. Four months after Japan's attack on Pearl Harbor, he enlisted in the army; soon after, she went to work at the
Office of War Information in New York, where she translated
U.S. propaganda into Italian for broadcasts beamed to her parents' homeland. He spent the war in combat in the Pacific until,
in the final days of the bloody Battle of Okinawa in 1945, he was
badly wounded in his left leg by a grenade tossed by a Japanese
soldier he shot to death. Army doctors amputated his leg below
the knee and outfitted him with a wooden replacement. Shortly
after returning to the States, he married Maria de Blasio, enrolled
in Harvard for a master's degree in economics, and then took a

job in Washington, D.C., as a budget analyst for the federal government. With his top-notch education, a good government job, an accomplished wife and growing family, and his record as a war hero, Warren Wilhelm's future seemed especially bright.

But in 1950 and again in 1953, allegations surfaced that both he and his wife were Communists. They were investigated by the FBI and called before a government loyalty board, one of several that President Truman had established in 1947 in response to growing anti-Communist hysteria in the land. Those boards routinely convened secret hearings aimed at identifying and rooting out possible leftists inside the government. More than 2,700 federal employees were dismissed as a result, while thousands of others ended up ostracized or had their careers derailed.[7]

The charges against Wilhelm were likely fueled by his wife's activities. Though both were supporters of Roosevelt's New Deal, she had always held more radical views than her husband. She not only joined the *Time* chapter of the nascent Newspaper Guild, the union founded by legendary columnist Heywood Broun, she eventually became the unit's chairperson at the magazine. There, she drew the animosity and suspicion of Whittaker Chambers, a new staff writer who would later become a key figure in the McCarthy-era investigations of dissidents. Chambers had been a Communist Party member himself and a Soviet spy in the 1920s and early 1930s but he subsequently renounced his earlier beliefs and turned virulently anti-Communist. By the early 1940s, he began reporting to the FBI and later to Congress on the presence of alleged Communists and their sympathizers within the government, and he was a key witness in 1948 before the House Un-American Activities Committee, accusing State Department diplomat Alger Hiss and other government officials of working secretly for the Communist Party.

Maria de Blasio was one of those Chambers singled out. Some of her colleagues at the OWI, where she was active in a local of the United Federal Workers of America, a Congress of Industrial

Organizations union, also accused her of slanting her transla-
tions during the war to favor Communist views. There seems to
be no doubt that de Blasio, like many young intellectuals of her
generation, was fascinated by Russia's socialist experiment. She
described her efforts to learn Russian and travel to that country
in an essay she wrote seeking admission to a doctoral program at
Radcliffe in Russian studies in the late 1940s: "I shall intensify
this studying if I am admitted to the Regional Program on the
Soviet Union. While in O.W.I., I applied for duty in Russia and
plans were under way when personal reasons forced a change of
plans.

"With our [my husband's and mine] combined background
in Journalism and Economics we expect little difficulty in being
assigned to Russia by a publication or a Government agency."[8]

But perhaps the greatest confirmation of Maria de Blasio Wilhelm's left-wing worldview was her involvement in the Progressive Citizens of America, a group whose Boston housing
committee she chaired for a time. Largely forgotten these days,
Progressive Citizens was a short-lived but influential mass organization founded by Henry Wallace, the steadfast New Deal cabinet
member and onetime vice president under Franklin Roosevelt. In
1944, the Democratic Party dropped Wallace as FDR's running
mate for being too liberal and replaced him with Harry Truman. Following Roosevelt's death and the conclusion of World
War II, Truman reversed the White House policy of alliance with
the Soviet Union and opted instead to embark on the Cold War.
That decision outraged Wallace, who then barnstormed across
the country in 1947 and recruited more than 200,000 liberals and
CIO union members to join his Progressive Citizens of America,
founding dozens of local chapters of the group. Among the new
group's best-known leaders were the historian W.E.B. DuBois
and the actor and activist Paul Robeson. The following year, its
members formed the core of Wallace's new Progressive Party,
which became the vehicle for his quixotic independent campaign

for president against Truman and Republican Thomas Dewey—an effort that ultimately attracted a mere 2.4 percent of the popular vote.

By joining Progressive Citizens of America, Maria de Blasio Wilhelm dared to take a firm stand with the idealistic, radical wing of Roosevelt's New Deal coalition and against the traditional Democratic Party machine. Her husband, Warren, meanwhile, was furious that, after returning home a wounded war hero, his patriotism had come under suspicion. "I consider my loyalty to the United States complete," he told the board, according to a transcript of his 1950 hearing. Although no allegations against the couple were ever substantiated, the board concluded they both harbored "a sympathetic interest in communism." As a result, Wilhelm was denied access to classified documents, and in 1953 he was passed up for a promotion at the Commerce Department.[9]

A Father's Descent, a Mother's Inspiration

The Wilhelms left Washington soon after for Connecticut, and eventually moved to Boston. By then Warren, bitter at how his own government had treated him and likely suffering from post-traumatic stress disorder from his experience in the Battle of Okinawa, had turned to alcohol. At first, neither his drinking nor his designation as an ultraliberal hampered his ability to land lucrative private-sector jobs, and those jobs gradually shaped his evolution from New Deal social liberal to proponent of a more muscular role for the United States during the Cold War. In 1950, while a consultant for Harvard's Russian Research Center, a think tank launched with financial help from the CIA, Wilhelm authored a paper on industrial development in the Soviet Union. He later worked for several years as a chief international economist at oil giant Texaco's Manhattan headquarters, and with the consulting firm Arthur Little in Boston. But his alcoholism escalated to the point that his wife, unable to convince him to seek counseling, filed for divorce in 1969, citing "cruel and abusive treatment." Their youngest son, Bill, was not yet eight at the time. In the years that followed, Warren Wilhelm spent little time with his sons.

"We were in touch, but it was kind of sporadic," Bill de Blasio has said of those days. "He was drunk pretty much every day so if I had anything to do with him it was in the context of that, some days a little less. Sometimes I would spend time with him earlier in the day when he was a little less drunk and you could have more of a conversation. It was very painful that this was the consistent reality."[10]

His father's spiraling decline affected de Blasio to such an extent that he later wondered if he could ever have a family of his own. "The pain he caused people, even if he didn't mean to, just so many people were badly affected," de Blasio told a *New York Times* reporter a month before his election as mayor. "I think I really was angered by that."[11]

By 1979, Warren Wilhelm was a broken man. He was not only alone and a hopeless alcoholic, he was terminally ill with cancer. That year, he fired a rifle into his heart as he sat in a car outside a Connecticut motel. Bill had just turned eighteen.

In stark contrast to his father's tragic unraveling, Maria de Blasio Wilhelm provided a steadfast and loving presence to her children. "She's the biggest influence on my life, without a doubt," Bill de Blasio said in late 2013, after publicly acknowledging his father's suicide and its impact on his family. Left to fend as a single mother, and forced to move her family to a succession of rented apartments, she devoted herself to raising her sons while still maintaining a career as a publicist.

She also never flagged in her support of the downtrodden and of left-wing social causes, always urging her sons to pay attention to politics. In the early 1970s, for example, as the oldest, Steve, approached draft age, she took a far different view of the Vietnam War than his father, Warren, who supported it.

"My mother, really like so many mothers in America, became increasingly anti-war, and sort of more and more objective about what was happening," de Blasio said. "And I always thought my father had this, you know he was an Army veteran, had this American-centric world view and talked about maybe we should be sending more troops. So he had that, a world view that I found a little out of step with what was happening on the ground."[12]

Her readiness to challenge authority rubbed off on her children. Steve joined in protests against the Vietnam War, while Bill, at the early age of twelve, launched a successful campaign to convince administrators at his Boston middle school to grant hearings to sixth and seventh graders before meting out discipline. After enrolling at Cambridge Rindge and Latin High School, Bill Wilhelm kept up his activism. Elected to student government, he gained attention in the Boston press as a representative to a statewide body of student leaders. And once he enrolled at New York University, he soon co-founded the Coalition for Student Rights and organized protests against tuition increases there.

By then, however, Bill Wilhelm was already grappling with his identity and family contradictions. "I had made the initial decision even in the senior year of high school that I was starting to think about the name," he once said in a radio interview. "I asked for one of the diplomas or one of the certificates to have de Blasio put in as a middle name. That was in May and he didn't die until July so already something was deep in me starting to feel like I really wanted to identify myself at least also with my mother's side. That was intensified from the time I went to see my grandfather's hometown in 1975. . . . It was obviously a very complicated reality."

A Long Lost Cousin

Bill de Blasio's initial encounter with his cousin John Wilhelm at the New York City Central Labor Council banquet in 1999 further underscored how dramatically different the de Blasio and Wilhelm families were. Like Warren Wilhelm, Donald Wilhelm also abandoned his family when his children were very young, but for a very different reason. "We went to Burma, the whole family, when I was seven," John Wilhelm said, "and my father was ostensibly working for a firm there studying the economic future of Burma. But we believe he had to have been in the CIA."

In fact, Donald Wilhelm was working as a consultant in Burma for the Point IV Program, which President Truman had created as a foreign aid program to counter the spread of Communism around the world. Wilhelm was stationed there even as CIA operatives were actively training Burmese soldiers to fight Communists along the border with China. In 1954, most Americans were forced to leave because of growing tensions with the Burmese public.

"They produced a multivolume report . . . which essentially says, Western corporations should exploit the natural resources of Burma, which was rubber, tin and oil and ivory, and they said that in so many words," his son John recalled, "and a few years afterward the generals took over the country."[13]

Donald Wilhelm's wife, Jane, would later be dubbed one of the early founders of Reston, Virginia, the suburb that came to be the preferred neighborhood for many of the nation's spy operatives.[14]

"My dad left us in 1954," John Wilhelm recalled, "literally in a matter of weeks after we had returned from living in Burma." His father gathered his wife, Jane, and their four children in their living room in Arlington, Virginia, and announced he was leaving to work as a visiting professor for a year at a university in Iran and wouldn't be taking the family with him. This was less than a year after the CIA, along with British intelligence, had organized the overthrow of Iran's democratically elected prime minister, Mohammad Mosaddegh, and installed the shah of Iran as the country's new leader.

"My father's one year in Tehran ended up being twelve or thirteen years," John Wilhelm recalled. "I never saw him again. He ended up becoming a member of the royal court of the shah and he even ghostwrote the autobiography of the shah. It was one of the most awful books written by anyone."

Donald Wilhelm died in London in 2001, but in recent years, as John Wilhelm came to know his cousin Bill de Blasio, and as the remaining members of the Wilhelm family began comparing their recollections of Warren and Donald, brothers who had both abandoned their spouses and children at an early age, they reached a common conclusion. "They felt very strongly that my father was a bad person," John Wilhelm said, "but that Bill's father was a really good person who had become really messed up by the war. Today we would say he had PTSD, but that wasn't acknowledged back then."[15]

Asked in 2013 about his uncle Donald, Bill de Blasio spoke with regret of "family lore" that he was "sort of a mouthpiece for the Shah."

"I think it was the wrong thing to do," de Blasio said. "The overthrow of Mosaddegh was one of the most profoundly negative, immoral, unfair acts of U.S. foreign policy in the last hundred years."[16]

Standing up for Nicaragua's Poor

Following his graduation from New York University in 1984, Bill de Blasio enrolled in a master's degree program at Columbia's School for International Affairs, specializing in Latin American politics. Much of that region of the world was in revolt at the time. Bloody civil wars were raging in Nicaragua, El Salvador, and Guatemala, with much of the violence inflamed by covert

CIA action, and tens of thousands of Central American refugees were fleeing to the United States to escape. Here at home, scores of religious and political groups opposed to the Reagan and then Bush administration policies in the region founded sanctuary centers for the refugees or sent humanitarian aid to the conflict zones. In 1987, de Blasio, by then a tall, bearded, and often-disheveled admirer of socialist ideas, took a $12,000-a-year job as an organizer with one of those groups, the Quixote Center in Maryland. Founded by Catholic nuns and priests who espoused liberation theology, the center was collecting donations of cloth-ing, household goods, and medical supplies to ship to towns and villages in Nicaragua. At the time, that country's left-wing San-dinista government was battling the Contras, a guerrilla move-ment that had the support of the Reagan White House. Despite a congressional ban, Reagan's aides had, via the National Security Council, established a secret network operated by the infamous colonel Oliver North to funnel weapons and aid to the Contras. De Blasio's job was to recruit volunteers to collect humanitarian supplies from various churches and synagogues and then arrange shipments of those supplies to Nicaraguan civic groups.

"We set out to match the amount of Contra aid the Reagan administration was sending," said Sr. Maureen Fiedler, one of de Blasio's supervisors back then, who praised him for arranging millions of dollars in shipments. "His work ethic was superb. He didn't just stop at five o'clock. It wasn't unusual for us to fill two or three containers a week."[17]

In 1988, de Blasio joined a ten-day trip to Nicaragua organized by the Quixote Center. He visited a government-run health cen-ter in Masaya, a city at the base of an active volcano about thirty kilometers southeast of Managua. It was there that he first began to realize the potential power of government to change people's daily lives. On the wall of the clinic was a map where doctors tracked the progress of an immunization campaign for every fam-ily in the city. "There was something I took away from that," he would later say, "how hands-on government has to be, how proactive, how connected to the people."[18]

Soon after his trip to Nicaragua, de Blasio left the Quixote Center and returned to New York. He became a volunteer with the Nicaragua Solidarity Network, a collection of liberals, Marxists, and anarchists that backed the Sandinista government. The network sought to change Bush administration policies toward Central America. And while he has since criticized the Sandinista repression of dissent before their government was voted from office in 1990, he has continued to praise the revolution's accomplishments. "They had a youthful energy and idealism mixed with a human ability and practicality that was really inspirational," he said in 2013.[19]

By 1989, however, de Blasio was already being drawn into local politics. Rev. Jesse Jackson and his Rainbow Coalition had made a strong showing in the 1988 Democratic presidential primaries—Jackson even captured the majority of the vote in New York City. That had emboldened the city's liberal Democratic wing, led by the powerful health care workers union, Local 1199, to mount a challenge against three-time incumbent mayor Ed Koch. They convinced Manhattan borough president David Dinkins, a longtime member of Democratic Socialists of America, to be their candidate. Dinkins's chief strategist was Bill Lynch, one of the unsung heroes of progressive politics in the city. A rotund, disheveled political organizer with a scraggly beard, an impish grin, and a razor-sharp mind, Lynch had cultivated strong ties with scores of neighborhood activists, labor leaders, and political radicals, and had coordinated the 1988 Jackson presidential run in New York. Following that campaign, he and his friend Dennis Rivera, then the charismatic new president of Local 1199, conceived the idea of turning that same Rainbow Coalition into the core of a Dinkins campaign. But they had to spend months convincing a reluctant Dinkins to declare his candidacy, and instead of the militant-sounding Rainbow Coalition, they opted for the more congenial campaign slogan of turning New York into a "gorgeous mosaic" of races and ethnic groups. In short order, Lynch began recruiting a ragtag group of radical organizers to work out of a makeshift campaign center in a dilapidated office building at West 43rd Street and Eighth Avenue, just down the street from the 1199 headquarters.

One of the early volunteers to the Dinkins campaign was Ken Sunshine, now a successful publicist to Hollywood stars like Leonardo DiCaprio, Barbra Streisand, and Ben Affleck. "Lynch had this coterie of young kids," Sunshine recalled. "Michael Gaspard was one of them, and there was Michael's brother Patrick Gaspard, and Scott Levenson. And there was this tall gawky guy with a beard, de Blasio."

Sunshine vividly remembers an elderly woman who often showed up to feed the volunteers. "Bill's mother would bring us Italian food," he said. "She was a pistol, a lively lady with clearly progressive views, and we would often end up talking politics."[20]

By then, Maria de Blasio had finally produced a book she'd been trying to write for decades. Published by Norton in 1988, it was titled *The Other Italy: The Italian Resistance in World War II*. In it she recounted the story of the various Italian partisan groups that rose up in 1943 in a people's war against German occupation following Italy's armistice with the Allies. Based largely on Italian documents and her own interviews with former resistance fighters, it not only depicted the various conflicts and alliances among Communist, socialist, Christian, and nationalist factions of the popular revolt, but also detailed the important role of female partisans. She ended the preface to the book with the words: "And finally I want to thank my son, Bill deBlasio-Wilhelm, for his constant interest and editorial support in this project, without which it might never have been undertaken much less completed."

A Mayoral Aide

In the September 1989 New York City mayoral Democratic primary, David Dinkins prevailed against Koch and two other contenders. He then defeated former federal prosecutor Rudy Giuliani in the November general election to become the city's first black mayor. Both contests resulted in historic voter turnouts, with more than 1 million people casting ballots in the Democratic primary and more than 1.8 million in the general election, where Dinkins edged out Giuliani by just 47,000 votes. After the election, both Patrick Gaspard, who was then twenty-two, and Bill de Blasio, then twenty-eight, landed jobs in city hall as low-level aides to Sunshine, who was appointed Dinkins's first chief of staff.

"There were all kinds of factions in that administration," Sunshine said. "I was part of the Lynch faction and there was the [First Deputy Mayor Norman] Steisel faction. Everyone was fighting with everyone else. One day Lynch told me, 'Spend less time with these kids. You have to worry about protecting the mayor and the only one of these kids worth anything is Gaspard and that tall bearded one.' "[21]

Dinkins would later lose his reelection bid to Giuliani. The lessons of that defeat were not lost on his brightest aides, Patrick Gaspard and Bill de Blasio, who became the closest of friends. Gaspard, of course, would go on to become a political director of 1199/SEIU and later a senior aide in the Obama White House and U.S. ambassador to South Africa. For while Dinkins espoused progressive ideals, he paid scant attention to the nitty-gritty details of governing the city. It was commonly known that one of his aides routinely accompanied the mayor wherever he went with a freshly pressed tuxedo so he could swiftly change into evening attire for the black-tie affairs he was constantly attending.

As for de Blasio, he was assigned to city hall's community assistance unit, which involved mostly responding to concerns of neighborhood leaders about city services or troubleshooting in times of neighborhood unrest. His new job not only exposed him to the intoxicating world of urban politics, it introduced him to the woman who would become his wife and closest political partner, Chirlane McCray, and to several other Dinkins operatives who decades later would play important roles in his own rise to power in city hall.

One of those people was a former reporter with the *Village Voice* named Maria Laurino. Bill Lynch recruited Laurino as Dinkins's main speechwriter and assigned her to work in the old Tweed Courthouse behind city hall. During visits to the main city hall offices, Laurino quickly bonded with "the tall bearded guy" with the quirky sense of humor. Like her, he was of Italian background, and he even offered her a signed copy of his mother's book on the Italian resistance. One day, the mayor's press office was short of staff. Lynch asked Laurino to lend one of her speech-writing aides to the pressroom. She promptly dispatched her assistant Chirlane McCray to city hall, which is how the young de Blasio first met his future wife.[22] He was immediately smitten with McCray, an outspoken feminist who was seven years older than him. Their first date was a lunch at Scallions, a vegetarian restaurant in Lower Manhattan that has long since closed.

Laurino also introduced de Blasio to Anthony Shorris, the man she was dating at the time. Shorris had been a veteran official of the Koch administration and was then serving as first deputy executive director of the Port Authority. "Maria spent every day with Chirlane and she spent many hours laughing and hanging out with Bill," Shorris recalled recently. He and Laurino married in 1993, and de Blasio and McCray exchanged vows a year later in Prospect Park. Each couple attended the other's wedding, but as the years passed they saw each other less frequently.

In 2013, Shorris's son Michael discovered that his favorite rock band, Vampire Weekend, had done an ad for de Blasio's mayoral campaign. Shorris had just received an invitation to a de Blasio fund-raiser. "'We have to go because maybe Vampire Weekend will be there,'" Shorris recalls his son saying. "'And I want to meet the candidate that Vampire Weekend supports.'" Shorris attended, donated $175, and reconnected with de Blasio. Several months later, after winning the election, de Blasio would immediately call Shorris, the veteran of the Koch administration, and offer him the job of first deputy mayor.

De Blasio, who for years had been inspired by his mother's radical idea of lifting up working people and the poor, who now championed government's role in ending urban inequality, was practical enough to understand that he needed seasoned aides at his side who not only shared his vision but knew how to effectively run a city as vast as New York.

Grappling with family ghosts and changing his name would be nothing compared to the battles that lay ahead.

2

Race, Class, and the Urban Growth Machine

The earth below, the roof above, and the walls around make up a special sort of commodity: a place to be bought and sold, rented and leased, as well as used for making a life.

—John Logan and Harvey Molotch[1]

How did the great metropolitan centers of the richest country in the world end up producing during the first decade of the twenty-first century the stark urban inequality that Bill de Blasio and the new crop of progressive municipal leaders have vowed to combat? What role did our government leaders play in widening both the economic and spatial divides between rich and poor, white and nonwhite?

This chapter sketches the rise of a "growth machine" that has dominated urban policy at the federal, state, and local levels since the 1920s. The machine was marked at first by conservative bankers and realtors, allied at times with liberal urban planners, and later by advocates of neoliberalism. Under either method, the growth machine has deeply exacerbated both urban inequality and racial segregation in housing. Its proponents, spurred by real estate, banking, and other wealthy interests in each major city, have historically coveted the finite and valuable land areas of our cities, especially those located closest to the central business districts—housing units in low-income neighborhoods, public parks, schools, streets, waterfronts, and the industrial sites left vacant after the flight of manufacturing—for their "exchange value," that is, for their potential to generate new high-end commercial development or to produce luxury housing.

The vast majority of city dwellers, however, are working or middle class or poor, and they typically view urban space, in general, and their neighborhoods, in particular, through a different lens. "The sharpest contrast," Logan and Molotch noted in their classic study of urban America, "is between residents, who use place to satisfy essential needs of life, and entrepreneurs, who strive for financial return ordinarily achieved by intensifying the use to which their property is put." Yet national leaders in both major political parties have generally adopted the growth model, with the only exception being a short period during the Kennedy and Johnson administrations. For the first half of the twentieth century, both federal government and the real estate and banking industries openly promoted racial segregation in urban housing as a way to maintain property values; they then subsidized the proliferation of all-white suburbs while they bulldozed inner-city neighborhoods in the name of urban renewal, encouraging local governments to corral a reduced number of the displaced poor into segregated high-rise public housing; and finally, in more recent decades, they systematically pushed the remaining minority groups as far away as possible from the downtown areas while promoting a massive back-to-the-city movement among affluent whites.[2]

At the center of this long-running conflict between the "use" model and the "growth" model has been the unanswered question: where and how will the nation provide affordable shelter for the masses of people who flock to our cities each year in search of jobs and a better life? This is hardly a new dilemma. Soon after the urban riots of the 1960s—a chaotic period that stunned the nation and raised deep concerns about the very future of big cities—one scholar noted: "since 1933, there has scarcely been a session of Congress without controversy and debate on the housing problem. And in the communities, there has been continuing conflict on what housing to build for whom—and where. In the background increasingly is the race issue."[3]

Yet those conflicts have been largely hidden from public view, to the point that most Americans have little idea how the actions of government leaders ended up shaping our modern cities. The public knows even less about the crucial role race and class bias have played in many of those policies. And while numerous scholars have unearthed and amply documented that checkered history over the years, those who govern our cities today keep ignoring the lessons of the past. So before we can examine why the current progressive urban reform movement represents such a radical break from prior ways of governing cities, we need to broadly sketch how those prior policies fostered the modern-day tale of two cities.

Segregating Cities with a Government Seal of Approval

Until the First World War, the federal government had no involvement in the cities or in providing housing to city dwellers. Home building was purely a private industry, dominated by small construction companies and by local banks and real estate agents who serviced a largely white population. But that all began to change once the United States entered the war. The nation's leaders, for one thing, confronted an immediate need to ramp up factory and shipyard production for the military effort, so the federal government rapidly erected sixteen thousand temporary homes in cities across America to house the swelling workforce of those industries. In addition, the sudden curtailment of European immigration during and after the war drew hundreds of thousands of African Americans from the South to the booming factories of the North. More than half a million blacks moved to the major northern cities just between 1916 and 1918, with Chicago's African American population, for example, skyrocketing from 44,103 in 1910 to 109,594 in 1920. The Great Migration would continue in a second phase during World War II and the Korean conflict, and by then hundreds of thousands of Mexicans and Puerto Ricans had also joined the vast trek northward of nonwhite labor, thus transforming the racial composition of the nation's urban areas.[4]

That migration also signaled the spread of racial conflict from the rural South to the urban North. Financial and real estate elites in the big cities began to systematically segregate the new arrivals into overcrowded and decrepit inner-city ghettos close to the factories where they worked, thus spawning separate and unequal housing markets—one for white workers and the middle class, another for the new nonwhite migrants. They achieved that at first with overt "racial zoning" laws that barred blacks from buying homes in white neighborhoods. But when the Supreme Court struck down such blatant discrimination in 1917, many cities resorted to a more disguised approach: they enforced private land covenants that forbade the sale of a home to nonwhite buyers, and they hired professional planners to zone specific neighborhoods within a city for distinct types of development. The zoning reform movement, as it was dubbed, began in New York in 1916 and had proliferated to 85 percent of American cities by 1936. Inspired by architects and urban planners who formed part of the City Beautiful movement at the turn of the twentieth century—Frederick Law Olmsted Jr., son of the designer of New York's Central Park, for example, and Chicago's master planner Daniel Burnham—zoning's proponents ardently believed that well-conceived, orderly urban spaces and physically attractive buildings could bring about social harmony from the sooty chaos of the modern city by taming the uncontrolled spread of industry and commerce. Before long, they had gathered political backing for their ideas from progressive politicians in both the North and the South. But the new zoning laws too often turned into a legal justification to keep excluding poor people and especially blacks from more affluent neighborhoods, and this was especially true in the Jim Crow South and in northern cities with growing black populations.

The result was a rising number of racial conflicts over housing. Those conflicts, in turn, fueled an upsurge of racial violence after the war, the worst of which was the Chicago Race Riot of 1919, which resulted in 38 deaths and 537 people injured, and left a thousand people homeless, almost all of them African American. An exhaustive study of that tragedy by the Chicago Race Relations Commission later highlighted the huge problem of housing discrimination. "Negroes are charged more than white people for loans, find it more difficult to secure them, and thus are generally handicapped in efforts to buy or improve property," the commission noted in words that still resonate nearly a century later.[5]

The 1920s were a boom period for housing in America, with an average of some 880,000 new units constructed each year, most of them on the outskirts of major cities. That boom, however, was followed by the economic crash of 1929, with the housing collapse a major factor in the intractable nature of the Great Depression. New home starts plummeted to just 132,000 by 1932, while home foreclosures soared to 250,000—an average of nearly 5,000 per week![6]

Soon after his election, President Roosevelt spearheaded a raft of government actions to aid the nation's cities through massive public work programs and with legislation to revive the housing industry by creating new jobs for some 2 million unemployed construction workers. The federal Public Works Administration built 21,800 units of public housing in its first four years, largely low-rise developments for the working class. In 1933, Roosevelt created the Home Owners' Loan Corporation to stem the epidemic of foreclosures. He launched the Federal Housing Administration in 1934 to boost lending by offering federal insurance of new mortgages, with the agency establishing and supervising standards for those loans. And in 1937, responding to pressure from big-city mayors like New York's La Guardia and Detroit's Frank Murphy, the president backed and signed the Wagner-Steagall Act that created the U.S. Housing Authority, the first federal agency to finance low-cost public housing. Between 1939 and 1943, the new agency produced 160,000 units of public housing. But once World War II began, opponents of public housing in Congress sharply reduced allocations for it.

Meanwhile, the new Home Owners' Loan Corporation was refinancing defaulted mortgages at low interest rates, often reducing the original principal, and granting delinquent home owners fifteen years to pay off the loans, a much longer time span than the private market allowed at the time. By 1935, HOLC had refinanced more than 1 million homes, 20 percent of all the mortgaged nonfarm dwellings in the country. By the end of the 1930s, the federal government had not only assumed a dominant role in the nation's housing and mortgage industries, it had spawned a two-tier class system: a handful of agencies, including HOLC, the FHA, and others, subsidized builders and lenders for the upper-tier, white middle-class home buyers, while the government sponsored public housing for working-class families that the private market would not service, except that the government allowed public housing to be built locally along segregated racial lines.[7]

From its inception, HOLC provided a government seal of approval to racial exclusion that until then had been practiced only by the private real estate market. It did so by secretly creating residential security maps for all cities and determining risks in every neighborhood, cataloging them not only by the condition of the housing stock, but by the income level, race, and ethnicity of their residents. The agency's color-coded system of maps ranked neighborhoods by desirability and assigned largely black neighborhoods the color red, signifying the worst risk, thus giving birth to the now-infamous term *redlining*. Officials at the FHA subsequently relied on HOLC's maps to establish their underwriting guidelines for federally insured mortgages. Several of those officials, in fact, had pioneered the specious real estate industry theory that "infiltration" by blacks into white neighborhoods led to social decline of those areas and lower property values.[8]

"There is one difference in people, namely race, which can result in very rapid decline [of property]," appraiser Frederick Babcock claimed in an influential real estate textbook he authored in 1932. "Usually such declines can be partially avoided by segregation," he noted. Babcock became the FHA's chief underwriter two years later and he subsequently penned the agency's underwriting manual, in which he directed that property values should be rated lower for "possible infiltration of inharmonious racial groups." The 1938 version of that manual specifically recommended "restrictive covenants" and "natural or artificially established barriers" to protect a neighborhood from "adverse influences," including "lower class occupancy and inharmonious racial groups." Ernest Fisher, a colleague of Babcock's at the agency, espoused similar views. "It is a matter of common observation that the purchase of property by certain racial types is very likely to diminish the value of other property in the section," Fisher had asserted in 1922. And there was Homer Hoyt, another top FHA official and one of the nation's most prominent housing and real estate economists. In a 1933 study he conducted before joining the agency, Hoyt concocted a hierarchical list of how various ethnic and racial groups affected land values, with "Negroes and Mexicans" at the bottom.[9]

Babcock, Hoyt, and Fisher were thus principally responsible for developing the underwriting and insurance standards that were later adopted by both the FHA and the Veterans Administration loan programs. The profound effect of those racially biased standards on urban development and on the economic status of nonwhite minorities cannot be understated. Since 1934, the FHA has insured a total of 40 million mortgages—an annual average of about 10 percent of all home mortgages issued. In addition, the government incentivized home buying by allowing owners to deduct mortgage interest and property taxes from their federal taxes. The combination of low-cost FHA and VA mortgages, together with direct federal tax subsidies, caused home ownership in America to zoom from just 44 percent in 1934 to 63 percent by 1972, and was the engine for the movement of the white middle class into America's suburbs.[10]

Yet between 1935 and 1953, less than 1 percent of new dwelling construction in the U.S. private housing market went to nonwhites, even though they comprised 10 percent of the population. Millions of blacks and Latinos, whether they were poor or middle class, were effectively shut out from home ownership and forced to remain in inner-city ghettos. Buying a home, after all, is the most important investment the average American will ever make, and it represents the biggest potential source of wealth accumulation for a family. Meanwhile, the public housing units where blacks lived were located at first in the inner city because local public housing authorities refused to admit them into units the government built in white communities. The effects of such policies continued for decades. As late as 1984, an investigation by the *Dallas Morning News* found that the nation's 10 million public housing residents were still segregated by race. The few projects that remained predominantly white were found to have better upkeep and superior services and amenities than those that were largely black. As one researcher noted, "examples nationwide abound of how public housing was used by federal, state and local governments to create the segregated metropolitan areas we know today."[11]

In 1948, the Supreme Court finally declared unconstitutional the enforcement by local governments of restrictive covenants banning the sale of property to African Americans. Until that landmark decision in the case of *Shelley v. Kramer*, the FHA had "actually encouraged its borrowers to give such guarantees and was a powerful enforcer of the covenants," notes historian Roger Biles. Covenants, however, continued in use as private agreements for years, and Biles ascribes the practice to "conventional racial prejudice characteristic of many middle class real estate men" of that era.[12]

Others have offered a much more blistering assessment. The FHA "adopted a racial policy that could well have been culled from the Nuremburg laws," one 1950s housing expert wrote, adding: "From its inception FHA set itself up as the protector of the all-white neighborhood. . . . It not only insisted on social and racial 'homogeneity' in all of its projects as the price of insurance but became the vanguard of white supremacy and racial purity— in the North as well as the South."[13]

The list of segregated neighborhoods that sprouted in the nation's cities and metropolitan suburbs by midcentury was astonishing. Of some three hundred private home subdivisions erected in New York's Queens, Nassau, and Westchester Counties from 1935 to 1947, for example, 83 percent had written deed covenants against the sale of homes to black people, with most citing Federal Housing Administration requirements for the restriction. The biggest of those, and the largest housing development ever established by a single builder, was Long Island's Levittown, where more than seventy thousand people lived by 1953. Not a single Levittown resident was black. Clause 25 of the standard contract for the first Levitt houses spelled out the whites-only policy. A second Levittown development in Bucks County, Pennsylvania, grew to 17,300 homes by 1958. Fifty years later, it was still 90 percent white.[14]

Such segregation was not limited to suburban areas. In New York City, Mayor La Guardia, faced with a dire housing shortage, announced in 1943 that the Metropolitan Life Insurance Company would build a new complex of private rental apartments for 25,000 middle-income people on the East Side of Manhattan.

The project, to be called Stuyvesant Town, was made possible by a twenty-five-year property tax exemption that city-planning czar Robert Moses had devised. Moses also agreed to condemn and demolish eighteen city blocks, including churches, stores, a school, and existing housing for ten thousand low-income residents and provide the land, including public streets, to the company at a discounted price, all of which made the claim that it was a "private" development somewhat specious. The tax exemption, worth an estimated $55 million, was considered then a novel way to spur private investment in slum clearance. Moses had used his influence with legislators in Albany and with Governor Thomas Dewey during the previous year to establish it. But very few of the people displaced by the condemnation could afford to pay the rents in the new Stuyvesant Town, since they were twice as high as prior housing costs in the area. And no black tenants were to be permitted even if they could afford to pay because, in the words of company president Frederick Ecker, "Negroes and whites don't mix." At a heated meeting of the Board of Estimate in June 1943 to consider the plan, only Ecker and Moses spoke in favor, the latter declaring the development "a good piece of business for the city." Ecker's racial policy sparked such a public furor that the city council passed a new ordinance in 1944 against housing discrimination, though by then it was too late to affect Stuyvesant Town. The Supreme Court eventually refused to hear an appeal of a state court decision upholding Stuyvesant Town's racial exclusion. More important, the city's use of eminent domain on such a massive scale proved to be, as we shall see, a precursor of the urban redevelopment model that Congress subsequently embraced with the pivotal Housing Act of 1949.[15]

So widespread had racial bias become in both home mortgage lending and the financing of multifamily dwellings that the U.S. justice department filed a complaint in 1946 against thirty-eight New York City banks and lending institutions, charging them with conspiring to "use their control of credit to cause the exclusion of certain minority racial and national groups from certain areas." The result, the department alleged, was that "Negroes and Spanish-speaking persons . . . have been compelled to pay higher rents than those charged for comparable dwellings in other sections of the city, and owners of properties occupied by Negroes and Spanish-speaking persons have been denied the mortgage financing required to maintain real estate in habitable conditions." The thirty-eight defendants did not even contest the claim, entering instead into a civil consent decree in June 1948.[16]

The Broken Promise of Urban Renewal

The nation's housing shortage reached crisis proportions immediately after the Second World War, as soldiers back from the battlefield joined the throngs of civilians who had migrated to the big cities during the fighting for jobs in manufacturing. The cost of urban rental housing soared, especially after wartime price controls ended. Soon big-city newspapers were filled with heartbreaking stories of homeless veterans and exposés of horrendous overcrowding in squalid slums. The nation's housing stock was in scandalous condition: 43 percent of units had no bathtubs and 35 percent no flushing toilets. The National Housing Agency reported in 1944 that 12.6 million new nonfarm dwellings were needed over the next ten years—an average of 1.2 million annually—and it urged that 22 percent of those be low-rent units. But conservative groups, especially home builders, realtors, and the chamber of commerce, rallied both Republicans and southern Democrats in Congress to block President Truman's call for more spending on housing.

The real estate and banking interests, however, wanted federal help to redevelop the cities. They were deeply worried about economic decline in the central business districts and the increasing minority populations around them. But land prices in those areas were so high, they claimed, that developers needed government

help. So the "growth" lobby, spearheaded by the National Association of Real Estate Brokers, began to advocate for a federal program of slum clearance, one that would subsidize building costs.

And while many New Deal public housing advocates agreed
that tenement slums should be torn down, they vowed to support
such a federal program only if it provided new units for those
who were displaced, and if it helped ease the overall postwar
housing shortage. NAREB and its allies in business, on the other
hand, bitterly opposed public housing as a "socialistic" intrusion
by the federal government into private business. They curried
backing from Dixiecrats in Congress by depicting public housing as a government-sponsored form of racial integration. Those
Dixiecrats, who controlled many key congressional committees, became the main obstacles in Washington to public housing
legislation.[17]

It took fierce political battles from 1945 to 1949 before President
Truman finally mustered congressional majorities for his housing plan. The landmark Housing Act of 1949 established a new
national policy of "the achievement as soon as feasible of a decent
home and a suitable living environment for every American family." With its passage, there was no longer any doubt that the
federal government would play a major role in urban policy and
housing construction for decades to come. But that role became a
contradictory one because the law, especially as amended in subsequent years, favored the private market's "growth machine" more
than the "use" model of public housing advocates. For example,
the bill's main provision, known as Title I, established a program
of urban redevelopment, later renamed urban renewal. It authorized $1 billion in federal loans to local redevelopment agencies
to demolish slums and blighted areas, and to make the cleared
land available to private developers, and another $500 million
in federal subsidies for two-thirds of the cost of the land write-
downs for those projects. A separate public housing provision,
Title III, set a goal of building 810,000 new low-rent housing

units over the next six years. That represented only 10 percent of what experts estimated the country needed, but the provision also required local housing authorities to *demolish one slum unit for every new unit built.* So even if the goal of 135,000 new units per year were met, there was to be no net increase in the nation's stock of low-income housing. Republican and Dixiecrat opponents of public housing soon crippled even that insufficient target by cutting annual spending for actual units. By the time Republican Dwight Eisenhower took office in 1953, a mere 156,000 units had even been started. Ike, a firm enemy of public housing, then proceeded to reduce the annual goal to a mere 37,000.[18]

Meanwhile, urban redevelopment turned into a steamroller aimed at black and Latino neighborhoods. In July 1952, for example, New York's rent commissioner Charles Abrams received a list from the Housing and Home Finance Agency (the umbrella group of federal housing agencies) of seventy urban redevelopment projects around the country that had been initially approved. According to that report, 45,450 families would lose their housing. Not one of the projects was on open land. "Of the 45,450 to be displaced, all but 13,650 were listed as 'non-white,'" Abrams noted. "If Mexicans, Puerto Ricans and other Spanish-speaking people were added, the figures would be much greater." Only 1,778 families were to be provided low-rent public housing.[19]

Those early urban renewal plans stalled in many cities due to bureaucratic delays and because private developers balked at the meager profits low-rent housing offered them. By 1953, only half the money allotted to urban renewal had been spent. So Congress amended the law to allow for more nonresidential projects on cleared land, a change that sparked increased private investment. Nowhere was the impact of that change felt more than in New York. In 1957, Moses and a private consortium led by John D. Rockefeller III proposed to demolish seven thousand tenement apartments and eight hundred small businesses in an entire neighborhood on Manhattan's Upper West Side known as San Juan Hill, where the residents were largely African Americans. The Rockefeller consortium planned to erect the new Lincoln Center for the Performing Arts, a downtown campus for Fordham University, a new high school, and 4,400 units of housing. The ambitious proposal soon won widespread support from the media. But Moses showed little concern for the fate of the site's original inhabitants. Of the 4,400 new units of housing to be built, 4,000 were slated to be luxury units.[20]

In his biography of Moses, Robert Caro estimated at perhaps half a million the total number of people Moses displaced with all his grand public works programs, adding:

> More significant than the number of the dispossessed were their characteristics: a disproportionate share of them were black, Puerto Rican—and poor. He evicted tens of thousands of poor, non-white persons for urban renewal projects, and the housing he built to replace the housing he tore down was, to an overwhelming extent, not housing for the poor, but for the rich. The dispossessed, barred from many areas of the city by color and income, had no place to go but into the already overcrowded slums—or into "soft" borderline areas that then became slums, so that his "slum clearance programs" created new slums as fast as they cleared the old.[21]

"Wrecking a Negro's building no longer had to be done by a mob," one critic lamented. Thanks to urban renewal, there "was a way to do it constitutionally."[22]

The same scenario was repeated throughout the country. Of 1,155 urban renewal projects approved between 1949 and 1966, 67 percent were predominantly residential when they were launched, but only 43 percent were residential by the time they were completed. In addition to New York's Lincoln Center, urban renewal brought new civic centers to Boston, Hartford, and St. Paul; it brought both a new civic center and a sports stadium to once-black neighborhoods around downtown Atlanta; it razed and rebuilt the area around Philadelphia's Independence Hall. In the end, less than 20 percent of all urban renewal land went for housing while over 80 percent was used for developing commercial, industrial, and public infrastructure.[23]

One study of Atlanta's urban renewal program concluded that the business community "deliberately promoted a policy of moving low-income blacks away from the center of the city into selected outlying areas," and city planners then ensured those areas would be segregated by placing relocation offices in neighborhoods that were already black, while placing none in Atlanta's largely white north side. Cities like Nashville, Savannah, and Baltimore went to even greater extremes; they got federal authorities to approve slum clearance projects that demolished homes occupied by African Americans only to replace them with public housing for whites.[24]

Everywhere the bulldozers of urban renewal or the federal government's highway construction program appeared, local community groups mounted opposition or legal challenges. Rebuilding housing did not require destroying entire neighborhoods and disappearing their residents, they insisted. Nor was it necessary to replicate past patterns of racial and class segregation. In 1961, a prophet of that neighborhood preservation movement, Jane Jacobs, derided in lyric terms the growth machine's grandiose claims of urban renaissance:

> Luxury housing projects that mitigate their inanity, or try to, with a vapid vulgarity. Cultural centers that are unable to support a good bookstore. Civic centers that are avoided by everyone but the bums. . . . Commercial centers that are lackluster imitations of standardized chain-store shopping. Promenades that

go from no place to nowhere and have no promenad-
ers. Expressways that eviscerate great cities. This is not
the rebuilding of cities. This is the sacking of cities.[25]

The Racial War over Housing

The nation was rocked during the late 1940s and early 1950s by
an epidemic of mob violence and terrorist bombings that targeted blacks moving into white neighborhoods, or that sought to
halt the construction of public housing projects for blacks outside
the inner cities. The sheer number of such racist incidents has
been virtually erased from the public consciousness since many
received scant attention in the mainstream press at the time and
few urban scholars later bothered to tally them. Far more attention has been devoted instead to the wave of rioting that erupted
in black communities during the 1960s. Yet that earlier organized violence by whites laid the basis for the urban uprisings
that would follow. As more nonwhites moved into the big cities
in search of jobs, the newcomers had a pressing need for housing, but everywhere they went restrictive covenants limited their
options. In Chicago, for example, 80 percent of the city's properties had such covenants during the 1940s, and before long, neighborhood property owners' associations popped up everywhere to
enforce them.[26]

In Detroit, tensions between whites and blacks over housing
escalated in early 1942, after federal authorities attempted to meet
the critical need for shelter among the city's defense industry
workers by opening two segregated public housing projects—
one for whites and another for blacks. They decided to erect
the black project, Sojourner Truth Houses, away from the overcrowded inner city, in an outlying area that was scarcely populat-
ed but racially mixed. Local white leaders immediately objected,
especially after the FHA announced it would no longer insure
home mortgages in the neighborhood if blacks were admitted to

Sojourner Truth. Joseph Buffa, a real estate agent opposed to the project, promptly founded the Seven Mile Fenelon Improvement Association to rally white residents against admission of blacks. Buffa and his followers claimed the federal government was violating existing racial restrictions on the land. They were joined by a local Catholic priest, Fr. Constantine Dziuk, who convened mass meetings of his largely Polish parishioners in which the good father warned that white girls would be in danger if blacks were admitted to Sojourner Truth. The project's opponents won crucial backing from the local Democratic congressman, Rudolph Tenerowicz, who pressured the federal housing agency to reverse its policy and designate the new public housing units for whites. But the switch from Washington prompted an even bigger uproar from civil rights and labor union leaders in Detroit who launched a campaign of picketing and lobbying of city officials and eventually forced yet another change, with those officials declaring that Sojourner Truth would, indeed, be housing for blacks. When the first twelve black families attempted to move in on February 28, they were met by a mob of five hundred whites wielding clubs and stones, and not enough police to ensure their safety. A crowd of black residents from a nearby black middle-class enclave soon gathered to confront the white mob and protect the new tenants. A pitched battle erupted between the two sides, with violent skirmishes continuing all that day and the next. By the time the fighting subsided 38 people had been hospitalized, 33 of them black, and police had arrested 104 people, only three of whom were white.[27]

As with the Sojourner Truth incident, countless urban neighborhoods "in transition" soon became tinderboxes when the urban renewal program of the 1950s pushed more low-income and minority residents out of the inner city. At least 350 incidents of racial violence related to housing were reported to the Chicago Commission on Human Relations between 1945 and 1950.[28] A subsequent study found hundreds occurred in the Windy City from 1949 to July 1952, including "bombings, fires, or organized assaults against Negro families." There was, for example, a hit-and-run arson that killed ten people, and the bombing of the home of Dr. Percy Julian, a prominent black scientist. In July 1951, Governor Adlai Stevenson had to declare martial law in nearby Cicero to quell several days of rioting by whites who were determined to prevent a black war veteran from moving into a rental apartment in the town. Historian Thomas J. Sugrue has estimated that more than two hundred similar incidents occurred in Detroit between 1945 and 1965.[29] Philadelphia witnessed 213 racial attacks just in the first six months of 1955. Meanwhile, southern cities became the scenes of even more horrific violence. In Birmingham, for instance, three homes of blacks were dyna-mited on March 26, 1949. Then in April 1950, bombs ripped through the homes of a black minister and a black dentist. That December the home of a black woman who had led a fight against the city's zoning law was blown up. And in 1951, a series of bombings and arsons rocked Miami, after city officials sought to open to black applicants an FHA-financed housing develop-ment. Built in a white area adjacent to the segregated black com-munity of Liberty City, the apartment complex was originally intended for whites but was virtually empty when the violence began.[30]

Racial Rebellion of the 1960s and the Great Society Reforms

By the 1960s a huge demographic shift had taken place in urban America. Whereas 91 percent of the country's 9.8 million blacks in 1910 lived in the South and only 27 percent were residing in America's cities, by 1966 the nation's total black population not only had grown to 21.5 million, two-thirds of it was now con-centrated in the cities, and nearly half of blacks were living out-side the South. In addition, some of the biggest cities, New York,

Los Angeles, and Chicago, now had significant populations of Mexicans and Puerto Ricans.[31]

Those newcomers faced rampant government-sanctioned racial segregation in housing, a practice, as we have seen, that was increasingly enforced by mob violence and terror. On top of that, urban renewal programs kept pushing tens of thousands of them from the inner city into adjacent neighborhoods. Panicked white residents promptly headed for the suburbs, and the "changing" neighborhoods they left behind then began to resemble the ghettos urban renewal had bulldozed. And to make matters worse, industries, especially those that paid the highest wages, had begun relocating to the suburbs as well, leaving fewer and fewer jobs available in the central cities and decimating municipal tax revenues.

The urban riots that swept the nation during the 1960s were in many ways a direct response by black and brown city dwellers to decades of segregation and mistreatment from government, police, and the real estate industry. Hundreds of violent incidents erupted throughout the decade, some of the biggest being the Watts uprising in Los Angeles (1965), Chicago's Division Street riot (1966), and Detroit and Newark (1967).

But the 1960s also marked the liberal reform era of the Kennedy and Johnson administrations. From his first days in office, John F. Kennedy promised a "magna carta" for the cities. He appointed Robert Weaver, a veteran of Roosevelt's New Deal, to run the Housing and Home Finance Agency. A long-standing advocate of public housing and a respected African American scholar, Weaver had spent decades fighting segregation, and had warned during the Truman years that "federal housing policies, more than any single factor, determine the racial patterns of the cities of tomorrow." At Weaver's urging, Kennedy signed an executive order in November 1962 to ban discrimination in housing financed by federal dollars and he fought unsuccessfully with Congress to create a cabinet-level Department of Housing and Urban Development. But Kennedy's legacy toward the cities was ultimately a mixed one. His executive order, for instance, applied only to new public housing, not to the existing stock, and he shifted a large percentage of new construction to units for the elderly, so that by 1964 one-fourth of all tenants in low-income public housing units nationwide were senior citizens. He also sharply increased funding for urban renewal, even if his administration did require more attention than in the past to providing housing for those displaced by the program.[32]

It was not until Lyndon Johnson declared his War on Poverty and his Great Society vision in 1964 that the federal government veered away from the growth machine model and started to address the actual needs of city dwellers. Faced with a growing urban crisis, Johnson vowed in March 1964 that "in the next forty years we must rebuild the entire urban United States. . . . Our society will never be great until our cities are great."

His landslide election victory over conservative Republican Barry Goldwater that November also gave him a veto-proof Democratic majority in Congress, and that majority, fueled by growing public concern over racial violence in the cities, then voted to approve much of Johnson's ambitious Great Society agenda. A remarkable stream of legislation ensued between 1964 and 1968 to address income inequality, civil rights, and the plight of the cities. The Urban Mass Transportation Act of 1964 and the High Speed Ground Transportation Act of 1965, for example, provided the first major federal aid for mass transit and high-speed trains, instead of just highway construction. The Housing Acts of 1964 and 1965 dramatically increased funding for public housing, urban renewal, and subsidies to house the elderly, veterans, and college students. In late 1965, the new Department of Housing and Urban Development was finally created, with Johnson appointing as its first secretary the public housing stalwart Weaver. Meanwhile, a provision of the Civil Rights Act of 1964 outlawed discrimination in any federally funded housing projects, and the Civil Rights Act of 1968 then extended that ban to private housing.

To combat poverty, Johnson created the Office of Economic Opportunity in 1964; he won passage of the Elementary and Secondary School Act of 1965, which provided special funding to poor school districts; and he secured approval of Medicare and Medicaid in 1965. He also signed the historic Voting Rights Act that same year, and over the next ten years black mayors swept into office for the first time in Gary, Indiana; Cleveland; Washington, D.C.; Newark, New Jersey; Detroit; Atlanta; Los Angeles; Cincinnati; Tallahassee, and a dozen other cities. Then in 1966, Johnson signed the Model Cities Act, which sought to foster greater grassroots participation by inner-city residents in government programs, but which ended up becoming the most controversial and least successful of all his Great Society efforts.

To help shape his vision, Johnson relied on a slew of commissions he appointed, including two that specifically addressed urban policy: the Advisory Commission on Civil Disorders, better known as the Kerner Commission, after its chairman, Illinois governor Otto Kerner Jr., and the Commission on Urban Problems, headed by Paul H. Douglas, the liberal former senator from Illinois. Both bodies delivered voluminous reports to Congress in 1968 with dire calls for immediate federal action to head off further racial and economic crisis in the nation's cities.

Each highlighted the grave danger facing urban America from the combination of a growing nonwhite population mired in poverty around the urban commercial centers and the massive white flight to middle-class suburbia. The Kerner Commission condemned both government and white institutions for fostering that divide. "What white Americans have never fully understood but what the Negro can never forget," the commission concluded, "is that white society is deeply implicated in the ghetto. White institutions created it, white institutions maintain it, and white society condones it."[33]

The Douglas Commission, as I will refer to it, saw inner-city housing problems as a major factor for urban decline, particularly decades of government urban renewal, code enforcement, and highway programs that "destroyed more housing for the poor than government at all levels has created." Such demolitions, it found, had eliminated 397,287 private units for the poor, while only 357,291 public housing units had been constructed in their place by 1967—a net loss nationwide of some 40,000 units. Its tabulation on a city-by-city basis was staggering. New York, for example, which received by far the largest share of public housing construction of any metropolis, counted 64,633 public housing units in existence by 1967, most of them having been built during 1950s and 1960s, but the commission also revealed that *56,414 private low-income units had been destroyed* since the 1930s either to make way for the new public housing or because of urban renewal and highway construction—for a net gain of just 8,219 units. Many big cities racked up significant net losses, including Philadelphia (-6,417), Detroit (-3,883), Baltimore (-7,136), Boston (-6,413), and New Orleans (-7,857). The result, the commission said, was an alarming concentration of people of color in ghetto housing, with nonwhite households occupying a third of the nation's substandard rental units in 1967 even though they made up just 16 percent of all rentals.[34]

The two commissions urged the federal government to embark on massive construction of low-income housing to improve the lives of inner-city residents. "To expect the free market to supply housing for all Americans without subsidy requires a flight from reality," the Douglas Commission concluded. "We have to turn to government at every level to help finance an adequate supply of minimum-standard housing, especially in the inner cities." It urged a goal of 2 million to 2.5 million total new housing units a year, with at least 500,000 of them set aside for low- and moderate-income Americans. Furthermore, it was essential to reduce segregation through construction in the suburbs and outlying white neighborhoods of scattered-site projects—small clusters of low-rise public housing units—and through increased federal subsidies for rental housing and for home mortgages, both groups insisted. Johnson's 1968 Housing and Urban Development Act set the lofty goal of 6 million low- and moderate-income units within ten years. It also pioneered the concept of public-private partnerships by offering government subsidies to private developers to build low-income housing. And while the goals of that legislation were not reached, it nonetheless achieved impressive results. Between 1969 and 1973, the federal government sparked production of 867,000 units of low-cost housing, more than had been built in all the decades since the New Deal. Of that total, only 359,000 were traditional public housing, while more than half (508,000) were government-subsidized private units for either rental or home ownership.[35]

Major corporate leaders, having recognized the potential for future civil disorder if social conditions in urban America did not change rapidly, agreed to join with the federal government to rebuild the inner cities. The Johnson era thus represented a historic attempt to devise policies for urban dwellers who were most in need. Between 1960 and 1973, the combination of economic prosperity and Great Society programs reduced by half the number of Americans living in poverty, with African Americans and the elderly recording significant economic gains. But such reforms would soon be cut short.[36]

The Nixon Era Brings Back the Growth Machine

The failure of his Vietnam War policies prompted Johnson not to seek reelection in 1968, and a backlash by white voters against his civil rights agenda then made possible Republican Richard Nixon's narrow victory over Democrat Hubert Humphrey in the race for the White House. The Nixon era signaled a return to power of the growth machine in national urban policy. Real estate and banking interests set to work immediately to either dismantle or privatize government programs that had been created during the Roosevelt or Kennedy and Johnson eras. Over the next few decades, through both Democratic and Republican administrations, that growth machine was largely triumphant. During his first two years in office, for example, Nixon slashed in half the budget of HUD, the main federal agency concerned with the cities. He shifted federal aid into revenue-sharing grants for states and cities to apportion as they saw fit. In 1973, he ordered a moratorium on all new federally funded housing construction, blasting many housing projects as "monstrous, depressing places" that were "crime-ridden and falling apart." His weakening of HUD, however, led to shoddy oversight of a key Johnson-era program meant to increase FHA home loans to inner-city minority buyers. Real estate speculators routinely abused the program and hoodwinked purchasers, and the result was a national FHA scandal. More than 20 percent of mortgages under the program defaulted and tens of thousands of inner-city homes ended up abandoned—as many as 36,000 in Philadelphia, 15,000 in Detroit, and 10,000 in St. Louis.[37]

In addition, Nixon rejected efforts by his own HUD secretary, the politically moderate former governor of Michigan George Romney, to cut off federal funds to local governments that were refusing to enforce the 1968 Civil Rights Act's ban on housing discrimination. The president even blocked HUD plans that were already in the works for new scattered-site public housing in suburban white areas. But with Democrats still in control of Congress, his efforts to reverse Great Society programs and to permanently end funding for public housing were temporarily stymied.

Not until Nixon's resignation in the wake of the Watergate scandal did Congress finally pass his most far-reaching plan for the cities, the Housing and Community Development Act of 1974. One of the act's key provisions began to shift responsibility for public housing even more into private hands. It authorized HUD and local housing authorities to contract with landlords and developers to supply low- and moderate-income units in return for either project-based or individual tenant-based federal rent subsidies. That program, known as Section 8, would later emerge as the main form of federal housing assistance. Another provision of the 1974 act dramatically reduced the federal role in cities by merging a host of existing projects like urban renewal and Model Cities into a block grant program for cities to use as they chose. And a third provision declared as a new federal goal "the spatial deconcentration of housing opportunities for persons of lower income and the revitalization of deteriorating or deteriorated neighborhoods."[38]

That new goal of spatial deconcentration soon engendered widespread opposition from black housing advocates and intellectuals who saw it as a veiled attempt to dismantle growing black political power in the cities. Its key proponent was Chicago economist Anthony Downs. A top housing and transportation consultant to federal agencies for decades, Downs had written portions of the Kerner Commission report and was appointed by Johnson to the Douglas Commission. Before that, he worked at the RAND Corp. and was on the board of directors of Chicago's Real Estate Research Corporation, one of the nation's most influential real estate consulting groups. RERC had been founded in 1931 by Anthony Downs's father, James C. Downs. The elder Downs worked closely at RERC with Homer Hoyt and other pioneers of the racially biased appraisal and risk criteria that FHA later adopted. During the 1940s and 1950s, James Downs also served as Chicago's housing and redevelopment coordinator; he spearheaded the city's construction of racially segregated high-rise public housing projects and such controversial urban renewal efforts as the new University of Illinois campus on the Near West Side, which displaced thousands of low-income residents, nearly half of them Mexican American.[39]

In 1961, the younger Downs began urging more deliberate measures to reduce the percentage of poor and minority populations in our cities. According to him, "middle-income and upper-income white families will not move into central cities in any large numbers unless cultural (not racial) homogeneity of local neighborhoods can somehow be reconstituted." Downs proposed, according to one urban planning expert, a "truly massive urban renewal program," one "so large that whole neighborhoods of high-school-district size would be demolished and replaced by newly constructed developments occupied by middle-class residents."[40]

While the goal of spatial deconcentration sounded similar to the liberal recommendations from the Kerner and Douglas commissions to integrate more blacks into suburban neighborhoods, its practical effect was to provide federal approval for removing even more blacks and Hispanics from the inner cities, while it did nothing to eliminate housing segregation. Both the Nixon and Ford administrations, after all, refused to press for subsidized low-income housing in the suburbs, so local housing authorities and private landlords were limited to using the Nixon-era Section 8 program within city boundaries—most often in neighborhoods adjacent to the inner city. Thus, those people displaced by commercial projects, by university expansion, or by new middle-income housing ended up reconcentrated in those new neighborhoods, which in turn became segregated as white residents fled.[41]

From Carter to Clinton, the Growth Machine Triumphs

The federal government's retreat from public housing soon turned into a stampede. The one-term presidency of Democrat

Jimmy Carter continued the budget austerity of Nixon and Ford toward low-income housing. Carter's signature initiative for the cities, Urban Development Action Grants, simply resurrected the old urban renewal approach with a new title. During its first two years, the federal UDAG program leveraged nearly $3 billion in private investment in 214 cities, but most of the money went to commercial projects like downtown and waterfront shopping complexes and hotels, with only 10 percent for residential housing.[42]

Once Ronald Reagan succeeded Carter, the White House effectively declared war on public housing and the urban poor. During his two terms in office, Reagan reduced the budget of HUD by two-thirds—from $33.4 billion in 1980 to $10.2 billion in 1988—more than any other federal agency.[43] His initial plan called for terminating all new public housing construction, demolishing or selling existing units, and moving instead to "vouchers" that tenants could use in the private market. Reagan also wanted existing tenants of subsidized housing to pay a higher percentage of their income for rent, and he sought to create "enterprise zones" in blighted inner-city areas, where businesses could receive huge tax credits and exemptions for creating jobs. Fierce opposition by a Democratic majority in the House stalled many of his most extreme proposals, but Reagan nonetheless intensified the dismantling of federal aid to cities begun under Nixon, Ford, and Carter. Annual starts for all federal low-rent programs, for instance, plummeted from 183,000 in 1980 to just 28,000 by 1985, and Reagan eventually succeeded in getting Congress to authorize both a voucher program and the selling of some public housing units to tenants. His policies were ardently backed by think tanks like the Heritage Foundation and the Brookings Institution, whose prescriptions for urban housing reform included the sale of all public housing and the elimination of HUD altogether.

Soon after Reagan left office, however, two colossal housing corruption scandals that originated during his tenure became public. One was the savings and loan industry collapse and the other involved HUD's low-income housing programs. The savings and loan debacle was made possible after Congress passed a 1982 law backed by the White House to deregulate the thrift industry. The law was meant to spur home lending, but its reduction of government oversight allowed speculators to gobble up thrift banks and recklessly lend money to hundreds of commercial projects and multifamily rental units, all backed by the Federal Savings and Loan Insurance Corp. Bailout costs eventually reached $500 billion. Meanwhile, Reagan's HUD secretary Samuel Pierce had turned the agency's dwindling housing program into a patronage piggy bank. A young executive assistant to Pierce doled out huge consultant fees to former cabinet officials like James Watt and John Mitchell, and steered funding for federally subsidized housing projects to former agency bureaucrats and developer clients of top Republican office holders on Capitol Hill. Those office-holders in turn pocketed large lobbying fees from their clients. Instead of building low-income housing, the agency financed "luxury apartments, swimming pools, golf courses and the like for the cronies of HUD officials." After years of investigations by a special federal prosecutor, seventeen people, many of them former HUD officials, were convicted of corruption, with Pierce forced to enter into a plea agreement in which he admitted "improper and even criminal conduct" by his subordinates but managed to avoid arrest.[44]

Reagan's successor, George H.W. Bush, continued the pro-business growth model toward cities. Along with his HUD secretary Jack Kemp, Bush pressed Congress to sharply cut any remnants of Great Society programs and to greatly expand rental vouchers for low-income people, to allow public housing tenants to purchase their units—a program labeled HOPE (Home Ownership for People Everywhere)—and to establish enterprise zones to subsidize business investment in the inner city. But the Democratic majority in Congress resisted the Bush agenda, so the housing bills that emerged marked compromises by both sides. The Housing Act of 1990, for instance, authorized funding for the HOPE program but also increased public housing funds for the homeless and for AIDS victims. Nonetheless, overall federal aid to cities kept plummeting. According to one report, the budgets of the nation's fifty largest cities rose by 90 percent between 1980 and 1990, yet federal contribution to that spending dropped from 17 percent to 6 percent.

In the two decades following the launch of Johnson's Great Society programs, the urban crisis deepened. The nation's stock of low-income housing dropped from 6.5 million in 1970 to 5.6 million in 1985, even as the number of low-income households increased sharply, from 6.2 million to 8.9 million. Both the number of homeless Americans and the poverty rate of the inner cities soared and racial segregation in housing saw little change, except for an increase in housing discrimination actions during the Bush years. Even as government tilted more toward the growth machine policies, efforts to revitalize the cities did little to help the working class and poor. When Nixon came into office in 1969, 30 percent of inner-city residents were poor, but by the time Bush lost his reelection bid to Bill Clinton in 1992, that rate had grown to 42 percent.[45]

Bill Clinton, much like fellow Democrat Jimmy Carter, crafted an urban policy that relied more on the private market and less on direct federal spending. Its centerpiece was the empowerment zone program that Clinton got Congress to approve as part of a 1993 budget bill. The empowerment zones—another version of the Reagan- and Bush-era enterprise zones—provided lucrative tax benefits for new investments in the inner city, including elimination of capital gains taxes. In effect, they were a more oblique way for government to subsidize the private sector instead of through direct spending. At the same time, Clinton's successful increase of the federal minimum wage, and his expansion of the earned income tax credit, along with the nation's overall economic prosperity during his two terms in office, did result in significant income growth for the nation's poor and for low-income workers. And during Clinton's presidency, HUD began funding local housing groups to monitor banks for fair lending practices, a program that soon opened the door for groups like ACORN and others to assume big roles in neighborhood housing battles in many cities.

Equally important in their impact on the cities were the historic crime and welfare reform bills that Clinton signed in 1994 and 1996 to stave off the growing conservative movement that brought Republican control of Congress. But the 1994 crime bill's huge funding ($30 billion) for more police, prisons, and crime prevention reduced the amount of money available for housing and for general aid to cities. And once the Republicans gained control of the House and Senate, they drastically cut HUD's budget, they eliminated all new Section 8 vouchers, and they demanded deep cuts in public housing. To save his agency from extinction, HUD secretary Henry Cisneros promised to begin tearing down the most distressed public housing towers under the Hope VI program and to give displaced tenants Section 8 vouchers so they could move to other neighborhoods. As a result, little remaining new public housing was built by the federal government. Those concessions eventually allowed the Section 8 program to survive, and it is now by far the largest federal housing program. Nearly 3.3 million privately owned housing units currently receive federal subsidies, either through personal vouchers or as part of multifamily Section 8 developments. By comparison, there remain only 1.1 million public housing units nationwide, with New York City's nearly 180,000 units by far the largest number. Five other cities, Philadelphia, Chicago, Boston, Los Angeles, and Baltimore, have a combined total of 65,000 units. And according to the Center for Budget Priorities, the $46 billion cost of all federal low-income housing programs in 2008 was dwarfed by the $144 billion in tax breaks the government gave that year to home owners.[46]

3

Radical Outsider
or Political Insider?

We ran a war room in the campaign against overturn-
ing term limits, and Bill was the quarterback. He quickly
became a leader of the opposition to Bloomberg and Quinn.

—Jonathan Rosen

In March 1995, less than a year after his marriage to Chirlane McCray, thirty-three-year-old Bill de Blasio took charge of his first successful political campaign, though he was not an actual candidate. The occasion was a special election for the sixty-eighth state assembly district from East Harlem, the city's most storied Latino neighborhood. Angelo Del Toro, the previous assembly-man, had held the seat for twenty years until he suddenly collapsed in late 1994 of a fatal heart attack. So influential had Del Toro become by the time of his death that many of the city's political elite showed up at his funeral, including Governor George Pataki, Mayor Rudy Giuliani, and former governor Mario Cuomo. But the deceased politician had also been a master of corruption, having amassed considerable wealth for himself and some of his family members over the years by controlling a web of poverty programs and patronage appointments.

The Democratic Party moved in short order to anoint his brother, William Del Toro, as its candidate to succeed Angelo in the special election, thus making William the presumptive favorite. In doing so, the party bosses ignored several inconvenient facts about him. Back in 1973, for instance, while directing a major East Harlem poverty program he and his brother had founded, William was charged with fraud and perjury in a $70,000 bribery conspiracy involving the federal Model Cities program. He was subsequently convicted and served nine months in prison, though the bribery count was later overturned. Nor did the bosses care that in 1989 a firm connected to William had owned an East Harlem brownstone for which they charged rents at double the neighborhood's average rate to several state-funded tenants—including his own brother Angelo's district office—thus producing thousands of dollars in profit for William and some of his partners in this venture. Or that in 1991, when William ran in the Democratic primary for city council, some of his supporters engaged in apparent election fraud. In that contest, Del Toro was initially declared the winner by thirty-five votes, until his main opponent, Adam Clayton Powell IV, challenged the results and documented more than a thousand irregularities in the balloting. Among them: twenty people who were listed as registered voters at William Del Toro's 106th Street brownstone home, including eleven Del Toros, even though many of them actually resided outside the district. It turned out that more votes were tallied on election day for Del Toro at several polling locations controlled by his supporters than the actual number of people who had signed in to vote. Based on that evidence, the courts promptly ordered a new election, and Powell then crushed Del Toro with 73 percent of the vote.[1]

Four years later, here was shameless Bill Del Toro running for office again as the official Democratic Party candidate. But this time a community leader named Francisco Diaz dared to challenge him. Diaz, the young and inexperienced manager of East Harlem's community board, was recruited to run for the seat by Bill de Blasio's old friend Patrick Gaspard, who was then handling political affairs for the powerful health care workers union,

1199/SEIU. The union was especially influential in East Harlem, as it counted many members who were employed at the nearby Mt. Sinai and Harlem Hospitals and who also were residents of the neighborhood. Gaspard recommended to Diaz that he hire de Blasio as campaign manager, and he threw the union's resources behind their effort. Their defiant bid received an added boost when Harlem congressman Charlie Rangel and Manhattan's liberal borough president Ruth Messinger decided to buck the Democratic Party and throw their support to Diaz.[2]

At the time, both 1199 and the Communication Workers of America were nurturing a new political group called the New Party. It was the brainchild of ACORN's Jon Kest and of former ACORN organizer Dan Cantor, and it sought to take advantage of state election law that allowed fusion tickets—the cross endorsement of a single candidate by more than one party—to forge an organized left wing among progressive Democrats. The effort won initial backing from several Democratic Party elders with close ties to former mayor Dinkins. Two of them, Bill Lynch and Harold Ickes, were still furious that Dinkins had lost his reelection bid in 1993 by a slim margin of fifty thousand votes that the tiny Liberal Party garnered on its ballot line for Republican Rudy Giuliani. Lynch and Ickes thus envisioned the New Party as their potential counterweight to the Liberal Party, and it would later evolve into the present-day Working Families Party.[3]

The Democratic Party in New York was at its nadir at that point and had nothing to lose. Not only had Giuliani prevailed over Dinkins in the 1993 mayoral race, but the following year, a little-known, first-time state senator from Peekskill, George Pataki, had pulled off an upset victory over Mario Cuomo, the state's three-time governor and liberal Democratic lion, all part of the Republican tide that also brought Congress under the control of Newt Gingrich.

Moreover, the grip of the old-line party bosses over the electorate had waned over the years. Tammany Hall, the infamous political machine with its corrupt control of city jobs and contracts, was by then the stuff of historical lore. The last of its bosses had been Carmine De Sapio in the 1960s with his Tamawa Club in Greenwich Village. Ever since then, liberal reform movements had arisen periodically within the separate county Democratic Party operations of Manhattan, the Bronx, Queens, Brooklyn, and Staten Island, each promising to do away with pay-to-play politics. But many of those reformers ended up co-opted. A young Ed Koch, for example, had wavered repeatedly between membership in De Sapio's Tamawa Club and its liberal reform competitor group, the Village Independent Democrats, before finally wresting leadership of the reform group. But when Koch faced off against Mario Cuomo in the historic 1977 Democratic Party run-off for mayor, he garnered the backing of key party bosses Pat Cunningham and Stanley Friedman in the Bronx, of Charlie Rangel, Percy Sutton, and the Harlem black leaders who controlled Manhattan Democrats, and of Brooklyn's gruff, cigar-chomping Meade Esposito, whom Koch had once labeled a "gangster." Esposito would boast years later to *Village Voice* writer Jack Newfield: "I get whatever I fuckin' want [from Koch]. I told him not to dump our captains, and he said no problems. He promised me access and that he would be a good mayor. He kept his word on both scores."[4] But the municipal scandals that erupted during Koch's third term as mayor ended up with several key party leaders indicted and convicted for corruption, including Friedman and Esposito.

In East Harlem in 1995, de Blasio and Diaz collected enough petitions to have their own newly declared Independence Fusion Party placed on the ballot in the East Harlem race. In New York, a state infamous for its arcane regulations for gathering valid signatures on a nominating petition, most insurgent candidates never make it on the ballot. They are often derailed by the expensive and time-consuming process of defending challenges to their nominating petitions in court, the very courts where all the judges owe their positions to the party bosses who select them to run for the bench. But young de Blasio was already displaying a skill that would be invaluable in his political ascent: his relentless attention to details. Once on the ballot, Diaz then stunned the political experts by capturing 59 percent of the vote against Del Toro. It was de Blasio's first experience with a come-from-behind victory, but it would not be his last.[5]

The lanky campaign operative so impressed Rangel and other New York Democratic Party leaders with his work for Diaz that the following year they entrusted him with the job of running the Clinton-Gore reelection effort in New York State. Admittedly, there was no danger of Democrats losing a traditional blue state like New York. "Harold Ickes hired Bill to run everything and choose his own staff but told him there was no money to pay them," recalled Peter Ragone, who served as the communications director under de Blasio for that campaign. Their work for Clinton-Gore would be the start of a two-decade friendship between the two men. There was a big advantage to their volunteer labor, however. Given New York's position as the country's media capital, President Clinton and Vice President Gore flew into town repeatedly for fund-raisers or to draw local press attention, and de Blasio would always be on the scene to greet them, thus ingratiating himself to the Clintons and top Democratic officials and getting to know some of the party's wealthiest donors.

Two months after Clinton and Gore's victory over Republican challengers Bob Dole and Jack Kemp, Secretary of Housing Henry Cisneros, the former mayor of San Antonio and the highest-ranking Latino in the administration, suddenly resigned following months of controversy over his possible cover-up of cash payments he'd made to a former mistress. Clinton selected Andrew Cuomo, an assistant secretary to Cisneros, as the new secretary of HUD. Not long after that, publicist Ken Sunshine called Cuomo, his friend of many years, on behalf of de Blasio and secured for him a job interview at HUD. "I remember yelling at

Andrew, you've got to hire this kid or he's going to go to some other organization and you're going to lose him," Sunshine said. Cuomo eventually appointed de Blasio director of HUD's New York–New Jersey region and later hired Ragone to run HUD's media office.[6]

The Rise and Fall of ACORN

It was while he was working at HUD that de Blasio came into regular contact with the Association of Community Organizations for Reform Now, better known as ACORN. The boisterous group was already a household name to many politicians across the country, and especially to President Bill Clinton. After all, ACORN was born in Clinton's home state of Arkansas and its leaders backed him in his races for Arkansas attorney general and governor. Once Clinton entered the White House, his administration secured two key reforms that helped spur ACORN's rapid growth—the 1994 Voter Registration Act, or Motor Voter Law, which required states to provide the public easier access to voter registration forms, and beefed-up enforcement of the Community Reinvestment Act by the Department of Housing and Urban Development. CRA was the Carter-era law that required federal oversight of whether banks were redlining minority neighborhoods for home mortgages. Under Clinton's toughening of the law, Secretary Cisneros began approving funding for local groups like ACORN to monitor bank-lending practices. This occurred just as a series of bank mergers were sweeping the financial industry, and it provided community groups new leverage to delay or block those mergers until the banks agreed to improve lending policies to inner-city neighborhoods.

One of New York ACORN's leaders by then was a mercurial African American activist named Bertha Lewis. A former theater producer turned tenant organizer, Lewis had been put in charge of ACORN's first-time home buyer's program in the late 1990s by Jon Kest. Before long, she got to know de Blasio as the man at HUD who was sympathetic to ACORN's efforts to get banks and real estate agents not to discriminate against blacks and Latinos seeking to buy homes in Brooklyn. Kest, Lewis, and several other ACORN leaders and former organizers—among them, Jon's older brother Steve Kest, Valerie Berlin, Dan Cantor, Emma Wolfe, Harold Miller, Peter Colavito, Jonathan Westin—along with successor organizations that ACORN spawned after the group's collapse in 2010 would later play pivotal roles in de Blasio's political ascent, and several landed roles in his city hall administration.[7]

ACORN's influence on today's progressive politics reached far beyond New York to the forgotten slums and rubble-strewn neighborhoods of North and West Philadelphia and Chicago's South Side, to Richmond, California, and all across urban America, as thousands of low-income African American and Latino workers suddenly started squatting in abandoned homes, marching outside of bank headquarters, disrupting city council meetings, and registering people to vote. The group's importance was perhaps better grasped by conservative Republicans, who worked tirelessly for years to undermine and discredit ACORN, than by its liberal allies, many of whom deserted the organization once it began to implode in 2008 from a combination of financial mismanagement and a withering campaign of McCarthy-like attacks from conservative groups and Republicans in Congress.

But ACORN's rise and fall remains a crucial subplot of our story. It is one that goes back to 1969, when Wade Rathke, a tall, lanky long-haired white student radical at Williams College in Massachusetts and a member of the Students for a Democratic Society, landed a job in Springfield as a community organizer for the National Welfare Rights Organization. NWRO itself had been founded in 1966 by African American civil rights leader and former chemist George Wiley, with its main goals being to secure for the inner-city poor all the welfare benefits allowed by federal law, and to achieve more political influence for its dues-paying members.

Rathke proved an adept student of his mentor Wiley. He organized well-publicized sit-ins at Springfield welfare offices by the female recipients and their children. Before long, Rathke started to dream of building an organization to tackle not just welfare benefits but a variety of issues faced by the country's working poor and the middle class. Inspired by the writings of the legendary Chicago organizer Saul Alinsky, and by Alinsky's fellow strategist Fred Ross, who had worked with Cesar Chavez to build the United Farm Workers Organizing Committee, Rathke convinced Wiley in 1970 to allow him to launch a similar group in Arkansas. Rathke called it the Arkansas Community Organization for Reform Now, and within a few years he had recruited dozens of former college students, many of them graduates of Ivy League schools, to work as organizers for it.

Rathke rejected, however, the Alinsky model of building coalitions among neighborhood churches and civic groups. He opted instead for a grassroots membership organization, and he sent his organizers door to door to recruit individuals to pay dues of $5 a month. He also emphasized civil disobedience, sit-ins, and disruptive protests by his members to pressure government and corporate officials to address their needs.[8]

Over the next forty years, ACORN mushroomed into the largest organization of poor people in the country. It boasted more than 400,000 members and had over 1,200 neighborhood chapters in more than one hundred cities. More important, its leaders cultivated relationships with liberal politicians and key labor unions, often coordinating voter registration and get-out-the-vote efforts that could help their allies.

In several cities, ACORN organizers led drives to win union recognition for low-paid workers. In New Orleans, Rathke himself organized service and hotel workers into Local 100, while in the Midwest ACORN leaders Dan Cantor and Keith Kelleher led drives for fast-food and factory workers in several states under the banner of the United Labor Unions. The various ACORN labor groups eventually affiliated to the Service Employees International Union in 1984. Meanwhile in New York City, the United Federation of Teachers hired ACORN leader Fran Streich in 2001 as a community organizer.

"We formed something called the Brooklyn Education Collaborative to fight for more science labs in Brooklyn's middle schools," Streich, the wife of Jon Kest, recalled. That group later became the Coalition of Educational Justice, which continues to advocate for improved public schools today. A few years later, ACORN joined with the UFT in the largest successful union organizing drive in New York City in half a century, with 28,000 home day care providers voting in October 2007 to join the teachers union. Streich helped to coordinate the drive as a UFT staff member, and ACORN members knocked on thousands of doors to mobilize the day care workers to vote.[9]

But even as ACORN grew rapidly, it failed to address glaring internal flaws. The biggest was the inordinate power Rathke wielded over the entire organization. On paper there was an elected board of directors that was in charge of the group's policy. But in reality, Rathke, as the chief organizer, made all major decisions in consultation with the inner circle of lead organizers who had been with him since ACORN's founding and who came to be known as "the bishops."

"Wade Rathke was God, everybody trembled in fear of him," said Bertha Lewis, one of the few African Americans who rose to become a lead organizer during ACORN's early years. But in June 2008, it came to light that ACORN's chief financial officer, Wade Rathke's brother Dale, had embezzled nearly $1 million from the group during the late 1990s. Even worse, Wade had kept the scandal secret from the board for more than eight years while his brother and the Rathke family sought to pay back the money. During that time, he had even kept Dale on the ACORN payroll.

"Everybody within the organization was traumatized," Bertha
Lewis recalled. "We just had no idea this was happening." The
board members felt especially betrayed because they were legally
responsible for ACORN's finances.

Beyond ACORN's authoritarian structure, an obvious racial
flaw had gone unaddressed for too long. The group's mass membership, even its board of directors, was overwhelmingly African
American, Latino, and poor, yet the organizers who had made
all the key decisions since ACORN's inception were almost all
white and middle class. "Once they felt betrayed by this embez-
zlement thing, the board members were determined the person
at the helm was going to be a person of color," Lewis said. The
board promptly fired both Wade and Dale Rathke and handed
control of ACORN to Lewis, who until then had been a co-
leader with Jon Kest of the New York City chapter.[10]

As soon as she took the helm, Lewis discovered even greater
financial problems. The organization owed more than $1 million
in payroll taxes to the IRS, it had failed for many months to pay
health insurance and retirement benefits for staff members, as well
as bills from vendors, and, even though it was handling tens of
millions of dollars in federal and foundation grants, there was no
indemnity insurance for the board of directors.

And the troubles kept mounting. ACORN's massive voter registration drive in the months preceding Barack Obama's
2008 race drew the ire of Republicans in Congress who lodged
unproven claims of voter fraud. Then came the now-infamous
series of undercover videos by right-wing filmmaker James
O'Keefe. Broadcast on Fox News in late 2009, they featured
O'Keefe, dressed as a supposed pimp, visiting various ACORN
offices around the country with a young woman, and asking for
tax advice on opening a sex trafficking business and other illegal
scams. In several of the videos, ACORN staff members appeared
to provide the couple counseling on what they could do legally.
Republicans in Congress seized on the sensational footage and

began cutting off federal funding to the group. By then, many of ACORN's foundation donors started to desert the group as well. In November 2010, Bertha Lewis, unable to stanch the financial losses, declared the organization bankrupt and closed its doors. Before that, however, several chapters in various parts of the country reincorporated under new names, and continued to do much of the same grassroots work they had done as part of ACORN.

From Community School Board to Hillary Clinton Campaign Manager

In 1999, when ACORN was still a growing force in New York City, Bill de Blasio resigned his post at HUD and ran for election to the school board in his Brooklyn neighborhood, Community Board 15, a nonsalaried post. His successful race received crucial support from ACORN members. School board elections, of course, are routine events across America, but they were not even permitted in New York City until 1969, when state lawmakers, responding to demands for community control that were sweeping the city's black and brown neighborhoods—especially in the aftermath of the racially charged 1968 teachers' strike—passed a school decentralization law that authorized elections for more than thirty new local school boards and granted those boards limited powers vis-à-vis the central Board of Education. While they could not make decisions on curriculum, the hiring of professional employees, or major service contracts, the local boards had the power to choose their own school superintendent. They also exerted influence over the hiring of school aides and minor purchasing contracts, and they determined how their school buildings could be used for evening community activities.[11] In the decades that followed, city school board elections drew tens of thousands of inner-city parents into battles over educational policy, and the boards emerged as stepping-stones to higher office for a slew of budding politicians, especially in minority communities. But many of them also became notorious both for petty corruption and for their abysmal parent voter turnout. One of the first reforms Michael Bloomberg achieved upon entering city hall in 2002 was to get the state legislature to abolish the local school boards, and replace the old central Board of Education, a majority of whose members had been named by the borough presidents, with a new Panel for Educational Policy, for which the mayor held the majority of appointments. In addition, the mayor was granted sole authority to appoint the schools chancellor. Henceforth, all power over the recentralized school system would be in the hands of the mayor. Many lauded the end of decentralization, but the change also signaled a major step backward in the ability of the school system's parents, most of them black and Latino, to hold their neighborhood schools accountable for performance—a right suburban parents have always wielded over their own school systems.

De Blasio's stint on the board thus took place in the twilight of the school decentralization era, but it gave him valuable direct experience with the nuts-and-bolts of public education and it helped shape his views on school policy. District 15, for example, has long been one of the city's most innovative districts. Stretching from the middle-class brownstone neighborhoods of Park Slope and Windsor Terrace, through Carroll Gardens and the more working-class area of Sunset Park, it boasts many high-achieving schools and active parent groups. Its administrators rebuffed for years the national stampede toward high-stakes testing as the only measure of student performance, opting instead for a more holistic approach that tracked the portfolio of a child's work throughout the school year. De Blasio's own children, Dante and Chiara, benefited from that philosophy while attending one of the district's best schools, P.S. 372. In addition, their father served on the school board when it selected as its district superintendent a highly regarded principal from Manhattan's Upper

East Side, Carmen Fariña, who espoused the same progressive philosophy. Even after he left the board to run for city council in 2001, de Blasio spoke often with Fariña. "He wanted Carmen to teach him everything that she could," one member of the school board, Dorothy Siegel, told *Politico*. "Bill was her pupil." Their relationship would later prove to be a pivotal one for de Blasio as a mayoral candidate, with Fariña, long an advocate of early childhood education, helping him craft his signature plan for universal pre-kindergarten classes.[12]

While de Blasio was still on the school board, First Lady Hillary Clinton decided in 2000 to run for the U.S. senator from New York. Clinton family confidant Harold Ickes, along with the president of 1199, Dennis Rivera, urged her to hire de Blasio as her campaign manager. One night, de Blasio called his cousin John Wilhelm, asking for advice on whether to take the job. "I don't personally have a high regard for the Clintons," Wilhelm recalls telling him, "but you should do it if you think it's the right thing to do." De Blasio took the job and was immediately surprised by how much time the president himself dedicated to plotting strategy with him. On election day, Bill Clinton even agreed to conduct numerous phone-in interviews with local New York radio stations to get out the vote for his wife. Hillary's victorious senate campaign solidified de Blasio's reputation with the most powerful Democratic Party couple in the country. In addition, his ties with the activists of ACORN, the Working Families Party, and 1199 provided him a formidable network of labor and community supporters.[13]

A New Progressive Voice in City Council

Soon after Hillary Clinton's senate victory, de Blasio called his old friend Ken Sunshine, shared his plans to run for a city council seat from Brooklyn, and asked him to host a fund-raiser. "Bill had it all scoped out," Sunshine recalled. "He wanted to invite all these Hillary supporters. So the first fund-raiser he ever held was at my old apartment, and a lot of the Hillary people showed up."[14]

But a de Blasio triumph was hardly assured. The 39th Council District snakes from the liberal and affluent areas of Cobble Hill, Carroll Gardens, and Park Slope to the largely Orthodox Jewish neighborhood of Boro Park, to some mostly Hispanic sections of Sunset Park. Moreover, the crowded field of six candidates for the Democratic nomination included several with far more impressive résumés as progressive activists than de Blasio. There was, for instance, Jack Carroll, a lifelong resident of the neighborhood and one of a dying breed of Democratic Party reformers. And there was Steven Banks, a well-known housing activist and Legal Aid attorney who had successfully sued city agencies on behalf of the poor for more than two decades. Others included Anthony Pugliese, an organizer for the carpenters union; businessman Paul Bader, who was the husband of U.S. representative Nydia Velazquez; and community board manager Craig Hammerman, the favored candidate of Brooklyn's borough president Howard Golden.

Unsavory ties from de Blasio's past dogged him as well. Some local press accounts noted that during his time as a school board member, he had continued defending Frank DeStefano, the district superintendent who preceded Fariña, despite revelations of massive misspending by DeStefano on expensive junkets for district executives and huge budget deficits. In addition, one of the big contributors to de Blasio's council race turned out to be Israel Spitzer, the deputy mayor of the upstate Hasidic village of New Square, who donated $2,500, the maximum amount permissible by campaign finance law. During Hillary Clinton's race for senate the previous year, her campaign had courted Spitzer, and the residents of New Square subsequently delivered to her the phenomenal vote margin of 1,400 to 12. Shortly after the 2000 election, President Clinton, in an astonishing act of political payback, commuted the prison sentences of four New Square civic leaders who had been convicted of fraud, a decision that subsequently touched off an investigation by the U.S. attorney's office.[15]

The council race also posed a dilemma for the nascent Working Families Party that ACORN, 1199, and other unions had formed. Several WFP leaders wanted to endorse Banks, while others favored de Blasio. "Jon [Kest] saw something in Bill and wanted to support him," Steve Kest recalled, but given the divisions within WFP, Jon settled for keeping the party neutral in the council race.[16]

The Brooklyn contest, however, was eclipsed by far bigger events in the city that summer of 2001. Most media attention centered on a tough Democratic mayoral primary that pitted the liberal public advocate Mark Green against three contenders, Bronx borough president Fernando Ferrer, city comptroller Alan Hevesi, and city council speaker Peter Vallone. The winner was almost certain to face Republican Michael Bloomberg in a general election to succeed Mayor Giuliani, who could not run for office again because of a two-term limit voters had approved in a 1993 referendum. More important, the primary was scheduled for September 11, a day that was to become the most infamous in American history. Once the magnitude of the devastating terrorist attacks on the World Trade Center became clear, city officials hurriedly canceled the voting.

In the midst of that terrible day, an act of kindness from de Blasio cemented his relationship with labor leader John Wilhelm, his recently discovered older cousin. At the time, Wilhelm was living with his family in California, but his son Vincent was a recent college graduate who had moved to New York City the week before 9/11 to pursue a career as a writer, and had settled in a small apartment in Williamsburg. Vincent had never met de Blasio, but Wilhelm convinced his son to volunteer for the city council campaign as a way to begin meeting people. "So Vinnie was in some precinct passing out leaflets on September 11, and the world ends," Wilhelm recalled. "Bill and Chirlane first went and found their children Dante and Chiara, who were maybe six and four back then. But then Bill went back out, found Vinnie, and took him into their home. As a result, my son really bonded with them, and so did the rest of our family."[17]

The postponed mayoral and city council primary took place two weeks later. But with New Yorkers still reeling from the toll of nearly three thousand dead at Ground Zero, and with rescue crews still digging around the clock through the smoldering rubble for possible survivors, the contest received far less attention than usual. On primary night, the tally in Brooklyn's 39th Council District showed Bill de Blasio the victor with 5,161 votes, and second-place finisher Banks registering just 3,529.

Once again, though, all media coverage was focused elsewhere, this time on the mayoral contest, where Fernando Ferrer finished with the highest vote total among the Democratic contenders but fell short of the 40 percent threshold required to avoid a run-off with his closest rival, Mark Green. Most experts had expected Green to win handily, but his popularity plummeted after he endorsed an extraordinary request by Mayor Giuliani to extend his term for ninety days in order to deal with the aftermath of the 9/11 attack. That request met widespread opposition from the public and the city council. The head-to-head contest between Ferrer and Green two weeks later turned into an ugly and divisive battle. In the white areas of south Brooklyn, last-minute robocalls and anonymous flyers appeared warning voters that Rev. Al Sharpton, the controversial black leader and Ferrer supporter, would end up running things in city hall if Ferrer prevailed. After Green was declared the winner of the run-off by a slim margin, Ferrer's top aides claimed that the racially tinged last-minute flyers had tipped the vote. They demanded Green fire those responsible. Among the people they targeted was Jon Kest, the head of ACORN and founder of the Working Families Party, who was also managing Green's field operations campaign. Kest had attended a pre-election meeting where the use of anti-Sharpton flyers was discussed, though he later claimed those flyers had been issued without his authorization by a rogue campaign operative. When Green declined to fire Kest, several angry black and Latino leaders in the Ferrer campaign then refused to support Green's candidacy, and their boycott became a pivotal factor in Bloomberg's narrow victory in the November general election, as nearly 48 percent of Hispanics cast ballots for Bloomberg. The incident also sparked mistrust toward both ACORN and the Working Families Party among some African American and Latino leaders, a rift that would take years to overcome.[18]

De Blasio, however, managed to avoid any fallout from his own close ties to Jon Kest and ACORN, even after hiring ACORN's political director Peter Colavito as his first city council chief of staff. The new councilman from Brooklyn quickly developed a reputation for being a vocal advocate for the city's poor. When council speaker Gifford Miller named him chair of that body's General Welfare Committee, de Blasio hired a young policy whiz named Josh Wallack as his policy director, and he sought to mend fences with Legal Aid attorney Steven Banks, his former opponent in the council race. Before long, de Blasio was sponsoring bills vital to the low-income clients Banks served, bills that preserved, at the same time, city funding for the Legal Aid Society that Banks directed.

"One of the first things I remember is the legislation relating to domestic violence," Banks recalled. "The city would say you're not eligible for shelter because you can't prove you are a domestic violence survivor. De Blasio passed a bill that limited the proof that was needed. It was really an important piece of legislation that undid this problem."[19]

A few years later, a major dispute over housing discrimination brought Legal Aid and ACORN together behind legislation sponsored by de Blasio. At the time, many city landlords were refusing to rent apartments to tenants who received Section 8

housing certificates. "Bill was almost like one of the organizers and strategists working with our groups to get the legislation
through council," recalled Jonathan Rosen, one of the architects of that campaign. A former aide to Democratic politicians
in Albany, Rosen launched a public relations company in 2005
along with Valerie Berlin, one of the early ACORN organizers.
The firm, BerlinRosen, eventually became one of the city's most
influential messaging and strategy groups, its clients ranging from
major real estate developers, to labor unions, to top city politicians, and it would play a major role during 2013 in shaping the
message of Blasio's mayoral campaign. But at its start in 2005,
BerlinRosen's first client was Jon Kest and ACORN.[20]

Two years later, the owner of Starrett City in East New York,
Brooklyn, a mammoth middle-income housing complex that had
been built in the 1970s under the state's Mitchell-Lama subsidized
housing program, was on the verge of selling the property for
$1.3 billion to a developer who planned to turn it into market-
rate housing. Jon Kest and Bertha Lewis were determined to save
the more than 5,800 apartments as affordable units, especially
since many ACORN members were residents at Starrett City.
They enlisted the help of their friend de Blasio, who by then was
in his second term in the council.

"We worked with every community and housing preservation
group in the city and built a huge campaign," Jonathan Rosen
recalled. "Bill was a very vocal and active elected official in our
Starrett City campaign." In June 2008, federal and state officials
finally approved $70 million in annual subsidies and tax breaks
to a new group of buyers for Starrett City, but required them to
maintain affordable rents. The Starrett City campaign became a
major victory for ACORN.[21]

A few months later Wall Street and world financial markets
crashed. On October 2, 2008, Mayor Bloomberg made the surprise announcement that he would ask the city council to amend
the municipal charter and remove the two-term limit on city

officeholders so he could run for a third term as mayor in 2009. The city needed his steady hand in the face of the financial crisis, Bloomberg insisted. He thus ignored the public's overwhelming support for term limits, as expressed in two previous referenda, and angered even many of his admirers. The mayor wasted no time in securing the backing of city council speaker Christine Quinn, a Democrat. Quinn took charge of rounding up a majority of her fifty-one members for the charter change. A fierce three-week public debate ensued before the vote, with Bloomberg lining up scores of nonprofit organizations to support his bid to remain in power. Many of those groups had benefited for years from sizable "anonymous" donations from the billionaire mayor's charity. That conflict turned into a defining moment for de Blasio. "We ran a war room in the campaign against overturning term limits, and Bill was the quarterback," Rosen said. "He quickly became a leader of the opposition to Bloomberg and Quinn."[22]

The council's vote on October 23 to overturn term limits was unusually close, twenty-nine in favor, twenty-two opposed. Bloomberg had prevailed. The next year, despite spending nearly $80 million on his reelection campaign, Bloomberg won a surprisingly tight race against his lackluster Democratic opponent, comptroller Bill Thompson. But the biggest loser of the term limits vote was Quinn. She was thereafter seen as Bloomberg's chief ally in circumventing the democratic will of the voters. It was an image that would dog her when she sought in 2013 to succeed Bloomberg as mayor. Meanwhile, de Blasio's unwavering opposition to overturning term limits won him new respect from activists across the city.

Another Upset Victory

By early 2009, the world was changing. The subprime housing crisis and Wall Street's financial collapse had led to the Great Recession. Unemployment soared, millions of people lost their homes, and economic inequality deepened. And while Barack Obama, himself a former community organizer, was now in the White House, ACORN, the nation's biggest organization of poor people, was under increased attack from Republicans in Congress. Jon Kest and the leaders of New York's Working Families Party were convinced that de Blasio was the best hope among the city's progressive politicians to lead a new fight against income inequality. At the time, Kest and his wife, Fran Streich, shared a home in Ditmas Park, Brooklyn, with Jon's brother Steve, and much of the planning for de Blasio's future occurred there in late-night meetings.

"Bill would come over often and there would be strategy sessions together with us and Emma [Wolfe]," Steve Kest told me. A tiny, slender woman with close-cropped hair and a keen-edged mind, Wolfe would become one of de Blasio's most trusted aides. Trained straight out of Barnard College as an ACORN organizer in 2001 by Fran Streich, she went to work for 1199/SEIU on John Kerry's 2004 presidential campaign in Ohio, then joined the Working Families Party as an organizer in late 2005.

When de Blasio announced in early 2009 that he would run for the citywide post of public advocate, WFP assigned Wolfe to be his campaign coordinator. Their run for the Democratic Party nomination was an underdog effort from the start. De Blasio faced three better-known or better-financed candidates: the liberal consumer advocate Mark Green, who had held the seat previously and had narrowly lost his bid for mayor in 2001 against Bloomberg; the famed civil rights attorney Norman Siegel; and fellow councilman Eric Gioia, from Queens, who had amassed a campaign war chest of $2.5 million. Once again, de Blasio pulled off a surprise win. After finishing slightly ahead of Green in the first round of balloting, he trounced him by a two-to-one margin in a run-off election, and then romped to victory in the general election. Once again, the ground troops of ACORN, the Working Families Party, and 1199/SEIU had proved their capacity to carry an election. Public Advocate de Blasio promptly named Emma Wolfe his chief of staff. By then, de Blasio's knack for simultaneously cultivating Democratic Party honchos, wealthy donors, and grassroots activists had become part of his political DNA. For the next three years, he, Wolfe, and the leaders of the Working Families Party quietly laid the basis for a 2013 mayoral run.

4

The High Cost of Michael Bloomberg's New York

[T]he Bloomberg Way proposed a corporate vision of the city: the mayor as a CEO, the government as a private corporation, desirable residents and businesses as customers and clients, and the city itself as a product to be branded and marketed.

—Julian Brash[1]

For the twenty years leading up to the election of Bill de Blasio, New York City government was the epicenter of a massive experiment in neoliberalism. Advocates of the neoliberal approach to running our modern cities claimed the private sector did things faster, better, and cheaper than public employees, that the ideal of any mayor should be to run city hall as a chief executive would a corporation, while devising innovative policies that promote economic growth. Meanwhile, the postindustrial information technology revolution had long promised a brave new world of human organization and commerce, along with uncommon profit to those who pioneered that revolution.[2] Not surprisingly, the contracting of many traditional government services to outside businesses—or privatization—has mushroomed throughout the nation over the last few decades, much of it driven by the notion that competition among private vendors would drive down the price of traditional government services, even as evidence mounted that such efforts only result in higher cost to government. Privatization was also driven by a fiery conservative ideology that saw big government and public employees, with their labor unions, as the enemies of progress.

This was especially true in New York City, first under Rudy Giuliani, and then under Michael Bloomberg, the latter the self-styled epitome of a nonpolitical, technocratic, data-driven manager. One study found that between 1996 and 2011, annual New York City expenses for outside contractors nearly doubled, from $5.7 billion to $10.5 billion.[3] But spending trends alone do not convey the extent of startling changes brought about by neoliberal urban policies of the past few decades, in both the way government functions and the way ordinary citizens and the public commons are treated. To understand the day-to-day impact of such policies we have a rich array of examples.

Rudy Giuliani not only advocated increased contracting out of government services, he gave unprecedented tax breaks to major city corporations to retain jobs and stay in the city. During his eight years in office, Giuliani negotiated eighty-four such deals, more than his two predecessors Ed Koch and David Dinkins combined. "Under Giuliani, companies [that received such subsidies] could in some instances lay off hundreds of workers and not be penalized," said Bettina Damiani, of the advocacy group Good Jobs New York.[4] But during his second term, several of Giuliani's biggest privatization efforts backfired. He attempted, for example, to unilaterally lease Brooklyn's Coney Island Hospital and two other public health facilities that were part of the municipal Health and Hospitals Corp. to a private health care firm. But in 1999 the state's highest court struck down the lease, ruling that only the legislature, which had created the public hospital network, could make such a change. Then in 2001 he sought to turn five poorly performing public schools in Brooklyn, Manhattan, and the Bronx into charter schools and turn over their management to the for-profit chain of Edison Schools Inc.

Founded as the Edison Project in 1992 by Christopher Whittle, a media entrepreneur and advocate of private vouchers from government for educating children, and a man whose critics have likened him to a snake-oil salesman, Edison was an early pioneer of for-profit ventures that sought to take over management of public schools and guaranteed improved student performance at lower cost. The company was the darling of conservative think tanks like the Hoover Institution and key officials in the Reagan and George H.W. Bush administrations, and its influence and presence spread across hundreds of schools around the country, but by the time Giuliani tried to bring it to New York, it was already under fire for delivering poor results. Community groups led by ACORN demanded a voice for parents at the five public schools, and in a subsequent referendum organized by the Board of Education 80 percent of the parents at those schools voted against the proposal.

Then there was the $104 million contract awarded to Maximus, a Virginia-based government services firm, which prompted allegations from the city comptroller of conflict of interests by a top Giuliani official, welfare commissioner Jason Turner, who had made his national reputation running welfare-to-work programs in Wisconsin before being brought to New York. In 2001, a damning report by the city's Department of Investigation found that Maximus had helped Turner's wife obtain a $50,000-a-year consulting job with Milwaukee's public schools, even providing matching funds for her job, at the same time the company was negotiating its huge New York City welfare-to-work contract with Turner.[5]

It was under Bloomberg, however, that privatization permeated every corner of government, often through no-bid contracts that received little public scrutiny. Management of many parks was handed off to private, philanthropic groups run by wealthy New Yorkers, while scores of public schools were closed and charter schools grew sharply in number. City planners rezoned

an extraordinary number of neighborhoods to spur construction
of more high-rise commercial buildings and luxury apartment
units, while the mayor's rent guidelines board permitted sharp
increases each year in rents for the city's rent-stabilized housing
stock, all of which accelerated displacement of low-income residents. At the same time, Bloomberg granted huge tax breaks and
subsidies for mega-developments such as Hudson Yards, Atlantic
Yards, and new stadiums for the Mets and Yankees, projects that
siphoned future property taxes from the city budget by creating
special tax districts and by using a speculative method called tax
increment financing.

Finally, there was Bloomberg's massive spending on information technology projects, an area that was supposed to be his
strength. Having amassed a vast fortune as a computer entrepreneur and salesman before his election—almost every financial
trading room, brokerage, and economic consulting firm relies
on a Bloomberg machine—Bloomberg promised voters to use
his expertise in media, finance, and technology to transform the
delivery of government services, to prove once and for all the
power of modern data-based management and the wisdom of
privatization. "In God we trust. Everyone else bring data" was
one of his favorite mottos. As mayor, he launched expensive,
new information technology projects at a raft of city agencies,
importing thousands of private computer consultants to directly
work inside those agencies and at times to actually run them. But
many of his signature projects turned out to be grossly misman-
aged, beset by years of delays and vast cost overruns. Several were
marked with waste and fraud. When it came to technology, the
Bloomberg era became a disaster for taxpayers.

In the end, the Bloomberg Way was a "deeply political" project that aimed "to restore the power of economic elites," says
anthropologist Julian Brash in his study of Bloomberg's neoliberal
policies. Geared to rebranding New York as a "Luxury City,"

it sought to attract maximum investment from global capital while convincing affluent professionals—those dubbed the new "creative class" by some scholars, but which Brash calls the new "professional managerial class"—to relocate en masse to the city and settle in newly gentrifying areas.[6] It was a vision, in other words, that regarded most of New York's lower-income residents, its small independent retailers or manufacturers in areas like the South Bronx or Greenpoint-Williamsburg or Long Island City, as expendable or even undesirable.[7]

Branding and Building the Luxury City

The main governing instruments for shaping the Luxury City were land use and housing policies: driving up the cost of private rent-regulated housing for low-income New Yorkers; rezoning of scores of neighborhoods to fuel private commercial development; and providing huge tax breaks, land giveaways, and direct public subsidies for marquee mega-development projects like Hudson Yards, Atlantic Yards, and the Yankees and Mets stadiums.

One recent housing study found that from 1990 to 2000 (roughly the Giuliani era), median rents citywide increased by only 1.9 percent, while they jumped by 18 percent from 2000 to 2010–14 (the Bloomberg era). And the picture was most dire in fifteen gentrifying low-income neighborhoods of Harlem, Upper Manhattan, the Bronx, and north Brooklyn. There, rents climbed by just 3 percent during the decade of the 1990s, but by an astounding 30.4 percent from 2000 to 2010–14! Throughout the Bloomberg era, the city's rent guidelines board approved increases that averaged 3.2 percent annually for more than 800,000 rent-regulated units.[8]

The federal government defines as affordable housing any unit that costs 30 percent or less of a family's gross income. Yet by the time Bill de Blasio entered city hall in 2014, one-half of the city's renter households were paying more than 33.8 percent of their income in rent, and an astonishing one-third were paying more than half their income to keep a roof over their heads.[9]

Faced with such a monumental housing crisis, the city chose instead to concentrate on more subsidies for commercial development. Anyone wandering along Midtown Manhattan's far West Side in the past few years would come across the dusty din of jackhammers, cranes, and construction crews lifting new hotels, condos, and office buildings into the sky. Hudson Yards, the twenty-eight acres in and around the Metropolitan Transportation Authority's West Side rail yards, has been touted for more than a decade as New York's next great commercial district. It is the biggest development of its kind in the nation. The scandalous subsidies taxpayers have shelled out since 2006 for this luxury mega-project are rarely mentioned, nor are the hundreds of millions of dollars in property taxes that will be siphoned for decades from the city's budget into the coffers of a little-known public authority called the Hudson Yards Infrastructure Corp.

None of this was supposed to happen when the city council agreed in 2005 to condemn and purchase more than fifty square blocks of the far West Side and rezone the entire area to make way for Hudson Yards. Back then, Mayor Bloomberg promised nearly 26 million square feet of prime office space, twenty thousand housing units of mostly market-rate housing, 3 million square feet of hotel and retail space, a new public school, and more than twenty acres of public open space. But to transform the long-neglected area of warehouses, light manufacturing, and parking garages into a virtual city-within-the-city, Bloomberg asked the council to also permit him to issue $3 billion in bonds through a new Hudson Yards Infrastructure Corp., mostly to finance an extension of the 7 subway line from Times Square to 34th Street and Eleventh Avenue, one that the state's own transit agency, the Metropolitan Transportation Authority, didn't see as necessary.[10]

Bloomberg's chief economic aide, Dan Doctoroff, assured the council at the time that all the new development generated by extending the subway line would soon unleash a stream of new property tax revenues—more properly called payments-in-lieu-of-taxes (PILOTs)—from real estate developers, and all those revenues not only would repay the money spent on the subway, they would fill the city's coffers with billions of dollars in additional revenue for years to come. This way of self-financing capital projects, usually called tax increment financing (TIF), is considered such a risky and speculative approach—since it is based only on new revenues that may occur but that are not certain—that some states like California have banned its use altogether.[11]

But there were two small wrinkles in Doctoroff's plan: in the unlikely event that new construction was slower than expected, the city would cover the debt service shortfall on the bonds from its regular operating budget until PILOT revenue from new buildings reached a sufficient level; and if the subway project went over budget, the city would pick up any extra costs. You can imagine what happened. A 2016 report by the city's Independent Budget Office found that new construction in Hudson Yards after ten years was so much slower than projected that the city has had to provide the Hudson Yards Infrastructure Corp. $358 million just to meet its interest payments, far more than even Doctoroff's worse-case scenario, and that more city support will be needed for years to come.[12]

But those interest payments are just part of the public subsidy. There were also cost overruns. In 2014, the Independent Budget Office (IBO) calculated some $205 million in additional infrastructure costs in the Hudson Yards area that the city had not previously acknowledged. And that was on top of $75 million that Bloomberg suddenly allocated during his last year in office for the Culture Shed, a new Hudson Yards performance venue for high-end cultural activities that Doctoroff created and chaired.[13]

And finally, there were hundreds of millions of dollars in

property tax abatements (or discounted PILOTs) that Bloomberg doled out to spur new construction and lure major commercial tenants to Hudson Yards, a practice that further weakened and delayed the project's ability to pay off the subway bonds.[14]

As economist James Parrot has noted:

> The magnitude of the Hudson Yards tax breaks only became widely understood when JPMorgan Chase sought an additional subsidy of $1 billion in October 2014 when considering constructing a new headquarters in the Hudson Yards district. In rebuffing the bank's request, the de Blasio administration pointed out that the bank would already get about $600 million in tax breaks under the as-of-right Hudson Yards program established by Mayor Bloomberg.[15]

In addition, as some critics have noted, the Hudson Yards financing scheme through PILOTs reduces democratic accountability. "Because they do not appear in the city's budget, these funds . . . are not subject to the city's annual budget process between the City Council and the Mayor, where spending of city resources is subject to oversight, openly debated and voted on by representatives of the whole city," Bridget Fisher notes.[16]

The total public price tag for the Hudson Yards project may not be known for years, but of this we can be sure: it will be far greater than its proponents ever conceded.

Bloomberg and Doctoroff used the city's power to rezone, to abate taxes, and to provide direct subsidies as leverage for other massive development programs in other parts of the city, most of them geared to more luxury housing or big-chain commerce.

Take Williamsburg-Greenpoint in Brooklyn. In a once-modest, ethnically diverse working-class neighborhood filled with three-story buildings, city hall proposed a phalanx of forty-story waterfront luxury condos that would bring in nearly forty thousand new residents, most of them well heeled. "These hyper development projects are going up all over the city," said Beka Economopoulos of the Creative Industries Coalition, a neighborhood group in Williamsburg, Brooklyn, in 2005. "City Hall keeps squeezing out residents and small businesses in favor of rich developers."[17] As in most low-income neighborhoods close to the center of a city, the first wave of gentrification to Williamsburg was largely of struggling artists, musicians, and liberal young professionals desperate to find affordable apartments, and the newcomers suddenly made the neighborhood a cutting-edge cultural space, while they coexisted with its older population of orthodox Jews, Puerto Ricans, and Dominicans. But as local landlords saw the immense potential for higher rents, they moved to displace the original residents, especially the Hispanics, who were less organized. Before long, real estate developers were eyeing former industrial sites along the waterfront for mega-projects, and Bloomberg's aides were more than willing to help.

There was also the Atlantic Yards development, where community groups battled for years to prevent the city and the state from handing the developer Forest City/Ratner land over the Long Island Rail Road for a twenty-two-acre development that would include the new basketball arena for the Brooklyn Nets and sixteen residential buildings, most of them market rate. The Barclays Center opened in 2012, though only a few of the residential buildings have yet been completed.

The Yankee Stadium Heist

No single project of the Bloomberg era more exemplifies how government ran roughshod over low-income New Yorkers, how city officials deliberately misled the public and circumvented the law, and how pay-to-play politics flourished even under the "nonpolitical" Bloomberg administration than the effort from 2005 to 2009 to erect a new baseball stadium for the Yankees in the South Bronx—a monument to luxury consumption smack in the midst of one of America's poorest congressional districts. More than a decade later, the total cost of the Yankee Stadium project, in both direct government subsidies and lost revenues, has been all but forgotten, yet the public tab has likely surpassed $1 billion and will continue to grow for decades.[18]

Bloomberg's predecessor, Rudy Giuliani, had attempted before leaving office in 2001 to provide up to $400 million to Yankees owner George Steinbrenner to build a new stadium, which was then estimated to cost some $800 million, but the city council balked at such direct support, and when Bloomberg came into office he initially declared his opposition to large public subsidies for sports arenas. A few years later, however, the mayor did a dramatic about-face when his deputy mayor for economic development, Dan Doctoroff, who convinced him to have New York City bid for the 2012 Olympic Games, began promoting subsidies for sports teams as smart economic development. With Doctoroff spearheading the effort, Bloomberg called for public subsidies for a slew of sports teams: for the Jets, as part of the city's ultimately unsuccessful bid to win the Olympic Games; for the Mets and the Yankees; even for the New Jersey Nets as part of a deal to lure them to the aforementioned new Atlantic Yards basketball arena in downtown Brooklyn.

None of those proposals proved more controversial than the Yankees deal. On June 15, 2005, Bloomberg and Governor George Pataki unveiled plans to turn over one of the largest public parks complexes in the South Bronx—twenty-two acres of Macombs Dam and Mullaly Parks—for the building of a new Yankee Stadium directly across the street from the historic venue where Babe Ruth, Joe DiMaggio, and Reggie Jackson had played ball, and for the building of an expanded parking system for nine thousand cars. The city and the state, they announced, would provide about $200 million to improve the neighborhood around the stadium, including $116 million for new parks and playgrounds to replace those that would be demolished. In a departure from so many previous stadium deals around the country, they said, the Yankees organization would completely pay for the stadium, the construction of which would be financed with tax-exempt bonds. The team would then repay the bonds over forty years with payments-in-lieu-of-taxes—in other words, with the same tax increment financing scheme that Doctoroff had proposed for Hudson Yards on Manhattan's far West Side. The state's $70 million contribution to the project, officials said, would solely finance one of the parking garages. Furthermore, they predicted, the new parking system—which was to be owned and operated by a separate private company—would generate for the city a minimum of $3.2 million annually in rent, plus millions more in property taxes.[19]

Both houses of the legislature promptly introduced bills on June 20, 2005, authorizing the transfer of the parkland, and the final vote came only three days later. For Albany, a place notorious for gridlock, this was lightning speed. Without a single public hearing or independent review of the deal, lawmakers voted to turn over control of twenty-two acres of parks for free to one of the richest sports franchises in the world. Meanwhile, the city council held a quick vote on June 20 on its own parallel approval, also without any public hearing. Neighborhood residents were not even informed beforehand that such a seizure of their parks was about to occur, nor was the South Bronx community board, which by law must be permitted advisory review of such land-use changes. Nor was much consideration given to the fact that increasing parking spaces from the previous 6,500 to 9,100, something the Yankees were demanding, could lead to higher pollution in an area that already had the highest asthma rate in the city. "There is absolutely no consideration for the residents who live here," South Bronx resident Joyce Hoigi said at the time. Hoigi and her husband had lived in the shadows of the old Yankee Stadium for thirty years and raised three children in the neighborhood.

She also worked at a nearby Catholic school, All Hallows High School, whose sports teams had used Mullaly Park for decades for all their games. "What are our kids supposed to do for the next few years while they build the stadium?" she asked.[20]

Hoigi and scores of her neighbors immediately began to organize a movement against the deal, but they received no help in their fight from the Bronx Democratic political machine, whose wheels had already been greased with money from the Yankees. Borough president Adolfo Carrion, one of the new stadium's biggest defenders, for example, received $11,850 in campaign contributions from executives of the team and its affiliate YES cable network between 2003 and 2005.[21]

So great was the outcry against the giveaway of parkland that the local community board opposed the plan by a vote of sixteen to eight with ten abstentions. Nonetheless, in 2006 the council ignored the board and overwhelmingly approved the rezoning of areas around the stadium and the issuing of tax-exempt bonds for the Yankees. A few months later, Carrion, who appoints the community board members, removed four who had voted against the plan. One of them, Mary L. Blassingame, lost her position as chair of the board's housing and land-use committee after twenty-one years of service. "It's called revenge," Blassingame said of her removal.[22]

But the rigging of the deal for the Yankees didn't end there. By the time the city's Industrial Development Agency was ready in late 2006 to issue the bonds, the amount the Yankees needed had climbed to $942 million, and the total price of the project had zoomed to $1.2 billion. It would take another two years before evidence emerged from internal city emails that top Bloomberg aides had maneuvered to inflate official tax assessment of market value of the new stadium site. Everyone knew what the stadium would cost to build, but what was the value of land under the new stadium? The combined assessment of the land and the new construction was crucial to the Yankees and their bond underwriters, since it established the maximum amount of money under IRS regulations that the team could pay in PILOTs for the bonds while still preserving their tax-exempt status.

In a July 15, 2005, email, for example, Assistant City Attorney Joseph Gunn notified Assistant Finance Commissioner Dara Ottley-Brown that "the Yankees have an interest in seeing that the assessed valuation will be high enough to generate as much PILOT for tax-exempt debt as is lawful and appropriate."

But on March 21, 2006, a few weeks before the city council's vote on the Yankees project, the city's chief assessor, Maurice Kellman, shocked city hall when he notified Ottley-Brown that his initial assessment pegged the value of the stadium site at $26.8 million, or about $35 per square foot—far lower than the Yankees wanted.

A series of frantic phone calls and emails ensued that day and the next between a half dozen city officials and the team's representatives, after which Ottley-Brown ordered Kellman to produce a new report. "Here is the write-up with the changes you requested earlier today," Kellman emailed to his boss on the twenty-second. By then, Kellman had pumped up his assessment to a whopping $204 million—$275 per square foot—almost eight times his original calculation. He accomplished that amazing feat, the records show, by resorting to comparable sales of vacant lands in gentrifying areas of Harlem, and even as far away as the Lower East Side—neighborhoods in wealthier New York County—instead of using vacant land prices in Bronx County, where the stadium was actually located.[23]

Less than a month later, in an application the city was required to submit to the National Park Service before it could convert the parkland for stadium use, the Parks Department gave a far different estimate. An independent appraisal the department commissioned had concluded that the land under the stadium was worth just $45 per square foot, much closer to city assessor Kellman's original assessment. Why such wildly different values for the same property? "Our assessors jacked up the numbers and the comparables for the Council to justify the stadium bonds," alleged a Finance Department official familiar with the project.[24]

Those contradictory assessments later prompted probes by committees of both the state assembly and Congress, but other than produce critical reports of the process, those investigations led to no charges of illegal behavior. In 2009, the Yankees gained city approval for an additional $360 million in tax-exempt bonds to pay for added costs of construction, thus bringing the stadium's final price tag to $1.6 billion.

The Finance Department's unusual treatment of the stadium continues to this day. In 2016, for instance, city assessors estimated the market value of Yankee Stadium at $2.06 billion, a 23 percent increase over its original value when it opened. Each year since then, the Yankees have sought the highest possible assessment from the city. Why? Because the higher the assessment, the more money the team gets to claim as its tax liability. Moreover, its carefully crafted lease agreement with the city allows the team not only to pay off bond debt, but also to pay for stadium maintenance, *as if they were tax payments*. Thus in 2016, Yankee Stadium's estimated market value, according to Finance Department records, was listed as greater than the combined value of the 102-story Empire State Building ($794 million) and the 44-story world headquarters of Goldman Sachs ($703 million).

In April 2009, the stadium opened on schedule for the new baseball season, with premium ticket prices starting at an astonishing $2,500 per seat. Even seats in the outfield were so expensive that attending a Yankees game was no longer feasible for ordinary families with children. Soon, however, the embarrassing spectacle of thousands of empty seats forced the team to lower its prices.[25]

Stadium revenues did soar in the first year from the new luxury skyboxes and from those higher ticket prices, but the flow from attendance sales has steadily declined every year since then, so that by 2015 it had dropped to nearly the same amount as the old stadium produced during its last year of operation.[26]

As for neighborhood residents, they were forced to wait more than five years before all the parks and ball fields the city had demolished were eventually replaced. The All Hallows High School baseball team, for instance, was reduced to constant pleas to the Parks Department for substitute playing fields for their teams. "I can get an answer from the Pope in Rome faster than I can from the Parks Department," said principal Sean Sullivan, who doubled as the school's assistant baseball coach. At one point in 2009, the Parks Department offered the All Hallows team a run-down field at Pelham Bay Park—a forty-minute trip by automobile to the other side of the Bronx. "The field looks like a lunar landscape," Sullivan said. "When I'm standing in the third base coaching box, I can't see my shortstop completely because he's playing in a ditch."[27]

But the biggest scandal of the Yankee Stadium project has been the system of garages and parking lots that surrounds the new stadium. In 2013, the specially created company that built and runs the parking system—in Wall Street lingo it would be called a special purpose entity—suddenly declared itself in default on $237 million in tax-exempt bonds that financed the project. It was the largest default of a New York municipal bond since the 1970s.[28] To understand why it failed, we need look no further than the original deal Bloomberg's aides negotiated with the Yankees. The team not only insisted on a minimum nine thousand spaces for the parking system, but it also demanded free use of six hundred valet-parking spaces year-round for its executives, staff, ballplayers, and VIPs in the new garage directly connected to the stadium. That perk alone represented up to a $40 million annual subsidy to the Yankees by Bronx Parking Development Company.[29]

Both the Yankees and city officials should have known from the start that it was financially unfeasible to arrange a bond deal for the garages that was separate from that of the stadium itself. But the team wanted no financial exposure to the garages. Emails later obtained by a state assembly committee show that team officials were directly involved in discussions over the structure of the garage deal, and that any change in parking capacity had to be approved by the Yankees. The cost of the garage system, however, ended up being far higher than originally projected, a whopping $340 million—or an average of nearly $38,000 per parking space. Even worse, the six hundred free spaces allotted to the Yankees meant that Bronx Parking Development would receive virtually no revenue from a second garage. And, of course, all the parking spaces would sit empty during the fall and winter months. It did not take a genius to realize this project was doomed from the start, yet city officials produced a glowing feasibility study that projected the parking company not only would cover its operating expenses and pay off the $237 million in bonds issued by the city's Industrial Development Agency, it would also provide millions of dollars in rent and taxes to the city for decades to come, and still make a profit.[30]

The "private" company the city chose to build and run the garages turned out to be a shell company with a majority of city representatives, one from the Parks Department, one from the city's Economic Development Corp., and another from the Bronx Overall Economic Development Corp., an arm of the Bronx borough president's office. In addition, the city ended up spending nearly $200 million for the project, largely to replace parkland that was demolished for garage construction, and the state added another $70 million for the garages.[31] Even with those subsidies, however, the garages swiftly turned into a financial sinkhole. The bonds, which were issued in December 2007, were so speculative that they had to be marketed as uninsured junk bonds. Once the garages opened in 2009, parking prices of $35 per game drove away so many fans that the system was soon averaging barely 38 percent of capacity, even during Yankees home games.[32]

In April 2013, Bronx Parking Development Company officially defaulted on its debt payments. Its creditors then took control
of its finances while they sought to negotiate a deal with New
York City on how to unravel the virtually bankrupt company. By
March 2017, nearly four years later, city officials and the creditors had still not resolved the issue. Meanwhile, Bronx Parking
has yet to pay a single penny to the public since opening for
business in 2009. As of mid-2016, the company owed the city
nearly $100 million in rent, property taxes, and penalties for the
twenty-two acres of city-owned land it occupies. Those arrears
keep growing every month, and there is almost no likelihood of
the city ever recouping its money, since the deal originally negotiated by Bloomberg's aides places the company's debt to the city
last in line behind all other creditors and operating expenses. All
that city-owned land with empty parking garages and lots thus
sits there, blocks away from the biggest mass transit hub in the
Bronx, unable to be used either for parks or for new affordable
housing or even for commercial development, while the Yankees use payments-in-lieu-of-taxes to pay for their stadium and
its maintenance.[33]

Class War in City Parks

Welcome to the $2 million soccer field. Actually, you can take
your pick of them at Randall's Island Park, an idyllic, 480-acre
oasis of picnic grounds and ball fields nestled on a spit of land in the
East River, beneath giant spans of the Robert F. Kennedy Bridge
that connect the Bronx and Queens to Manhattan. Randall's
Island housed for decades the executive offices of Robert Moses,
when he managed both the Parks Department and the powerful Triborough Bridge and Tunnel Authority. Until recently,
the island's only connection by foot to the rest of the city was a
pedestrian bridge at East 103rd Street in Manhattan, which meant
that the park offered much-needed open space for residents of

East Harlem's teeming tenements and public housing projects. But years of constant cuts in the Parks Department budget had caused a marked decline in the island's upkeep. Under Bloomberg, however, the park emerged as a glaring symbol of efforts to privatize public space for the benefit of the city's wealthiest residents.

In 2006, Bloomberg's aides and the Randall's Island Sports Foundation, a public-private partnership in charge of managing the park (and now known as the Randall's Island Park Alliance), developed a plan to renovate the entire park, nearly doubling the number of playing fields to sixty-five and erecting new comfort stations and lighting for night games, at an original estimated cost of $130 million, though it ultimately surpassed more than $165 million. The upgrade, however, was part of an agreement city hall had quietly negotiated with a group of Manhattan's twenty richest private schools to grant those schools exclusive use of many of the fields every weekday afternoon. In exchange, the private schools would make annual payments over twenty years of about $52 million. The proposal infuriated East Harlem residents who received no advance notice of the deal. Those residents wanted, at a minimum, proportional access to the fields for the city's public school teams. Neighborhood leaders, joined by the area's city councilwoman Melissa Mark-Viverito and park advocates, promptly labeled it a naked "pay-to-play" scheme for the mayor's rich friends.

City hall, meanwhile, defended the plan as an innovative public-private partnership—one of many that mushroomed under Bloomberg, with private nonprofit groups taking over management of the city's most desirable parks. "The foundation doesn't have any neighborhood representation on that board, they never advertise their concerts in East Harlem and you rarely see black and Latino faces at their concerts," said Marina Ortiz, of the East Harlem Preservation group. "They forget this park is part of our neighborhood." The foundation's board of directors, in fact, boasted some of the city's wealthiest figures, including billionaire corporate raider Carl Icahn and even Bloomberg himself before he became mayor. In a sign of its elitism, Ortiz noted, the foundation twice closed the only footbridge to Randall's Island during the summer of 2005 for concerts by the Dave Matthews Band. And every year around July Fourth weekend, the footbridge was closed again for a huge private party and fair sponsored by Bloomberg LP for its employees.[34]

Opponents challenged the lease agreement in court, claiming the mayor had failed to seek approval from the city council for such a significant change in the use of public parkland. Over the next few years, both the state supreme court and an appellate court ruled in favor of the community, forcing the city eventually to agree to pay for the entire renovation and to adopt a somewhat more equitable division of playing time on the fields between public and private schools.[35]

But that was not the only example of the selling off of Randall's Island. City hall pursued a separate plan with the foundation to lease twenty-six acres of the island to a politically connected private firm to create a $168 million Six Flags–style outdoor water park and indoor beach club. If built, it would have been the first such theme park in a major American city. The deal eventually fell apart when the firm failed to find sufficient financing. Then in 2009, the foundation handed a lease for a section of the park to the private Sportime Tennis Center, where matches of the professional World Team Tennis league were to be scheduled, and where tennis legend John McEnroe's brother runs a private tennis academy named after the former star. Court fees at Sportime were not exactly affordable to most New Yorkers. They ran from $72 to $102 per hour, and that was on top of the required annual membership fee of $500 to $750. Finally, there was the annual New York tour of Cirque du Soleil, with its performances occupying a section of the park for up to two months at a time. In the fall of 2016, the Cirque's ticket prices ranged from $54 to $225 each.[36]

Other examples abounded throughout the city. In the middle of Union Square Park in Manhattan, for example, a location famous for decades as a gathering space for labor and other dissident groups, the Bloomberg administration took the landmark colonnaded pavilion, where neighborhood children had been accustomed to playing under a gorgeous Spanish tile roof for decades, and turned it instead into a swanky 120-person restaurant concession. This even though more than 150 restaurants and bars were already in operation within two blocks of the park.[37]

And in the far reaches of the southeast Bronx, city officials hired Donald Trump to build and run the most expensive municipal golf course in the nation. Erected at a cost to taxpayers of $230 million, the Trump Golf Links at Ferry Point Park opened in April 2015, only months before Trump launched his successful run for president. Unlike other city-owned courses, however, which charged local residents an average of $43 on weekdays for eighteen holes of golf, fees at the Trump course were more than three times higher—$141 per round. For a mere $10.8 million investment, not only did Trump receive control of the course for thirty years, but the city even agreed to supply him free water, a perk worth at least $300,000 annually.[38]

All of these transactions might have been fine, of course, had they occurred between private firms operating in a competitive free market, but all involved the use of public lands and taxpayer subsidies, so that New York City's most desirable parks were suddenly transformed under Bloomberg into playgrounds for the city's wealthy.

Urban Corruption 2.0—CityTime and Other Boondoggles

In December 2010, Preet Bharara, the U.S. attorney for the Southern District of New York, announced the first in a series of stunning criminal charges against a group of computer consultants who had been employed for years by the Bloomberg administration on a project called CityTime. Bharara would later describe that project as the "single biggest fraud ever perpetrated on the city of New York," and the scandal surrounding it would turn into the biggest blot of Michael Bloomberg's tenure.

A year before those arrests, I began exposing in the *Daily News* CityTime's extraordinary cost overruns and delays, its outrageous salaries, and even allegations by project whistle-blowers of phantom workers and corruption orchestrated by the project's top managers. CityTime's origins went back to 1998, when the Giuliani administration hired an outside IT firm to modernize the city's vast and archaic timekeeping and payroll system. The original vendor proposed using a combination of state-of-the-art biometric hand scanners and specially designed software to track the hours of employees on their desk computers, all of which was supposed to end the age-old occasional abuse of city workers punching time clocks for friends, something that both Giuliani's and Bloomberg's aides believed was rampant. The overhaul was projected to take five years and cost $63 million. In 2000, defense contractor SAIC took over the original contract. But by 2009, more than a decade after work on CityTime began, the company had managed to roll out the system to only a third of the 145,000 city employees targeted to use it, while the price tag had ballooned to more than $700 million—over ten times the original projection! At first, only a few lonely voices questioned the mushrooming costs and delays, among them John Forster, a leader of the public employee union local that represents the city's architects and technicians, and councilwoman Letitia James, who chaired the council's contracts committee.[39]

In early 2010, I reported that some 230 CityTime consultants were being paid an average salary of $400,000 a year, with several project managers raking in more than $600,000 each, yet the project was nowhere near finished. The scandalous cost overruns prompted the city's Department of Investigation and the U.S. attorney's office Public Corruption Unit to take a closer look, and soon the magnitude of the theft became clear, with investigators tracing millions of dollars in bribes, no-show jobs, and payoffs to a gang of corrupt consultants, some of whom were project managers, who had laundered the money through a web of phantom companies and bank accounts they set up from Russia to India. Federal prosecutors eventually charged eleven CityTime consultants or members of their families with fraud and money laundering. Eight were later convicted or pleaded guilty, one died before trial, and the remaining two fled to India with millions of dollars before authorities could arrest them. Bloomberg's head of payroll, Joel Bondy, who had overseen and defended this debacle, was forced to resign. As for SAIC, the company entered into a deferred prosecution agreement with the justice department and repaid the taxpayers a whopping $500 million.[40]

The waste uncovered in CityTime, however, paled when compared to another, far more vital project, the city's effort to modernize its mammoth 911 system. Launched in the summer of 2005, the Emergency Communications Transformation Project was one of the signature initiatives of the Bloomberg era. It was supposed to centralize call-and-dispatch operations for vital police, fire, and emergency medical services into a single state-of-the-art computerized system.

But the project was plagued from the start by massive cost overruns and major failures by giant firms like Hewlett-Packard and Verizon to deliver properly functioning systems. As the years dragged on, frustration grew from emergency responders over the troubled overhaul, and union leaders for the city's fire, police, and ambulance workers claimed repeated failures of the new system's operation were creating slow emergency response times and endangering the public, a claim Bloomberg's aides repeatedly denied. A scathing report issued by the city's Department of Investigation after Bloomberg left office found that the upgrade had fallen ten years behind schedule, was nearly $1 billion over budget, had been woefully mismanaged, and suffered from a persistent battle of the badges between the FDNY and the NYPD over which agency would control it. More than $200 million of those costs had not previously been disclosed because Bloomberg aides buried them in the budgets of other agencies, investigators found, and those aides rewrote monthly reports of 911 project managers or pressured them to "sanitize" and "soften" negative news so as to "improve the spin" on its progress.

The litany of ECTP management failures seemed endless. Layers of private consultants and vendors virtually ran the overhaul with little supervision from city employees, the report found, with some consultants marking up their bills to the city as much as 600 percent. During one eighteen-month period, city hall kept canceling meetings of the interagency city group that was nominally in charge of the project, which caused the city's own quality control firm to complain: "The most senior members of the administration simply failed to pay attention."[41]

Before you conclude CityTime and the 911 project were aberrations, consider the case of Willard "Ross" Lanham. From 2002 to 2008, Lanham was in charge of Project Connect, the federally funded program to wire public schools for Internet service—an effort on which New York City alone has already expended more than $1 billion. Federal agents arrested Lanham in 2011 and charged him with fraud and theft. Investigators alleged he approved payments for no-show jobs for family members, arranged kickbacks from contractors, and then hid all of this from city Department of Education officials by using layers of other phantom companies. He hired his brother, for example, to work from home reviewing electronic files of school phone bills and paid him $40 an hour. Lanham's company then charged a Verizon subcontractor $175 an hour for the brother's labor. The subcontractor, in turn, billed Verizon $192.50. And Verizon then marked up the final price to the city's department of education to $225 an hour—a white-collar version of the vig (or vigorish), the underworld system of paying interest on illegal bets or loans, only this time it was the city that was paying. All the major companies that colluded with Lanham and the DOE supervisors who hired and oversaw him claimed they had no clue all this was going on. Meanwhile, the accused was convicted of stealing $1.7 million and sent to prison, and the federal government later fined the city $3 million for its gross mismanagement, plus it required the city to forfeit $123 million in Project Connect funds.[42]

Then there was Future Technology Associates, which collected more than $74 million over nearly six years in a no-bid contract from the city's school system for developing a new computerized purchasing system for schools. FTA headquarters was a mail drop at a Jacksonville, Florida, UPS store. The firm employed more than sixty programmers on the project and billed the city $110 an hour for the services of each—only many of its employees were secretly working from Turkey and India, and being paid only $10 an hour, with the owners pocketing the rest through their Turkish shell company. The scam was made easier because the top DOE official in charge of supervising FTA later admitted to investigators a romantic affair with one of the firm's owners. She subsequently resigned after being questioned about the relationship and the firm's contract was canceled.[43]

There were similar hair-raising examples of massive technology programs gone awry at other agencies. Bureaucrats at the New York City Housing Authority, for instance, gave their new $36 million computerized rent-collection system the Orwellian acronym NICE (NYCHA Improving Customer Experience). But for landlords and public housing tenants, the system became a cyber-monster run amok. Launched in February 2011, it immediately turned the annual certification process for 100,000 tenants who received Section 8 rent subsidies into a hellhole of disappeared documents, erroneous payments, and baseless eviction notices. "It's total chaos beyond belief," said one Brooklyn building owner. "Landlords are being mixed up and getting wrong checks. Sometimes the computer automatically sends termination notices to every tenant in a building. Transfers get held up for months. The whole thing gets worse every day."[44]

Then there was the $500 million public safety wireless network that Northrop Grumman constructed for the city's Department of Information Technology and Telecommunications. It proved to be so unreliable that the police department balked at using it, and the network, known as NYC-WIN, was eventually relegated to regulating traffic lights and reading water meters. In 2012, even Bloomberg's aides grew so frustrated with the system's problems that they offered to sell it back to Northrop but the company declined. Three years later de Blasio's technology aides, in an effort to end the network's spiraling maintenance costs, announced plans to put it up for sale.[45]

As these IT projects proliferated in every city agency, many marked by inevitable delays, cost overruns, and abysmal oversight by city officials, they became a new-age version of capitalism feeding at the government trough, providing high-priced employment for thousands of computer-savvy members of the "creative class" and windfall profits for those firms with the political connections to secure new contracts. In one of the great ironies of modern urban politics, New York City taxpayers were bilked for hundreds of millions of dollars under a mayor who had boasted of being an expert in technology and management.

5

Urban Neighborhoods in Revolt: The First Wave

I learned you often don't need a majority to get things done. What you need is a bloc that sticks together and has a solid message.

—Nick Licata

Gayle McLaughlin is a soft-spoken teacher and former anti-war radical who defied and bested the mighty Chevron Oil company in Richmond, California. Nick Licata lived for decades in a Seattle commune, grafted his own unique blend of environmental activism with comical theatrics and poetry, and founded an anti-nuclear group called Legs Against Arms. Wilson Goode Jr., the son of Philadelphia's first black mayor, spent his college years organizing fellow students to oppose the apartheid South African government before challenging discriminatory practices in his own City of Brotherly Love. They seem, at first glance, unlikely heroes of a modern movement to remake the nitty-gritty world of American urban politics. But along with kindred activists like San Francisco's John Avalos and New York's Letitia James and Melissa Mark-Viverito, they were among the first wave of progressive leaders to win city council elections during the late 1990s and 2000s. Several were products of 1960s radicalism on college campuses or were the children of former radicals. For the most part, they were propelled to upset victories with the help of independent grassroots movements. Their initial triumphs took place before the Great Recession, when neoliberal urban policies reigned supreme, yet they managed to achieve groundbreaking legislation to combat economic and racial inequality. A few years later came the Wall Street crash and the Occupy Wall Street protests, events that fueled a second and even stronger progressive surge and led to the mayoral victories of New York's de Blasio, Pittsburgh's Peduto, Newark's Baraka, Minneapolis's Hodges, and Boston's Walsh.

A note of caution, however: our cities have seen radical movements flare up before during periods of social turbulence. Precisely because the United States is such a vast country and has such a multitude of local governments, innovative political trends inevitably start at the municipal level, some of them spreading later to state capitals and to Washington, D.C., itself, but many burning out right where they began. More than a hundred years ago, in the aftermath of the economic depression of the 1890s and amid rising public outrage against the nation's robber barons, an unwieldy coalition of progressive reformers, immigrant and labor groups, and left-wing radicals captured a startling number of elected posts. At one point during the early 1900s, more than twelve hundred members of the Socialist Party held office, including seventy-nine mayoralties in cities like Milwaukee, Buffalo, and Minneapolis. They sought to tax the wealthy, hold down transit fares, and create municipal water and electric utilities. Progressive Republican reformer Hazen Pingree, for example, served four terms as mayor of Detroit and then as governor of Michigan. Pingree fought for the eight-hour day, against child labor, in defense of immigrants, for an income tax, and against private monopolies of utilities. And while some of its cherished reforms eventually became part of Franklin Roosevelt's New Deal, that vibrant urban progressive movement eventually waned, many of its followers consumed, no doubt, by the convulsions of two world wars and a depression, its leaders co-opted into the federal bureaucracy Roosevelt created, others repressed and marginalized by postwar McCarthy-era hysteria. It would take the urban rebellions of the 1960s and expanded voting rights for the fast-growing African American and Latino populations of the cities to bring new radical ferment and a new generation of progressive officials to power during the 1970s and 1980s.[1] Urban elites, however, soon reasserted control through neoliberal economic land use and financial policies and through massive privatization of government services, until, at the turn of the twenty-first century, yet another surge of progressive politics emerged.

Read Me a Poem: Nick Licata's Unusual Journey

Nick Licata is often called the elder statesman of the new progressive movement in Seattle. Now seventy years old, he is short and wiry, with an angular face, a neatly trimmed beard, and wisps of white hair encircling his balding head. His mother was a factory worker, his father a barber and truck driver, and in the blue-collar area of Cleveland where the family lived Licata developed little patience for esoteric political views from the left or the right. During his sophomore year at Bowling Green University, with the Vietnam War raging, Licata was drawn to political activism. "A friend of mine said, let's form an SDS [Students for a Democratic Society] chapter, so we did," Licata recalls. "All of a sudden I was a Communist in other people's eyes, and that's when I started to see how the power of labeling people can distort reality." He was no ideologue, however. After attending a national SDS conference in Ann Arbor, he quickly decided that many of the radical group's leaders were "misguided and elitist."[2]

Licata soon displayed an uncommon ability to mix his anti-authoritarian politics with humor, showmanship, and nuts-and-bolts organizing, winning election as Bowling Green's student body president in 1969 and campaigning for such prosaic improvements as allowing beer to be sold in the student union.[3]

By the 1970s, he was attending graduate school at the University of Washington and deeply immersed in Seattle's anti-war movement through a small group that dubbed itself the Provisional Revolutionary Action Group. The group's members purchased a big house and founded the PRAG commune, one that eventually included as many as eighteen people. "I lived there for twenty-five years, got married, raised a daughter there, but it never became a cult and never became far left," Licata said. "I did throw a lot of parties, though, which built a progressive network." It remains one of the few surviving collectives from that era.

Along the way, Licata produced several gadfly publications and organized popular annual twenty-four-hour dance marathons he labeled "Give Peace a Dance." He also joined the Green Party and at one point founded an anti-nuclear group he called Legs Against Arms. His experience earning a living as an insurance broker led him to organize a community coalition against redlining of inner-city neighborhoods by Seattle banks. In the mid-1990s, he spearheaded Citizens for More Important Things, a group that opposed demands for massive public subsidies for new sports facilities by three Seattle professional teams—Major League Baseball's Mariners, the NFL's Seahawks, and the NBA's Supersonics. Despite an initiative in which county voters rejected the Mariners' stadium, the state legislature authorized public funding for it, even though the old stadium, which had been built only eighteen years earlier with public subsidies, still had to be paid off![4]

The stadium battles turned Licata into a Seattle folk hero. In 1997, he parlayed that fame into a run for the city council. At the time, the council's nine members were all elected at-large. Outraised financially by two to one and staunchly opposed by the city newspapers' editorial boards, Licata startled the establishment by winning. Green Party activists Peter Steinbrueck and Richard Conlin also scored council victories that same year, and the three soon formed a new progressive wing. "I learned you often don't need a majority to get things done," Licata said. "What you need is a bloc that sticks together and has a solid message."[5]

In his early years, Licata pushed Seattle City Light, the municipal electric company created by voters during the 1890s progressive era and still regulated by the council, to demand higher rates from Nucor Steel, the utility's biggest customer, thus saving other ratepayers more than $750,000. He fought successfully to do away with a vehicle impound law that was disproportionately affecting black residents. And he began the unconventional tradition of opening every council committee meeting he chaired—even public safety hearings—with poetry readings by local residents that he dubbed Words Worth.[6]

His bohemian politics aside, Licata also cultivated a reputation for doing his research on legislation and asking the toughest questions in council hearings, traits that would get him reelected repeatedly over the years. In 2006, less than a month after becoming city council president, Licata began his biggest showdown against professional sports, the mayor, the chamber of commerce, and the state legislature. The Supersonics were demanding $200 million in new subsidies for renovations to the team's Key Arena or they threatened to move elsewhere. Licata was outraged. Only ten years after taxpayers had poured $75 million into building the arena, the team wanted more money. He secured a council majority against such a large subsidy, prompting the team's owners to pack up and move to Oklahoma City and cementing his notoriety as a progressive who would not bend to corporate welfare demands.[7]

In the years that followed, Licata worked with a "progressive bloc" on the council that kept pressing a social justice and environmental agenda. They passed a series of reforms to improve civilian oversight over the police department. They approved a twenty-cent plastic bag and paper tax, and when voters overturned it in a referendum—one that the American Chemical Council spent $1.4 million to win—the council responded in 2012 with a total ban on single-use plastic bags. That ban survived all challenges, and in its first four years it reduced the volume of plastic bags in city landfills by 50 percent.[8]

But the most intractable problem facing Seattle progressives has been housing. Given the city's rapid growth in population, "it's the number one issue, even more important than the economy," Licata says. "We have a huge homeless population, and a lot of people, minorities, are literally being forced out of the city for lack of affordable housing." Back in 1981, Seattle launched an innovative property levy to fund affordable housing construction. At a median cost to home owners of $65 a year, it has been repeatedly reauthorized and has funded more than ten thousand affordable apartments. But it scarcely addresses the growing need. In 2015, the council passed landmark legislation that levied an affordable housing fee on all new office and apartment construction. Ranging from $8 per square foot in lower-income areas to $17.50 per square foot downtown, it is expected to generate nearly $200 million over ten years to fund thousands of low- and moderate-income units.[9]

But turnover in the council and deepening class and racial divisions in the city have made it harder to define a "progressive." The election of socialist Kshama Sawant to the council in 2013 made that quite apparent (see chapter 9). "The cutting edge in Seattle is between the liberal urbanist and the social justice liberal," Licata insists. "Social justice liberals are very interested in things like rent control, inclusionary zoning, development fees, all things that tap the revenue stream from developers and siphon off some of that money for those who can't afford the housing market. The liberal urbanists, and I'm not sure they even understand it, argue the Reagan theory of trickle-down economics:

if you have a big enough supply you will be able to find enough housing because it will be cheaper per unit. What they miss is that more people are moving into the area and that keeps [the price of housing] up."

Licata retired in 2015 after serving five terms on the Seattle city council. By then, he'd become a fixture in city politics and had founded and co-chaired Local Progress, the national alliance of progressive urban officials. Meanwhile, Seattle had changed its council elections from at-large seats to individual districts. With Licata's backing, his longtime aide Lisa Herbold then ran for one of the new district seats and eked out a narrow victory.

Gayle McLaughlin and the Rise of Richmond's Radicals

The rest of the nation has long regarded the northern California cities of San Francisco, Oakland, and Berkeley as isolated liberal enclaves. But in 2004, the gritty East Bay city of Richmond, in western Contra Costa County, suddenly emerged as ground zero for the new urban progressive movement. Richmond had been a center for shipbuilding, automobile, and petroleum production during World War II, drawing tens of thousands of black and white migrants from the South to its industrial plants. More than 20 percent of workers in the town's Kaiser shipyards were African American by the war's end. But most of those plants fled during the next half century, except for the sprawling Chevron refinery, which stretches across nearly three thousand acres, employs twelve hundred workers, processes some 240,000 barrels of oil per day, and has been for decades the biggest employer and most influential force in the city.

Industrial flight brought inevitable economic decline, with Richmond's population shrinking drastically after the war. It would take until 2000 for the city to regain its 1950 population of 99,000. By 2010, more than 75 percent of its 107,000 residents were Latino,

African American, or Asian, according to the U.S. Census Bureau. With economic decline came the usual social problems: abandoned factories and toxic waterfront sites, high unemployment and poverty, poor schools, soaring crime rates, and the spread of youth gangs. A 2004 national survey ranked Richmond as the most dangerous city in California. On top of that, the town was beset with racial tensions between police and the growing Latino community and teetering on the edge of financial collapse—forced at one point to lay off three hundred employees—following years of mismanagement and corruption by officials tied to the police and fire unions. In 2001, Darrell Reese, the longtime president of firefighters union Local 188, and the city's real political boss, was convicted of income tax evasion. Soon after, grassroots activists came together to form a new political organization, the Richmond Progressive Alliance (RPA), and began to challenge the establishment political machine allied with Chevron and the chamber of commerce.[10]

Green Party activist Gayle McLaughlin became the group's first success story when she won an upset victory for a council seat in 2004. McLaughlin, then fifty-two years old, hardly fits the image of an upstart rabble-rouser. Shy, with a soft, soprano voice, she often exudes an infectious smile, and, like Seattle's Nick Licata, hails from modest Midwest working-class stock. The daughter of a carpenter and a factory worker from Chicago, she dropped out of DePaul University in the 1970s and drifted into anti-war and anti-racism activism. During the 1980s, she worked at a string of jobs in nonprofit organizations throughout the Midwest, while pursuing her passion, opposing U.S. involvement in the wars in Central America through groups like the Committee in Solidarity with the People of El Salvador (CISPES). "I really found in many ways that work to be so fulfilling," McLaughlin said. She also organized for Jesse Jackson's Rainbow Coalition and was a member of North Star, a short-lived political network founded by Peter Camejo, the socialist and Green Party leader who later ran several times for governor of California and as Ralph Nader's vice presidential candidate in 2000. McLaughlin eventually finished college and worked as a teacher before moving to Richmond in 2001.[11]

From the start, however, the Richmond Progressive Alliance was not simply a political vehicle for the Greens and white radicals. Cofounder Andrés Soto was a well-known leader of the Latino community, a UC Berkeley graduate and worker in statewide anti-violence efforts. Soto and his two sons had been victims of police brutality in 2002 during a Cinco de Mayo celebration. As they and some neighborhood children approached a street where cops had set up a blockade, they were threatened, then tackled by some officers and pepper sprayed. One of the cops asked Soto's youngest son, then a Berkeley undergraduate, what gang he belonged to. The son responded: "I claim UC Berkeley."[12] The Sotos later won a civil rights lawsuit against the city. They and other progressive Latino Democrats who joined the family's campaign against police abuse subsequently decided to join RPA; so did advocates for the homeless and pro-labor organizations like the local ACORN group, later renamed the Alliance of Californians for Community Empowerment (ACCE).

So when the Richmond Progressive Alliance decided to back both Soto and newcomer McLaughlin as its candidates for the 2004 race, Soto was initially considered most likely to win. The city's business and political elite managed to successfully target him for defeat with a series of inflammatory, last-minute ads, but that allowed McLaughlin, with her quiet, diligent door-to-door campaign style, to "fly under the radar" and pull off an upset.[13]

In the years that followed, McLaughlin and the RPA achieved one stunning success after another. In 2006, she won an upset race for mayor, making her the Green Party's biggest success story nationwide. Two years later, a second RPA member won a council seat, and in 2010 McLaughlin was reelected mayor, while a third RPA member, Panamanian-born Jovanka Beckles, captured another seat on the council. Term limits prevented McLaughlin from seeking reelection in 2014, so she ran instead for another seat on the council and won. Then in 2016, two more RPA members won election to the council, giving the group a clear super-majority of five on the seven-seat council.

Many of the reforms McLaughlin and RPA secured have been similar to those of other progressive local governments around the country. They created, for example, a municipal identification card, ended police department license checkpoints that targeted the undocumented, passed a "ban the box" ordinance to curb discrimination against former felons, and in 2016 won passage of a referendum to institute rent control in Richmond, a measure that rolled back rents to what they were in July 2015.

But some RPA initiatives have broken new ground in tackling long-standing social problems. Take violent crime, for example. Richmond had a homicide rate eight times the national average in 2007. That year, Mayor McLaughlin and the council created the Office of Neighborhood Safety, which dispatched counselors to the most troubled neighborhoods and sought out former felons with offers of fellowships. "The fellowship pays them up to $1,000 a month as long as they follow their program, whether it's job training, anger management, substance abuse, and education," McLaughlin said. "It's amazing. Only one or two out of about 50 have gone back to the life." The result during her time as mayor was a sharp drop in homicides from forty-two in 2006 to eleven in 2014.[14]

The issue that has attracted the most national attention, however, has been McLaughlin's long-running battle to get oil giant Chevron to pay its fair share of taxes and be held accountable for its pollution and safety lapses at its refinery. In 2008, the RPA organized a citizens' referendum, Measure T, that imposed a special tax on large manufacturers, predominately on Chevron. The company, with its allies in the police and fire unions, campaigned vigorously against it, and when the voters approved it by 54 percent, the company went to court. A settlement was ultimately reached in which Chevron agreed to pay an additional $114 million in taxes over fifteen years, thus dramatically easing the city's financial problems.[15]

Wilson Goode, Helen Gym, and the New Philadelphia Story

In 1983, W. Wilson Goode Jr. was an eighteen-year-old freshman at the University of Pennsylvania's Wharton School of Business when his father, Wilson Sr., was elected Philadelphia's first black mayor. The elder Goode had ridden the wave of a grassroots black and Latino empowerment movement that only a few years earlier had toppled the legendary Frank L. Rizzo, the authoritarian mayor and former police commissioner whose cops had terrorized the black community in a city where African Americans comprised more than 40 percent of the population. During Wilson Sr.'s term as mayor, his son became embroiled with other black students in protests on the Penn campus against South African apartheid. One of Wilson Jr.'s close friends and fellow campus protesters was Pedro Ramos, the younger brother of 1970s Philadelphia Young Lords leader Juan Ramos. Pedro would later go on to become Philadelphia's city solicitor and its managing director. After graduating from Penn, Wilson Jr. went to work for a black-owned firm on Wall Street, before returning home a few years later as an economic development aide in several Philadelphia city agencies.

In 1999, Goode decided to follow his father into politics by running for a city council seat. Few expected him to succeed, especially when many top Democratic leaders declined to back him, but he narrowly pulled off an upset as the black empowerment movement that had brought his father into office in 1983 propelled John Street to victory as the city's second black mayor.

By then, however, Street, a former militant grassroots activist, was already becoming the crafty leader of a new business-friendly elite in the black community.

Young Goode earned a reputation from the start as a policy wonk who would produce periodic reports documenting racial inequities in the city's economy. His first, the Greater Philadelphia Capital Access Report, used data compiled by the federal Community Reinvestment Act to reveal that 90 percent of small-business lending by banks was occurring in the region's middle- and upper-income neighborhoods. Goode convinced the council to pass an ordinance requiring banks that held city government deposits to submit goals and strategic plans for lending in poor communities.[16] Those institutions that did not would lose their city deposits. A few years later, Philadelphia mayor John Street rejected legislation that councilman Angel Ortiz, a Goode ally on that body, spearheaded requiring specific goals for use of minority- and women-owned firms on city contracts. The new law, Street claimed, violated the city charter. After Ortiz lost a reelection bid, Goode countered by leading a successful campaign to amend the charter. "We moved participation by minorities from single digits to now what is about 25 to 30 percent of contract dollars to businesses owned by women and people of color," Goode said recently.[17]

In 2005, long before living-wage provisions had become a cause around the country, Goode successfully sponsored a living-wage bill for all city government employees and their contractors. His bill's language pegged the city's living wage to 150 percent of the state minimum wage, making the Philadelphia rate back then $7.72 an hour. But as the state minimum rate rose, so did Philadelphia's living wage, reaching $12 an hour in 2016. Moreover, in a state that has long rejected limits on campaign donations to political candidates, Goode managed to make Philadelphia the first city in the commonwealth to pass such limits for local races.[18]

Goode also locked horns with both Mayor Street and his successor, Michael Nutter, over their efforts to expand Center City's convention center. He held up the council's approval of the expansion until the mayor's office addressed the lack of workforce racial diversity on major construction projects. Mayor Nutter eventually agreed to an annual report that would track hiring and set goals for diversity. And while employment of minorities did improve, the most recent report revealed that no minority workers were being employed in nearly half of 369 construction projects in the city.

During four terms on the city council, Goode became known as that body's most effective progressive voice, sponsoring and passing more than 145 bills while building alliances beyond the city's insular black political establishment. "There are a lot of old school [black] politicians who still view progressives as being [white] liberals and aren't comfortable with that label," he said, "but that is changing." In 2012, Goode joined with Seattle's Nick Licata as one of the founders of Local Progress. Three years later, Goode lost his bid for a fifth term on Philadelphia's city council. He then accepted a post as senior policy adviser to the council's majority leader.

While Goode was making his mark as a progressive policy maven in the council, another Penn graduate, Helen Gym, was leading grassroots revolts against the neoliberal policies pursued by mayors John Street and Michael Nutter. Born in Seattle to Korean-immigrant parents, Gym grew up in Columbus, Ohio, where her mother worked in food services at Ohio State University and her father was a computer technician for Nationwide Insurance. She moved east in the late 1980s to study at Penn, where she wrote for the campus newspaper, the *Daily Pennsylvanian*. After graduation, she took a job as a business reporter in Mansfield, Ohio, and was stunned—even before Congress approved the North American Free Trade Agreement in 1993—by the sheer number of factories leaving Ohio and relocating to Mexico.

When the Rodney King riots erupted in Los Angeles, the scenes of the violence shook Gym. "Watching that on TV, and really struggling with why I was in Mansfield doing this work, being on the outside, believing that reporting things would actually create change, I began to realize the vitality of life was in these big cities." Gym moved back to Philadelphia, started working with a Korean-American community agency there, and eventually landed a job as a teacher at Lowell Elementary School in the Olney section of northern Philadelphia. Those experiences would spark her advocacy work with both Asian American immigrants in Chinatown and the public education movement.[19]

Philadelphia's Chinatown, which straddles the northeast fringe of Center City, dates back to the 1870s and still counts more than two thousand inhabitants. It had been a fulcrum of social activism decades before Gym's arrival, when radical Chinese American college students established a group called Yellow Seeds, at 10th and Winter Street. Between 1972 and 1977, Yellow Seeds members published a community newspaper by the same name, organized against poor housing conditions, against incidents of police abuse, and mostly against repeated efforts by city officials and the real estate industry to demolish Chinatown for commercial development and highway projects. But like many left-wing groups of that period, Yellow Seeds disbanded after a few years.[20]

By the late 1980s, a new group formed in defense of Chinatown. Its founders called it Asian Americans United (AAU), and they took over the old nonprofit status of Yellow Seeds, seeking to continue the legacy of grassroots advocacy for a new generation. In one of its early campaigns, AAU tried unsuccessfully to stop construction of the Vine Street Expressway, a main downtown thoroughfare that ended up demolishing portions of the Chinatown neighborhood. Gym, who joined AAU in the mid-1990s, credits the group with shaping her political outlook. "We really took on big issues: everything from racial profiling, immigrant rights, welfare rights, police brutality, economic development, and gentrification," she said. "It's this little tiny organization that always punched above its weight class."

At no time did that become more evident than in early 2000, when newly elected mayor John Street announced plans to build a new baseball stadium for the Phillies in the middle of Chinatown. AAU and other Chinatown organizations and businesses launched an all-out campaign to oppose Street's plan, with Gym playing a visible role as the campaign's spokesperson. Stadium opponents packed city council meetings, organized street protests of more than a thousand people, orchestrated a one-day strike of neighborhood restaurants and businesses, and at one point even blocked traffic on the Vine Street Expressway, and they eventually forced Street to back down and build the stadium in South Philadelphia. Eight years later, AAU waged a similar successful campaign against Street's successor, Mike Nutter, when he attempted to install a twenty-four-hour slot machine parlor in Chinatown.[21]

But while Gym's advocacy for Chinatown made her a wellknown activist, her work to improve public schools proved her to be a formidable political leader. She helped to launch the citywide organization Parents United for Public Education and for several years edited *Notebook*, a respected news organization about the city's schools. In 2001, the Pennsylvania legislature imposed a state panel to administer Philadelphia's debt-ridden and academically troubled school system of 220,000 pupils. It was the largest such state takeover of an urban school system in the country.[22]

The state's Republican governor, Tom Ridge, sought to turn management of the entire system over to the private for-profit Edison Schools Inc. A year earlier, Ridge had taken over public schools in the nearby city of Chester and handed most of them to Edison to manage. But after 9/11, President George W. Bush named Ridge to run the new federal Department of Homeland Security, and Ridge's successor as governor, Mark Schweiker, encountered massive opposition against Edison from Philadelphia public school parents, good government groups, and labor unions. "The plan was for Edison Schools to come in and do the for-profit model, prove that we can do more with less," Gym recalled. "We said 'no,' you can only do less with less. The only person that gets more is the for-profit company taking an overhead, charging management fees, and exploiting a state's refusal to fund schools properly."[23]

Gym helped lead a parent sit-in at the school district headquarters against the takeover, only this time she had allies in Mayor Street and many of the city's elected officials, who were furious at the state seizure of their schools. Street eventually reached a compromise with Governor Schweiker for some city representation on the new state control panel and for Edison to play a far smaller role. "They were reduced to managing only 20 elementary schools, and they were out of the district totally by 2008," Gym said. "Today they manage nothing in Philadelphia."[24]

The lesson for Philadelphia's many parent activists from such reckless privatization and overinflated promises was clear. Too often, when these companies fail and their experiments fall apart, they leave town after taking their financial cut. "And it's us, the communities, who have to pick up the pieces," Gym said. "We have to fight them with everything we've got, and when we do, we can win. And off of that we have to build."

It would not take long for Gym to put the lessons of her battles against a Chinatown stadium and the Edison Schools to use. (See chapter 9.)

John Avalos and the San Francisco Progressives

In the last months of 2000, the city of San Francisco produced the first surprise electoral victory by a grassroots progressive coalition against the growth machine in a major U.S. city. That year, a slate of candidates opposed to the policies of Mayor Willie Brown captured a majority of seats on the eleven-member San Francisco board of supervisors. Brown had been the powerful speaker of the California assembly for fifteen years before winning election as San Francisco's mayor in 1996. He became a relentless promoter of tax breaks and public subsidies for giant commercial developments, for the burgeoning dot-com industry, and for luxury housing, all of which drove up the price of San Francisco housing and caused the city's homeless population to soar.

In a city that has long had a reputation as a bastion of liberal Democrats, class divisions had been sharpening for years between "growth machine" moderates and progressives who sought a reduction of income inequality, more affordable housing, and greater civil liberties. The city's shift that year to district instead of at-large voting for supervisors no doubt helped the insurgents unseat Mayor Brown's moderate allies on the board. In one district, Sophie Maxwell, an African American union electrician, defeated Brown's handpicked candidate. In another, Chris Daly, a twenty-four-year-old advocate for the homeless and tenant organizer from the Tenderloin and Mission Bay area, became the youngest person ever elected to the board of supervisors.[25]

Daly emerged as the most vocal and effective of the new supervisors, repeatedly battling Brown and later Gavin Newsom, Brown's successor, to produce more affordable housing and stem displacement from gentrification. Two years after they swept into office, the progressive majority turned San Francisco into the first major city to use ranked choice voting, thus eliminating costly run-off elections, but the coalition never succeeded in getting one of its own elected mayor.

One of Supervisor Daly's early aides was John Avalos, a Mexican American labor activist. Avalos had grown up near Long Beach, gotten his master's in social work at San Francisco State University, and worked at a counseling program for at-risk youth before becoming an organizer with the Service Employees International

Union and helping to lead the union's famous Justice for Janitors Campaign.[26]

In 2008, Avalos decided to run for a supervisor's seat himself, utilizing his strong ties in the labor movement and among Latino groups to fuel his campaign. He won his election along with two other progressive candidates, Guatemalan immigrant and Harvard Law graduate David Campos, and college professor and Asian American community activist Eric Mar. "We came in with a solid seven- to eight-member progressive majority who could override the mayor's veto at any time," Avalos recalled. Over the next few years, their bloc kept pressing to reduce the city's income inequality. Avalos secured passage of the country's toughest local hiring laws on city contracts. "We were able to move thousands of African Americans and Latinos into publicly funded construction jobs, so that, by 2016, 40 percent of these jobs went to local residents who have brought their wages back to the community." In 2013, Campos pressured the city's Municipal Transit Authority to provide free passes to low-income youth, a project that became permanent in 2014. That same year, the board of supervisors also made San Francisco the second major city, after Seattle, to approve a $15-an-hour minimum wage, to be phased in by 2018.[27]

In the city elections of 2010, however, the progressive bloc lost its majority, a harbinger, perhaps, of the growing number of professionals escaping Silicon Valley for a more urban lifestyle. "We've been on the defensive since then, trying to stop wealth inequality and displacement," Avalos said. "Between 2011 and 2016, we saw tax cuts for the wealthy, including a big tax break for the tech industry. When Ed Lee was serving as interim mayor, he got through our board a tax break for companies willing to settle on a neglected part of Market Street. The loophole was tailor-made for one company, Twitter—we called it the Twitter tax break. Once Twitter and other tech companies started moving in, the displacement of everyday people and mom and pop businesses went out of control. We're in a situation right now where economic growth for one sector is overwhelming our housing supply."[28]

Avalos, Campos, and Mar were all term-limited in 2016 and thus could not run for reelection. But even fewer progressives won supervisor contests to replace them. By early 2017, San Francisco's moderates had regained control of the board of supervisors. The radical movement that had shown so much promise back in 2000 found itself in disarray.

Upstart Women in New York's City Council

The early years of the twenty-first century gave birth to a new generation of political leaders in New York City's black and brown communities, a shift best symbolized by the rise of two outspoken and radical women activists, Brooklyn's Letitia James and East Harlem's Melissa Mark-Viverito, both of whom would later play crucial roles in Bill de Blasio's progressive coalition.

When they first gained elected office, however, neither attracted much attention from the media or the city's political establishment. James, the daughter of working-class parents, had grown up in the southern portion of Park Slope, Brooklyn, before gentrification swept away the neighborhood's largely black and Latino residents. As a teenager, she volunteered to work with a group of nuns in a storefront on Fourth Avenue that would later become a center for ACORN. "The nuns provided services to the neighborhood, including food, social services, housing, and I helped out," James said years later. She graduated from Lehman College, got a law degree at Howard University, and came back to Brooklyn, where she worked for a time as a Legal Aid attorney. She eventually took a job as general counsel to state assemblyman Al Vann. By the mid-1980s, Vann was still considered the godfather of the black empowerment movement in central

Brooklyn. He had come to prominence in the late 1960s during the infamous Ocean Hill–Brownsville battle for community
control of schools, and later, along with another radical assembly-
man, Roger Green, and U.S. Representative Major Owens, had
formed part of a group of militant black reformers who dared to
challenge the corrupt Brooklyn Democratic Party machine and
even the establishment black Democrats from Harlem, such as
U.S. Representative Charles Rangel and David Dinkins.[29]

James eventually worked for Attorney General Eliot Spitzer
before deciding in 2001 to run for an open city council seat in
central Brooklyn on the ballot line of the Working Families Party. She narrowly lost that race to police officer James Davis, but
two years later Davis was tragically shot to death during a city
council meeting by a disgruntled former campaign fund-raiser.
James then ran again in the special election even though the
Democratic Party opted to give its nomination to the dead councilman's brother, Jeffrey Davis. Dan Cantor and Bill Lipton, the
leaders of the nascent Working Families Party, convinced her to
run on their line again, with Lipton even managing her campaign
and lining up important labor union support. This time, James
prevailed and she became the first New York politician elected
solely as a Working Families Party candidate.

Before long, she found herself battling city hall, the real estate
industry, building trades unions, and even powerful groups in
the black community over the massive Atlantic Yards Development Project in Brooklyn. "My very first week in office, Atlantic
Yards was presented to me," she said. "The sixteen skyscrapers,
the twenty-thousand-seat arena, the displacement of residents,
the use of eminent domain. I didn't have to consult with anyone.
I just knew in my heart that the community would oppose it. So
I came out in opposition, primarily because where the arena now
stands is where homes once existed. So I ran into conflict with
everybody. Everybody except my constituents."[30]

At first, Bertha Lewis and the powerful ACORN group, along

with other black leaders from Brooklyn, were neutral toward the project. But James recalled that after she began in hearings of the city council to challenge the lack of affordable housing in the initial plans, developer Forest City/Ratner rushed to amend them and increased the number of affordable units, going so far as to offer ACORN's nonprofit housing arm a managing role for those units. Forest City/Ratner even devised a community benefits agreement with a previously nonexistent nonprofit organization, BUILD, and then directly funded the group.[31]

At a boisterous public hearing at Brooklyn Technical High School that attracted thousands of supporters and opponents of the project, ACORN and the building trades unions mobilized their members to jeer and threaten James. "It was very nasty," she later recalled. "I had to be escorted out by NYPD as well as some members of the coalition who disagreed with me but nevertheless respected me. The trades union guys then locked me in my car, they jumped on top of it, right after the meeting."[32]

Despite persistent opposition to her by the building trades unions, which bankrolled an opponent against her, James was overwhelmingly elected to a full term on the council in 2005.

That same year, Melissa Mark-Viverito won election to the city council from East Harlem in another political upset. She was an unlikely choice for representative of the city's most famous Latino neighborhood. Born and raised in Puerto Rico in an upper-middle-class family—her father was a doctor who founded and ran a hospital in the town of Bayamon—Mark-Viverito had moved to New York City in 1987 to study at Columbia University. After graduation, she worked for the Puerto Rican youth leadership group Aspira and helped produce a weekly radio talk show, *Con Sabor Latino*, on WBAI, the local affiliate of the progressive Pacifica Radio Network. She then went to work as an organizer for the powerful Local 1199 of the Service Employees International Union.

It was while on the union staff that Mark-Viverito first became involved in electoral politics, running unsuccessfully in 2001 for the East Harlem council seat held by Phil Reed. She was still a relative newcomer then to the byzantine political world of East Harlem's El Barrio. This was, after all, the neighborhood where the legendary socialist congressman Vito Marcantonio had built a radical base of Italian immigrants and newly arrived Puerto Ricans into a formidable voting bloc in the 1940s; where many of the city's first Hispanic leaders got their start in politics. It was also the nexus during the 1960s and 1970s of militant Puerto Rican groups like the Young Lords and the Real Great Society, and in the 1980s of social service fiefdoms out of which emerged the infamous Del Toro brothers, and in the 1990s was the scene of tense conflicts between the old established black leaders of central Harlem and the younger Latino leaders of El Barrio over the apportionment of city services to both communities. In 2001, in fact, Reed's main challenger had been one of the figures from El Barrio's past, Felipe Luciano, the charismatic onetime television news reporter, cofounder of the Last Poets, and former leader of the Young Lords. Four years later, when Reed vacated the seat because of term limits, Mark-Viverito ran again, and once again she faced off against Luciano. This time, she surprised many when she narrowly defeated the former Young Lord by just twenty-six votes.

On the council, as chair of the Parks Committee, Mark-Viverito took to challenging further privatization of parks by Mayor Bloomberg, especially when it came to Randall's Island. A few years later, she became cofounder of the council's Progressive Caucus.

The small group of radicals elected to office around the country in the first years of the new century held a tenuous grasp on municipal power. Except for Richmond, they were confined to city council seats, where they were forced to craft alliances with moderate majorities to get progressive legislation passed. But they were acquiring important experience in governance. And when Wall Street crashed in late 2008 and thrust the world into the Great Recession, they were ready.

6

The Wall Street Crash and the 99 Percent

The whole order of things today is absolutely upside down.
Tax breaks for millionaires, working people suffer, and no
jobs for these kids.

—labor union leader John Samuelsen

Ana Rosado, a veteran New York corrections officer, was thrilled when she and her husband finally managed to pull together enough cash in December 2004 for the closing costs on a $410,000 two-family home in the Throggs Neck section of the Bronx. Despite their spotty credit history, some smooth-tongued real estate broker had somehow arranged a mortgage for them with zero down payment and a low initial interest rate. But their dream house soon turned into a horrid nightmare, as their monthly payments skyrocketed and the Rosados found themselves trapped—along with millions of other Americans—in a subprime mortgage they could not afford.[1]

The meltdown of the subprime mortgage market, rife as it was with fraudulent no-documentation, no-income-verification loans, ballooning adjustable rates, and inflated appraisals, would later spark the Wall Street crash of 2008 and a worldwide recession. "Neo-liberal economic orthodoxy that ran the world for 30 years suffered a heart attack of epic proportions" is how *The Guardian* newspaper described the cascading series of events toward the end of 2008.[2] The massive unemployment and home foreclosures that ensued also led to growing public fury over corporate and political corruption, to new protest movements like Occupy Wall Street and the Fight for $15, and to demands for more regulation over the banking industry. Meanwhile, the Great Recession became the excuse in New York City for Mayor Bloomberg's naked ploy to overturn term limits so he could remain in power. That action, in hindsight, did more to pave the way for Bill de Blasio and his progressive coalition a few years later than any single act of the Bloomberg era.

The Great Recession and the Battle over Term Limits

When I first interviewed Ana Rosado in early 2007, few outside the real estate and banking industry had even heard the term *subprime loan*. The great wave of home foreclosures was just beginning. Rosado's initial interest rate, for example, had ballooned from 6.6 percent to 9.9 percent only a few months earlier, driving her monthly payment from $2,800 to $3,500, an amount she could not possibly afford.[3] Her story was being repeated all over the city. During 2006, banks initiated nine thousand foreclosure actions against New York City home owners, a 50 percent increase from the previous year. And in just the first three months of 2007, the number of new actions soared past three thousand. By then, as many as ten homes per block were facing foreclosure in some areas of south Jamaica, Queens, and Brooklyn's Bedford-Stuyvesant; a nonprofit housing group plotted those foreclosures with red dots on a map of the city, and the result was a virtual outline of the major African American and Latino neighborhoods. The same was true in other northern cities including Chicago, Philadelphia, and Cleveland. And while Sun Belt states such as Florida, Arizona, California, and Nevada suffered far greater foreclosure rates, the disproportionate impact on blacks and Hispanics showed up everywhere. By 2009, an estimated 11 percent of African American home owners nationwide and 17 percent of Latino home owners had already lost or were likely to lose their homes—compared to 7 percent of non-Hispanic whites.[4]

With the nation's financial industry reeling from the growing number of subprime loans, and with panic spreading among Wall Street executives over the fate of trillions of dollars in derivatives and collateralized debt obligations tied to housing mortgages, Michael Bloomberg, then near the end of his second term in office, suddenly decided that the city and its financial community needed his steady hand at the helm of local government. He quietly began plotting an effort in the summer of 2008 to get the city council to extend the two-term limit on elected city officials, even though that limit had been approved by voters in a 1993 referendum, upheld in a second referendum in 1995, and still enjoyed widespread support—and even though Bloomberg himself had repeatedly endorsed it. In July 2008, a city official tipped me that the mayor had done an about-face and was secretly meeting with top corporate and media executives to broach overturning the law. I mentioned this to several of my editors at the *Daily News*, who immediately dismissed it as an unlikely rumor. The following month, the *New York Times* reported that Bloomberg had met separately with *New York Post* owner Rupert Murdoch, *Daily News* owner Mort Zuckerman, and *Times* chairman Arthur Sulzberger Jr. to seek their support for his plan. In a stunning revelation of how the city's elite operate, the *Times* story added: "Many of the city's top business executives have privately said they are dissatisfied with the field of candidates who are likely to run for mayor next year, and are seeking a way to keep Mr. Bloomberg in office. Mr. Bloomberg is hoping that newspaper publishers—and their editorial boards—will back a campaign to ease the limits, giving him some political cover in what would certainly be a contentious battle."[5]

In early October, Bloomberg made it official. Given the deepening economic crisis, he was asking the city council to amend the charter and allow all municipal officials to run for a third term, including council members—an incentive he figured most of the fifty-one-member council wouldn't be able to resist. By then, he'd also convinced the council's powerful speaker, Christine Quinn, to expedite the legislation that would be needed. That this was a blatant attempt to circumvent the will of the voters seemed not to matter to the city's economic elite. Stephen Ross, the chief executive of the Related Companies and the Bloomberg administration's most favored developer on city-subsidized projects, reflected their view: "He has the confidence of the business community and the executive ability to run the city," Ross said. "This is a good time for him to do this. People are scared."[6]

Within days, Bill de Blasio, then a little-known council member, emerged as leader of the campaign to stop Bloomberg's move. He was joined by city comptroller Bill Thompson and U.S. Representative Anthony Weiner, two city officials whose own plans to run for mayor would be imperiled should Bloomberg succeed. But only de Blasio had a direct vote in the council, where the fate of term limits was to be decided. Only he could galvanize opposition among his colleagues, exhorting them to risk the ire of the mayor by blocking his power grab. Scores of community groups testified against the proposal during two hastily convened, marathon public hearings. A surprising number of nonprofit organizations, many of which had benefited from Bloomberg's charitable donations over the years, spoke in favor. Not surprisingly, business leaders rallied to the mayor's side, while the editorial boards of the *New York Post*, the *Daily News*, and the *Times*, just as Bloomberg had hoped, all called for removal of the limit. Despite that immense pressure, the final vote in the council on October 23 was closer than anyone had expected, twenty-nine to twenty-two in favor of Bloomberg's plan. "The people of the city will long remember what we have done here today," a defiant de Blasio said afterward. "We are stealing like a thief in the night their right to shape our democracy."[7]

What Price for City Hall?

Once term limits were discarded, Bloomberg prepared in early 2009 to cruise to victory in a third race for mayor. Given his willingness to unleash limitless amounts of his own money—he'd already spent a record $74 million in his 2001 election and another record $85 million to get reelected in 2005—few politicians had the courage to challenge him. Queens congressman Anthony Weiner, then a popular figure and rising star of the Democratic Party, vowed to do so initially, but eventually reconsidered and dropped out of the race. In the end, only Comptroller Thompson, the city's highest-ranking African American official, and Tony Avella, an iconoclast councilman from Queens, dared to try. And while Thompson easily defeated Avella in the September Democratic mayoral primary, most experts expected Bloomberg to crush the comptroller in the general election. In truth, Thompson was a weak candidate from the start. An affable member of the old-style Brooklyn Democratic Party, he was a moderate politician who had rarely clashed with Bloomberg during eight long years as city comptroller, and had expected to inherit the front-runner status for mayor once Bloomberg's two terms were over, except that the overturning of term limits changed everything. Subsequent public opinion polls indicated voters were deeply angry about Bloomberg's maneuver, but they also showed those same voters generally approved of the way he managed city government.

Bloomberg embarked on an unparalleled advertising blitz to bury Thompson. From June 1 to September 20, his campaign aired more than 4,700 television advertising spots—an average of 42 commercials per day—while Thompson produced a mere 14 spots for the entire period. And in the final two months after the

Democratic primary, Bloomberg's attacks took on the character of a shock-and-awe campaign, as he threw an average of $1 million per day into his bid.[8] News accounts during the campaign continually underestimated the amount of money Bloomberg spent to keep control of city hall. Not until the city's Campaign Finance Board released its annual report the following year was the exact figure known: the mayor had spent the astonishing total of $108,371,688 to win reelection, the board reported. Thompson had spent just $9,352,416—a margin of eleven to one for the winner. On top of that, all the public opinion polls before the election predicted Bloomberg would coast toward a landslide. Some reported a margin as high as 25 percent, and even in the final days, the Marist College and Quinnipiac University polls showed Bloomberg with margins of 15 and 12 percent, respectively. Yet the final result on election night was remarkably close. In near record-low turnout for a mayoral race, Bloomberg barely defeated Thompson, garnering 50.7 percent of the vote to the latter's 46.3 percent. For every vote he collected, Bloomberg had spent $185.[9]

In the same election, five city council members who had voted to do away with term limits were themselves ousted by challengers. Among the victorious newcomers were Jumaane Williams, a young community activist from Brooklyn, and Daniel Dromm, a veteran teacher and public school advocate from Jackson Heights and Elmhurst in Queens. A few months later, Williams and Dromm joined with several other council members to launch a new Progressive Caucus. Its twelve founding members elected as their caucus co-chairs East Harlem's Melissa Mark-Viverito and Brooklyn's Brad Lander. With steady backing from the Working Families Party, caucus members soon began pressing for a raft of new bills, such as paid sick leave and living wages for low-income workers. Outgoing councilman de Blasio never got to join the caucus. In 2009, as mentioned earlier, he left the council to run for public advocate, a citywide post with considerable visibility but little real power, and one that has always been seen as a stepping-stone for future mayoral contenders. He won that race at the same time that John Liu, another vocal opponent on the council of Bloomberg's extending term, prevailed in the race for city comptroller. Thus, de Blasio, Liu, and the progressives on the council all emerged from the pivotal 2008 battle over term limits in stronger positions than ever. As for Bloomberg, even though he had managed to secure a third term as mayor, he had irreparably tarnished his image as a practical reformer above the political fray. By strong-arming the council so he could run for office again, and by expending vast amounts of money against a lackluster opponent, then barely winning the vote, he had revealed a typical politician's lust for power. As one voter told the *New York Times* afterward: "I feel he [Bloomberg] bought himself the election and ran a smear campaign against a nonexistent opponent."[10] The business community had imposed its choice in city hall, but, as the Great Recession deepened and as anger over income inequality swelled, all the moral authority was shifting to Bloomberg's opponents, to de Blasio, to Liu, and to those progressives on the council who had dared to stand up for home owners, renters, and workers and against domination by the city's corporate elite.

"We Are the 99 Percent!"

On September 17, 2011, a group of young radical activists began camping out in Zuccotti Park, a block-long concrete plaza of trees and benches wedged between towering office buildings in Manhattan's financial district. Inspired by the mass protests of the Arab Spring earlier that year and by the movement of the *indignados* that erupted that May in Spain, where tens of thousands of people occupied public squares to protest high unemployment, the domination of big banks, and government austerity, the Zuccotti Park rebels dubbed their own version "Occupy Wall Street."

The media and many of the area's financial industry workers

ridiculed the ragtag protesters, at first, as a minor and inconse-
quential nuisance but, as the size of the encampment kept growing, Zuccotti Park rapidly turned into a boot camp for social
activism, its rhythmic chant of "We are the 99 percent!" echoing
across the nation and drawing unexpected converts.

There was, for instance, the wide-eyed couple I met at the
encampment in early October, Colin Muth and Taylor Anderson,
both twenty. They were newly arrived from Catasauqua, Pennsylvania, still clutching backpacks and sleeping blankets under
their arms. "We came because we've got to do something to
reduce the wealth gap," Muth told me. His girlfriend Anderson had dropped out of community college, unable to afford the
tuition. "We're here to learn how this is done so we can go back
home and occupy Bethlehem," she said, smiling. Did they tell
their parents before they left home? "Sure," Muth said. "And my
dad said, 'Go for it.'"

Before long, tens of thousands of labor union members began
organizing support rallies for Occupy and providing financial
aid to the young protesters. "The whole order of things today is
absolutely upside down," John Samuelsen, the burly, no-nonsense
president of the Transport Workers Union Local 100, said. "Tax
breaks for millionaires, working people suffer, and no jobs for
these kids."[11]

By early November, the Zuccotti Park rebellion had spread
across the country, with makeshift twenty-four-hour camps pop-
ping up in scores of city squares, parks, and college campuses.
Some contained just a handful or a few dozen people, but many
turned into teeming, liberated enclaves that featured nonstop radical debates, 1960s-type communal living, daily marches against
banks and major corporations, and occasional confrontations with
local police. In Oakland, protesters even succeeded one evening
in shutting down the city's busy port. That followed a day of raucous picketing outside major Bay Area banks.[12]

Occupy's lasting impact, however, was on the national conversation over wealth inequality. Media accounts suddenly started to highlight the wealth divide and the failure of political leaders to address it. One of those aroused to action by the protest was Alvin David, a middle-aged, well-dressed black man I met at Zuccotti Park. He told me he hadn't been able to find much work in months. "I come here two or three days a week to join the marches," he said. "This movement is waking the country up, and I want to be a part of it."[13]

Someone else who showed up to express his support was the city's public advocate, Bill de Blasio. The protesters were "speaking to what people feel all over this country," de Blasio said. His remarks were starkly different from Mayor Bloomberg's. "I don't appreciate the bashing of all of the hard working people who live here and pay the taxes that support our city," Bloomberg said after Occupy activists marched to the homes of several Wall Street executives. "The reality is our city depends on the jobs that the financial services industry provides," he added.[14]

It soon became apparent that the standoff at Zuccotti Park would not end peacefully. Shortly after midnight on November 15, 2011, nearly two months after the Occupy protest began, police acting under Bloomberg's orders used pepper spray to clear the site, tore down the tent city that had been erected, and arrested more than two hundred people.

Low-Wage Workers and Small Businesspeople Speak Out

In late November 2012, some two hundred fast-food workers in New York City risked dismissal by walking off their jobs in a one-day strike demanding a $15-an-hour minimum wage. There is, of course, no more immediate and direct way to reduce the gap between rich and poor in America than by dramatically raising federal and state minimum-wage provisions. But when they launched their movement that day outside a Burger King on

West 34th Street in Manhattan, what impressed me most about the strikers was how old they were. These were not teenagers holding down their first part-time job while attending school, as the fast-food industry would have us believe. They included fifty-two-year-old Mary Lopez, her close-cropped hair sprinkled with gray. "I've never been so low in my life," Lopez said, rattling off a list of a half dozen maintenance jobs she'd held earlier in her life at far higher pay. Lopez had lost a unionized job when the state shuttered its Off-Track Betting Corporation in 2010 and all the workers were laid off. She ended up toiling at Burger King for $7.25. Standing next to her was Linda Archer, fifty-nine, a cashier at the McDonald's at Times Square. "I've only gotten an 80-cent raise in the past two and a half years," Archer told me. "It's just me and my mother at home, and she's retired. I've got bills to pay. How are we supposed to make it in this city, with everything so expensive?"[15] It was a tiny protest in a city that counted more than 4 million wage workers and where labor protests are a daily fact of life, but this one attracted unusual media attention because fast-food workers had never before organized such a walkout.

Their action was hardly spontaneous, however. It had been months in the planning by the workers, together with leaders of New York Communities for Change, one of ACORN's local offshoots, and a group of organizers hired by the powerful Service Employees International Union. ACORN had disbanded by 2010, but Jon Kest remained in contact with former ACORN leaders Madeline Talbott in Chicago and Amy Schur in California. "They had all been experimenting with some low-wage workers organizing," Jon Kest's brother Steve Kest recalled. "Jon said, maybe we should organize fast-food workers. I pulled together a meeting with Jon and the organizing director at SEIU, Scott Courtney. Jon, Madeline, and Amy came in and we pitched to SEIU to give us the funding to start. The Fight for $15 slogan came later. It was Madeline Talbott in Chicago who thought of it. We didn't do any research on it. It just sounded good because it was twice what the minimum wage was."[16]

SEIU president Mary Kay Henry initially agreed to pay for forty full-time organizers to jump-start the movement and added scores of others afterward, many of them recruited from the ranks of Occupy Wall Street activists. One of the first New York politicians to publicly seize the moment and back the fast-food workers was Bill de Blasio. He was joined by several colleagues who would later become his main rivals for the New York mayoralty, John Liu, Christine Quinn, and William Thompson. Cynics at the time speculated that all were seeking to curry favor with the Service Employees International Union. Still, one thing is undeniable: upon becoming mayor, de Blasio followed up his words with actions.

In similar fashion, de Blasio carefully cultivated an image while he was public advocate as a vocal defender of the city's small business owners, a group the Bloomberg administration had routinely ignored, except to target them for enforcement of city regulations and escalating nuisance fines. De Blasio issued a scathing report in February 2012 that concluded that 90 percent of New York's 400,000 immigrant-owned businesses had never received any kind of assistance from city hall, even as Bloomberg kept providing multimillion-dollar tax breaks for large companies.[17]

The report also revealed that fines to small businesses from the Consumer Affairs Department had more than tripled, from $4 million in 2002 (Bloomberg's first year as mayor) to $14 million a decade later. And while overall inspections had nearly doubled in the city's outer boroughs during that period, they had inexplicably dropped by 14 percent in Manhattan, where most high-end retail stores were located. More than a year later, I uncovered in a series of *Daily News* articles a startling quota system that pressured city inspectors to generate daily violations and thus greater revenue for the city. There were numerous examples of outrageous fines of up to $90,000 for small immigrant retailers who had been slapped with minor infractions. "We're going after places like hair-weave salons that the department doesn't even license for not having a customer refund policy posted on their walls," one whistle-blowing inspector told me. "We never used to do that." De Blasio immediately denounced the practice. "Before an inspector even walks through the door, the fix is in," he said. His stance was obviously welcomed by those businesses.[18]

By the time the campaign to choose Bloomberg's successor began in early 2013, the Great Recession, the fight over term limits, and the Occupy Wall Street movement had all deeply affected the public's outlook. Many voters were furious at the abuse of power by the 1 percent and at the spread of racial and income inequality. The main themes of de Blasio's platform, in other words, had already taken shape.

7

Insurgents Capture City Hall

[T]he City's highest officials have turned a blind eye to the evidence that officers are conducting stops in a racially discriminatory manner. In their zeal to defend a policy that they believe to be effective, they have willfully ignored overwhelming proof that the policy of targeting "the right people" is racially discriminatory and therefore violates the United States Constitution.

—U.S. District Judge Shira Scheindlin, *Floyd v. City of New York*

In a press conference in front of his three-story row home in Park Slope, Brooklyn, on January 27, 2013, public advocate Bill de Blasio made it official: he was entering the race for mayor. Flanked by his fifteen-year-old son, Dante, and his wife, Chirlane, who introduced her husband as "an outer-borough working dad," and cheered on by hundreds of supporters, de Blasio revealed the main theme of his campaign: the "Tale of Two Cities," one where "city hall too often has catered to the interests of the elite rather than the needs of everyday New Yorkers."

"One in five of our fellow New Yorkers lives in poverty, and that's not acceptable," de Blasio said as he pinpointed what he planned to change: "Too many working parents lack the basics:

childcare and afterschool programs they can afford, paid sick days they need, because no New Yorker . . . should have to choose between going to work when they're deeply sick or staying home and losing a day's pay . . . or maybe even losing their job." He blasted the city's "broken stop-and-frisk policy" and criticized Mayor Bloomberg's "demonizing [of] teachers" and the city's "unfair" water bills.[1]

At the time, few political experts gave de Blasio any chance of victory. A Quinnipiac University poll two months earlier had proclaimed that council speaker Christine Quinn had a "commanding" lead among mayoral hopefuls. Among registered Democrats, 32 percent favored Quinn, according to the poll, with only 10 percent preferring her closest potential rival, former city comptroller Bill Thompson, while both de Blasio and the current comptroller, John Liu, were lagging behind in the paltry single digits. Despite Quinnipiac's New York polls being notoriously unreliable in the past, especially when gauging sentiment among black and Hispanic voters, the results prompted media reports to anoint Quinn as the front-runner, especially given her close relationship to outgoing mayor Bloomberg.[2]

Ken Sunshine, the publicist and friend of de Blasio, recalls that that "the finance committee meetings for his mayoral campaign were held in my old office and I was the richest guy in the room. And that shows it wasn't the kind of finance committee you need."[3]

But de Blasio enjoyed advantages that were not apparent at first: his clear message of opposing income inequality, his consistent opposition to the privatization policies of the Bloomberg era; his loyal group of grassroots and labor activists, along with liberal operatives with experience in the Obama campaigns and other national Democratic races; a close-knit multiracial family whose members would play pivotal roles in winning voters to his side.

The Core Group

Many of the key players in de Blasio's mayoral run came from ACORN or the Working Families Party or labor unions like the Service Employees International Union and the Communications Workers of America. But there was another group of people who joined the campaign in its early stages, veteran operatives of liberal Democratic campaigns, either Barack Obama's two presidential victories or other races. Nick Baldick, of Hilltop Public Solutions, for example, had been a campaign manager for John Edwards's presidential run in 2008 and was a friend of de Blasio dating back to their days working on the 1996 Clinton-Gore effort. Baldick's partner at Hilltop, Bill Hyers, who had not known de Blasio previously, was hired to be the campaign's manager, while Rebecca Katz, another Hilltop employee, began handling press duties. John Del Cecato from AKPD Message & Media, the firm founded by Obama strategist David Axelrod, took charge of creating television ads, including the blockbuster commercial that would feature de Blasio's son Dante and that would later be credited with marshaling significant support among the city's black voters. Meanwhile, de Blasio's friend Jonathan Rosen of BerlinRosen, the consulting firm for both liberal nonprofit groups and some of the city's biggest real estate development companies, became the campaign's main policy strategist.[4] In early 2013, Wisconsin resident Phil Walzak, who had worked for Obama in 2008 and for the losing effort to recall Republican governor Scott Walker, joined the de Blasio team, soon after completing a stint as spokesman for the successful 2012 U.S. Senate race of Wisconsin's Tammy Baldwin, the nation's first openly gay senator.[5] Arnie Segarra, a veteran political operative who worked in the Lindsay administration and who had served as an advance man and confidant for both Mayor David Dinkins and Bronx borough president Fernando Ferrer, became the first major Latino leader to join de Blasio's circle of mostly white and black supporters.

This unwieldy combination of radical neighborhood activists and traditional political operatives would go on to engineer de Blasio's come-from-behind victory, then help spearhead his ambitious agenda to reduce income inequality during his first year in office. But several members of that same core group would also become enmeshed within a few years in widening probes by federal and state investigators into potential conflicts of interest and influence peddling within the de Blasio administration. Those probes tarnished the mayor's image as a progressive reformer, and they threatened throughout all of 2016 to damage his reelection effort, until prosecutors announced in March of 2017 that they had decided none of the allegations warranted criminal charges (see chapter 10).

Paid Sick Leave, Horses, and Unions

Of all candidates in the 2013 mayoral race, city council speaker Christine Quinn was closest to incumbent mayor Michael Bloomberg. Though Quinn was a liberal Democrat from Manhattan's Chelsea and West Village neighborhoods, and Bloomberg a Republican turned Independent, the two had cooperated for years, with Quinn serving as the mayor's loyal lieutenant in promoting massive development projects at Brooklyn's Williamsburg-Greenpoint waterfront and the Atlantic Yards, at Yankee Stadium in the Bronx, and at Manhattan's Hudson Yards. Most important, she had orchestrated and spearheaded the 2008 vote in the council to extend term limits so that Bloomberg could seek a third term as mayor. As a result, the mayor had practically designated her his chosen successor.[6] But shortly after she officially declared her candidacy for mayor on March 10, 2013, Quinn was forced to permit a vote in the council on legislation that Bloomberg and the city's business community vehemently opposed, a bill mandating that private employers provide at least five days of paid sick leave per year to their workers. The council's Progressive Caucus had been pushing the measure since 2010 and had secured a veto-proof majority of the council's members behind it, but Quinn had stubbornly used her power as speaker for nearly three years to block any vote on the floor.[7] Now, however, the Working Families Party and several major unions whose endorsement she hoped to secure were making the sick leave measure a litmus test for all mayoral candidates, and rivals like de Blasio had made it part of their platform and were blasting her for opposing it. So in late March, Quinn negotiated a compromise bill, one that covered fewer workers. Under her plan, the law would only take effect a year later and at first it would only cover businesses with twenty or more workers. That would mean up to 1 million low-wage employees would finally be entitled to a few paid sick days, but hundreds of thousands of others who worked in small restaurants and retail stores would be excluded. The compromise then passed with enough votes to override the expected Bloomberg veto.[8]

The Working Families Party celebrated Quinn's turnaround as a partial victory for progressives, but de Blasio dismissed the compromise as insufficient and vowed if elected mayor to enact a tougher version. "Bill was very disappointed with us for backing discharge on a weaker sick leave bill," WFP director Bill Lipton recalled.[9]

In early April, Quinn faced another major problem: a shadowy political action group named New York City Is Not for Sale launched a blitz of television commercials against her for refusing to support a ban on horse carriages in the city, which the animal rights group NYCLASS was advocating. The commercials, produced by the Advance Group, a lobbying firm, severely damaged Quinn's image. Over the next two months, her support in public opinion polls plummeted from 32 percent to 18 percent. "You can argue about what percentage we contributed to [Quinn's fall]," Scott Levenson, the veteran political operative who runs the Advance Group, said, "but you cannot deny that we were one of, if not the major contributing factors."[10] Fund-raising for that advertising campaign by NYCLASS would later lead to FBI and state attorney general investigations for possible campaign law violations, after clear links were uncovered between the horse carriage group and key de Blasio supporters.[11]

By late April, with Quinn dropping in the polls, Anthony Weiner, the disgraced former Queens congressman who had resigned his seat two years earlier over a sexting scandal, suddenly emerged as a potential new candidate for mayor. Weiner sought to position himself as a rival to de Blasio among the left-liberal wing of Democratic Party voters. But only a day after Weiner made his official announcement in late May, the de Blasio campaign sought to undercut it by unveiling a major endorsement from the city's biggest and most influential health care labor union, 1199/SEIU.[12]

The Fight over Stop-and-Frisk

While the growth of income inequality and the crisis of affordable housing were dominant issues in the early months of the mayoral primary, many Democratic voters found it hard at first to distinguish between Quinn, Thompson, Liu, Weiner, and de Blasio on those issues. But de Blasio clearly stood apart from his rivals when it came to police-community relations and the NYPD's notorious stop-and-frisk policies.

Under Bloomberg's police commissioner Raymond Kelly, the targeting of young African Americans and Latinos for questioning and searches on city streets had turned into an epidemic of police harassment and a flashpoint in black and brown neighborhoods. Between 2001, the year before Bloomberg took office, and 2011, the annual number of police stops skyrocketed by more than 600 percent, from 97,296 to 685,724, according to records compiled by the New York Civil Liberties Union. The mayor and Commissioner Kelly defended stop-and-frisk as a critical tool for confiscating illegal guns and reducing murders and gun violence. But the facts told a different story. During those same years, the number of shootings barely changed from 1,892 annually to 1,821, and murders declined just 19 percent, from 649 to 526. Meanwhile, black and Latino residents, who were half the city's population, made up close to 90 percent of those stopped by police; and in about 88 percent of the stops—more than 3.8 million—no one was charged with any crime. Even in predominantly white neighborhoods, blacks and Latinos were more likely to be stopped and searched. In Brooklyn's Park Slope, for example, where they comprised 24 percent of the population, they were 79 percent of those stopped in 2011.[13] For minority youth, police harassment had become a frustrating and daily fact of life under Bloomberg. In 2012, a *New York Times* editorial noted: "Young black and Hispanic men continued to be stopped in disproportionate numbers. They are only 4.7 percent of the city's population, yet these males, between the ages of 14 and 24, accounted for 41.6 percent of stops last year. More than half of all stops were conducted because the individual displayed 'furtive movements'—which is so vague as to be meaningless."[14]

Kelly's continued defense of stop-and-frisk made him a lightning rod in the mayoral race, especially after reports surfaced that Quinn had agreed to retain him as police commissioner if she won the race.[15]

"Bill was the only candidate out there early in city council on the police accountability issues," de Blasio's campaign strategist Jonathan Rosen said, "and our campaign was the first to say Ray Kelly would not stay on as police commissioner."[16]

De Blasio, Weiner, and Comptroller John Liu emerged as the mayoral candidates most critical of stop-and-frisk. Only Liu called for its total abolition, but Liu's candidacy had been crippled by an ongoing federal probe of his campaign finances.[17] Quinn was more moderate in her criticisms of stop-and-frisk, and Thompson, despite being the only African American in the race, became the most vocal defender of the policy, eventually winning the endorsement of police unions for his conservative stance but damaging his image in the black community.[18]

By March 2013, *Floyd v. City of New York*, a class-action civil rights lawsuit by victims of stop-and-frisk that the Center for Constitutional Rights originally filed in 2008, came to trial in Manhattan federal court before U.S. district court judge Shira Scheindlin. The twenty-week trial focused renewed public attention on the issue, though the NYPD had already begun to dramatically reduce stop-and-frisk after Judge Scheindlin ordered a trial of the facts to go forward. But before Scheindlin rendered her decision in the case, the city council's Progressive Caucus forced Speaker Quinn's hand on two police account-ability bills collectively known as the Community Safety Act, which caucus members Jumaane Williams and Brad Lander had sponsored. One bill proposed the creation of an independent inspector general to review police department policy, while the other expanded the definition of bias-based profiling and allowed individuals to sue police officers who violated the new law. Bloomberg and Kelly vehemently opposed both, and Quinn initially sought to stall any action on them. But when her col-leagues rebelled and forced a floor vote, Quinn ended up sup-porting the oversight bill while opposing the profiling bill. The fifty-one-member council nonetheless passed both measures with veto-proof majorities, and Bloomberg subsequently chal-lenged them in court. By the summer, stop-and-frisk was the most emotionally charged issue of the mayoral race, with aides to Bloomberg even taking the extraordinary step of trying to discredit Judge Scheindlin by claiming she was biased against the police.[19]

Dante, the Judge, and a Turning Point

In late July, a second scandal erupted involving Anthony Weiner, with photos of him publicized that were connected to his sexting with three additional women. That effectively ended Weiner's mayoral hopes, though he refused to bow out of the race, and de Blasio suddenly started to rise in public opinion polls. A few weeks later, a series of events marked the turning point of the mayoral primary.

On August 8, the de Blasio campaign aired one of the most remarkable television ads of any political campaign. Only thirty seconds long, it featured a fifteen-year-old kid with an oversized 1970s-style Afro haircut, who was identified only as Dante, and who talked succinctly and sincerely about candidate de Blasio's platform. "He's the only Democrat with the guts to really break from the Bloomberg years," Dante said. "The only one who will raise taxes on the rich to fund early childhood and after-school programs. He's got the boldest plan to build affordable housing. And he is the only one who will end a stop-and-frisk era that unfairly targets people of color. Bill de Blasio will be a mayor for every New Yorker, no matter where they live or what they look like, and I'd say that even if he weren't my dad."[20]

The stunning tag line reinforced for every New Yorker who didn't know already—and at that point many did not—that the de Blasios were a multiracial family, that their teenage son was an enthusiastic, telegenic, and articulate backer of his father, and that stop-and-frisk, the police tactic dreaded by many black and Latino parents, would be overhauled under a de Blasio administration. Four days later, Judge Scheindlin ruled in a landmark decision that stop-and-frisk as practiced by the NYPD violated the Fourth and Fourteenth Amendments for its illegal use of search and seizure and its subversion of the Constitution's equal-protection clause. "The City adopted a policy of indirect racial profiling by targeting racially defined groups for stops based on local crime suspect data," Scheindlin wrote in her decision. She went on to say:

> This has resulted in the disproportionate and discrim-
> inatory stopping of blacks and Hispanics. . . . I also
> conclude that the City's highest officials have turned a
> blind eye to the evidence that officers are conducting
> stops in a racially discriminatory manner. In their zeal
> to defend a policy that they believe to be effective,
> they have willfully ignored overwhelming proof that
> the policy of targeting "the right people" is racial-
> ly discriminatory and therefore violates the United
> States Constitution.

The judge then ordered, in a separate remedy decision, the appointment of an independent monitor to oversee the NYPD's reform of its stop-and-frisk policies.[21]

A week later, on August 19, de Blasio and his wife, Chirlane, appeared in another televised campaign ad. Titled "Dignity," it directly referred to stop-and-frisk, with de Blasio saying: "Chirlane and I have talked to Dante many times about the fact that someday you will be stopped." A narrator's voice followed with the words: "Bill de Blasio, the only candidate to end a stop-and-frisk era that targets minorities." The ad went on to mention his plans to tax the rich to pay for after-school programs, but its main message was clear: de Blasio was the anti–racial profiling candidate.

The Bloomberg administration immediately appealed Scheindlin's rulings and a federal appeals court later remanded her "remedy" decision back to the district court for review by another judge. But de Blasio's voter support in most polls had zoomed past 30 percent by the end of August and it continued to climb, while Quinn's had gone into a tailspin from which she never recovered.

On September 10, de Blasio captured 40 percent of the vote in the Democratic primary against eight other candidates, thus avoiding a run-off with his closest rival, Thompson, who garnered 26 percent. Quinn finished a distant third at 15 percent, with Liu at 7 percent and Weiner under 5 percent. Two months later, de Blasio romped to a landslide victory in the November general election against Republican Joe Lhota, capturing more than 70 percent of the vote.[22] In a city where Democrats outnumber Republicans by six to one, two previous Republican mayors, Giuliani and Bloomberg, had somehow managed to buck the odds by marketing themselves as nonpolitical and liberal on social issues. But Lhota proved to be a more traditional conservative candidate whose message never resonated among independent voters or moderate Democrats.

While de Blasio coasted to victory in the Democratic primary, other candidates supported by the Working Families Party prevailed in a series of contests. Councilwoman Letitia James won a hard-fought run-off election for public advocate. Manhattan borough president Scott Stringer, a traditional liberal Democrat who also enjoyed WFP support, captured the city comptroller's seat. And of the more than twenty new council members, nearly half won with the backing of the Working Families Party. In the days after the election, membership in the council's Progressive Caucus jumped from twelve to nineteen. The final victory came in early January 2014, when the Working Families Party, the Service Employees International Union, and Mayor de Blasio secured enough backing from old-line Democratic Party leaders to get East Harlem councilwoman Melissa Mark-Viverito elected speaker of the city council.[23] The combination of de Blasio, Mark-Viverito, Stringer, and James had produced the most radical municipal government in New York's history.

8

New Day in Gotham

The city just took a hard turn. It wasn't like slow or methodical. It was like, Aiiyee! There are going to be growing pains.

—Jumaane Williams, New York City councilman

At his inauguration as mayor on that cold New Year's Day of 2014, Bill de Blasio spoke bluntly both to Democratic Party stalwarts, many of them angling for patronage jobs or city contracts now that one of their own was in power, and to the many skeptics who had already started dismissing his vow to tackle the city's yawning income inequality as just naive and unattainable campaign rhetoric. "There are some who think now, as we turn to governing—well, things will continue pretty much like they always have," de Blasio declared to them all. "So let me be clear. When I said we would take dead aim at the Tale of Two Cities, I meant it. And we will do it."

It was the first inkling the public had that de Blasio was serious about transforming how government bureaucracy serves its residents, that he was serious about ending the conservative market-oriented policies that for decades had favored the city's wealthy elite. It is, of course, far easier to criticize what is wrong with government than to devise effective and imaginative ways to reform its operation. Yet over his first hundred days, and certainly during the first two years of his administration, de Blasio and his allies in the city council produced a stunning array of new laws and regulations, programs, and labor agreements, the biggest of which, their launch in September 2014 of universal, free pre-kindergarten for New York City's public schools, should be judged one of the truly extraordinary educational accomplishments by any municipal government in modern U.S. history. Moreover, the combination of de Blasio's early reforms resulted in a sudden and enormous infusion of income and new economic benefits to the city's working and middle classes. The extent of that infusion has yet to be definitively tabulated, but as documented in this chapter, it almost certainly surpassed $21 billion, and its size will continue to grow for years to come. In short, de Blasio dramatically moved New York City back to its early twentieth-century role as the nation's trendsetter for progressive and radical social reform.

But the new mayor did more than redirect the mission of local government by launching or expanding a raft of reforms that included universal pre-K and after-school programs, long-overdue wage increases for municipal workers, paid sick leave for all, a virtual freezing of tenant rents, and a municipal ID system now utilized by nearly 1 million city residents. He sought, as well, to dispel the notion that liberals are simply tax-and-spend politicians who can never make the trains run on time, collect the garbage, or keep crime rates low. While Giuliani had filled the top ranks of his administration with criminal prosecutors, and Bloomberg with corporate executives who had little prior experience in government, de Blasio consciously recruited his top staff from the ranks of two entirely different sectors, combining skilled technocrats who had racked up decades of experience managing major public agencies, some as far back as the Koch and Dinkins eras, with a slew of progressive labor and community activists, and then he directed them all to pursue twin goals of equity in city services and effective governance.

The result was felt in more than dollars and cents or better garbage pickup. At times it involved simple decisions that garnered little public attention. In September 2016, for example, the city administered flu shots for the first time in its history to its 300,000 employees. "No one ever did that," said Dean Fuleihan, de Blasio's no-nonsense budget director and a veteran of more than thirty years of crafting budgets in Albany for the state assembly. "Businesses always did this but the city never did this. It wasn't that kind of relationship with their employees." Such a seemingly small change, Fuleihan noted, would more than pay for itself through increased productivity from city workers and reduced health care costs for the city.[1]

Then there was the directive that Health and Human Resources commissioner Steven Banks sent just before Christmas 2015 to the city's various homeless shelters. De Blasio had put Banks, the former activist and attorney for the Legal Aid Society, in charge of overhauling the troubled shelter program. One issue homeless advocates had complained about for years was the city's policy of emptying shelters each morning and forcing residents to stay out on the street until the evening. "I told the shelter directors we expected people to be permitted to remain in the shelters throughout the day, and that there should be programming in place for them," Banks said, noting, "this was actually something [police commissioner Bill] Bratton called to my attention before."[2]

The speed with which the de Blasio coalition moved on its progressive platform caught the city's conservative circles by surprise, and it soon sparked fierce opposition from several quarters, including police unions, the charter school movement and its Wall Street hedge fund backers, and even Governor Andrew Cuomo, de Blasio's fellow Democrat and onetime boss. That resistance, in turn, led to several embarrassing setbacks for the new mayor in his first year. Meanwhile, most media coverage of the new administration seemed to focus more on de Blasio's personal foibles and miscues than on the enormous economic impact of his policies. Stories even appeared of how insulted New York's social elite felt because de Blasio and First Lady Chirlane McCray rarely attended high-profile soirees like the Metropolitan Museum's annual costume gala, as previous mayors had done.[3]

Recruiting a Team

Ever since the days of Fiorello La Guardia, the mayoralty of New York has often been referred to as the "second toughest job in America," surpassed only by that of the president. New York's municipal government raises and spends more money annually than the central governments of most nations, including Iran, Pakistan, Romania, and Chile. Yet at the time he became mayor, de Blasio had never run anything bigger than the public advocate's office, with fewer than one hundred employees. Now he was suddenly in charge of 300,000 city workers and a massive budget that reached nearly $70 billion in Bloomberg's last year. This was no place for on-the-job training, and de Blasio knew it. Sensing from the start that lofty ideals would mean nothing in a bureaucracy as large as New York City's unless his top administrators could effectively translate those ideals into everyday action, he made sure to surround himself with a group of older, more experienced government managers he had come to know over the years. But in a pattern that was becoming his trademark, he also sought to combine establishment liberals with advocates for long-neglected communities, who had little government experience. In long personal interviews with each potential aide, he sought to determine if they shared his overriding goal of ending the Tale of Two Cities.

Anthony Shorris, the slightly built, soft-spoken technocrat he chose as first deputy mayor, was typical. The son of famed author and social critic Earl Shorris, he had served as a city budget aide under Mayor Ed Koch, a top executive at the Port Authority under both Governor Mario Cuomo and Governor Eliot Spitzer, and a health industry executive. Soon after de Blasio's victory at the polls, Shorris received a call inviting him to dinner with Bill and Chirlane. A few weeks earlier Shorris had shared some ideas with de Blasio on what a progressive administration in New York City might look like. This time they met at Bar Toto in Brooklyn, de Blasio's favorite neighborhood haunt. They were joined there by McCray, who more than any New York first lady in memory has played a pivotal role in all of the mayor's major decisions and hiring. "We do everything as a couple—we think as a couple," de Blasio would later say of his wife. During the mayoral race, he had even placed McCray's name at the top of his campaign's organizational chart, alongside his.[4]

The dinner turned into a long evening, with the mayor-elect wanting to know everything about Shorris's life story. As the latter described it:

> When Bill interviews, he likes to go back to the beginning and understand what your personal motivations are. He was doing something that he and I then did throughout the staffing of the government, which is, you want to have people with competence, but it was very important to him and to me that there be alignment on perspective and political point of view, and ideology. And that has to be not just a new suit you put on because there's a new guy in city hall, it has to be something that is very core to your values.[5]

A few days later, de Blasio announced that Shorris would be his second-in-command as first deputy mayor. He then chose veteran managers to fill two other key positions, police commissioner and schools chancellor. He brought back sixty-six-year-old William Bratton, the city's police commissioner during the early 1990s under Rudy Giuliani and former police chief in both Boston and

Los Angeles, to run the police department a second time; and he convinced seventy-year-old Carmen Fariña, the veteran teacher, principal, and former superintendent of de Blasio's own Brooklyn school district, to leave her retirement home in Florida to run the whole school system.

Widely admired by both the business community and rank-and-file cops, Bratton was credited with modernizing the NYPD and masterminding an astonishing drop in the city's crime rate, at least until he was forced to resign in a clash with Mayor Giuliani. But many leaders in the African American and Latino communities were skeptical about Bratton's return. They warned that his "broken windows" policing practice—cracking down on low-level misdemeanors as a way to prevent bigger crimes—would only exacerbate the stop-and-frisk abuses that had mushroomed under Bloomberg's police commissioner Ray Kelly.

De Blasio, on the other hand, had vivid memories, from his stint as a junior mayoral aide during the Dinkins era, of that unforgettable day in 1992 when tensions between police and the city's first black mayor exploded, when more than ten thousand white cops surrounded city hall and staged a near riot, blocking traffic, assaulting reporters, and hurling epithets and racial slurs at Dinkins. That event had been organized by the Patrolmen's Benevolent Association (PBA) to protest the creation of a civilian complaint review board, and it had featured the shocking sight of former federal prosecutor Rudy Giuliani egging on the mob.[6]

De Blasio recalled, as well, that soaring crime rates during the Koch and Dinkins eras had been accompanied by a huge scandal within the police department. The scandal erupted that same year of 1992, after several cops were arrested and accused of corruption. It prompted Dinkins to appoint a special commission to examine the extent of the problem. For the chairmanship of the commission, he chose Milton Mollen, a highly respected state supreme court judge. The Mollen Commission, as it came to be known, soon uncovered a frightening story. In the 30th precinct in Harlem alone, its probe led to the arrest of fourteen officers on corruption charges, and it found major criminal gangs of officers operating in several other police stations, including the 75th and 77th precincts in Brooklyn, the 46th precinct in the Bronx, and the 9th precinct in Manhattan's East Village.

Exhibit A was the infamous Michael Dowd of the 75th precinct in East New York, the city's most crime-ridden neighborhood. Dowd not only stole drugs, guns, and money while conducting unlawful searches, the commission concluded he was "part of a gang of cops that raided drug locations almost daily for the sole purpose of lining their pockets with cash." His crimes went on for years, with Dowd being paid up to $8,000 per week by a group of drug dealers to provide protection and information. He drove to his police job in a new red Corvette, threw lavish parties for his friends, and made frequent trips by limousine to Atlantic City to gamble, yet none of his NYPD supervisors ever questioned the source of his money. It would take an arrest of Dowd by the Long Island police to finally expose his crimes.[7]

Such police corruption "has flourished," the Mollen Commission found in its final report, "because of a police culture that exalts loyalty over integrity; because of the silence of honest police officers who fear the consequences of 'ratting' on another cop no matter how grave the crime; because of willfully blind supervisors who fear the consequences of a corruption scandal more than the corruption itself . . . because of a hostility and alienation between police and community in certain precincts that breeds an 'Us vs Them' mentality."[8]

There was, for example, Officer Bernard Cawley of the 46th precinct, a 230-pound bruiser nicknamed "The Mechanic," who, like Dowd, ended up in prison for corruption. Cawley testified to the commission that he routinely beat up innocent civilians in housing projects, raped prostitutes, stole drugs, and burglarized homes. Asked at a public hearing if he ever worried that fellow cops would report his crimes, Cawley boasted instead about the

"Blue Wall of Silence." "Cops don't tell on cops," he testified. "If
a cop decided to tell on me, his career is ruined . . . he's going to
be labeled a rat."[9]

By the time the Mollen Commission's preliminary report was
made public in late 1993, however, Giuliani had narrowly defeated Dinkins in his quest for a second term—and a big reason why
Dinkins lost that election was public concern, especially among
white voters, over the mayor's failure to reduce the crime rate.
By appointing Bratton as his police commissioner, de Blasio not
only chose someone with a proven track record, someone who
agreed with his plan to sharply reduce police use of stop-and-frisk
tactics in minority communities, he also hoped Bratton's presence
would reassure ordinary cops and business leaders that the city's
law enforcement structure was still in good hands. All of that, de
Blasio expected, would give him time to roll out his major initiatives against income inequality. He never realized, though, how
short that time would be.

Shorris, Bratton, and Fariña were not the only "elders" de
Blasio recruited to his cabinet. There was sixty-seven-year-old
Lillian Barrios Paoli, who had run five agencies under three separate mayors and whom he appointed deputy mayor for health
and human services. And there was sixty-eight-year-old Carl
Weisbrod, whom he tapped to co-chair his transition team and
then to head the city's powerful Planning Commission. One of
those obscure city agencies that rarely gets attention from the
daily press, the Planning Commission is a crucial instrument
of city land policy. Its staff and commissioners determine the
future of whole neighborhoods through zoning changes they
fashion, dictating what kinds of uses—industrial, commercial,
residential, public—any designated areas will have. Bloomberg's
Planning Commission chair Amanda Burden had presided over
massive land-use changes through 124 separate rezoning actions
that affected 40 percent of New York City land. But Burden's
actions had a clear class character—using zoning to tighten use

restrictions in largely white and higher-income neighborhoods, thus preserving those neighborhoods, while loosening use restrictions in lower-income and minority neighborhoods and industrial areas, thus opening them up to more commercial and higher-density luxury development.[10] Weisbrod had worked in the Lindsay and Koch administrations and was well known to all the city's major land developers, since he had headed the vast real estate empire of Lower Manhattan's Trinity Church for many years. Weisbrod, in turn, was instrumental in convincing de Blasio to hire Dean Fuleihan, who for more than thirty years had been the state assembly's main negotiator on state budgets, to run the city's Office of Management and Budget.[11]

These were all experienced government operatives. They were there to make sure the novice de Blasio would succeed in the prosaic art of getting things done. But the new mayor also recruited from the ranks of activists and advocates. The most prominent was Legal Aid attorney Steven Banks, his former rival for a Brooklyn city council seat, whom he appointed to run the city's welfare agency, the Human Resources Administration. "HRA was the first government agency that I sued when I became a Legal Aid lawyer," Banks noted. "Over the years, I sued them for cutting people off from food stamps without providing prior notification; for failure to provide rent arrears benefits; for failure to provide education training; for putting people in workfare programs who had disabilities—a whole range of things around how people were treated."[12] Now, in a startling move, de Blasio appointed Banks to run the very agency he'd spent his career fighting.

He also selected Nisha Agarwal, a dynamic immigrant rights lawyer and former deputy director of the liberal Center for Popular Democracy, to run the city's Office of Immigrant Affairs; and Mindy Tarlow, a tiny woman with a limitless mastery of data, who had spent twenty years running a national nonprofit group that found employment for ex-prisoners, to run the

mayor's office of operations; and Mary Travis Bassett, a graduate of Columbia's College of Physicians and Surgeons, who had
spent seventeen years in Zimbabwe working on AIDS prevention
programs and then as a foundation program officer specializing in
public health programs for Africa, to be the new health commissioner. He plucked Maya Wiley, a civil rights attorney who had
worked with the NAACP Legal Defense and Education Fund,
and daughter of the legendary George Wiley, the founder of the
National Welfare Rights Organization, to be his chief counsel
and to spearhead his effort to bring affordable broadband Internet
to all city residents by 2020.

In early March 2014, de Blasio also appointed Richard Buery
as deputy mayor for strategic policy, and put him in charge
of implementing the massive expansion of free, universal
pre-kindergarten. The son of Caribbean immigrants, Buery had
been raised in Brooklyn's impoverished East New York section,
had gone on to graduate from Harvard College and Yale Law
School, then worked as a staff attorney for the liberal Brennan
Center for Justice before becoming the youngest president of
the venerable Children's Aid Society of New York. Buery had
turned down repeated phone calls and entreaties from de Blasio
to join the administration, and then one night in early 2014 he
was suddenly summoned to city hall, where both the mayor and
McCray sought unsuccessfully to convince him once again. But
they wouldn't give up, Buery recalled. They insisted Buery and
his wife come to dinner at Gracie Mansion a few days later; it was
then that Buery realized he could no longer refuse the mayor's
offer to head the history-making pre-K launch.[13]

From his first days in city hall, de Blasio made clear to his agen-
cy heads that he expected quick action on his progressive agenda.
"He really believed you needed to do big transformational things
in the first hundred days," said Jonathan Rosen, his close adviser.
"He talked a lot about [former mayor] Harold Washington in
Chicago showing people, immediately and physically, change,

how trash pickup immediately changed in Chicago's black neighborhoods after Washington became mayor."[14]

The most ambitious—though not the first—was universal pre-kindergarten.

It Can't Be Done

Who would have thought that a political revolution would hinge on four-year-olds? But that's exactly what happened in the spring and summer of 2014, when de Blasio mobilized everyone in his administration to launch his signature campaign promise of free, universal pre-kindergarten classes. Those accustomed to the "growth" model of urban governance, who judge a city's leadership by how many mega-projects it stimulates, how many jobs it retains or creates, how much commercial activity it spurs, how much it causes land values to rise, rarely pay attention to the needs of young children. De Blasio's extraordinary expansion of pre-K, however, didn't just offer a full year of educational enrichment for every child in the nation's largest school system—an investment almost certain to improve overall achievement levels for the city's future workers—it also freed tens of thousands of working parents from having to pay the annual cost of private childcare for their four-year-olds.

During its first year of operation, universal pre-K enrolled 53,000 pupils, more children than attended the entire public school systems of Seattle or Cincinnati, and nearly three times the 18,500 who had been served by a more limited initiative at the end of the Bloomberg administration. The following year, New York's pre-K enrollment jumped to an astonishing 70,000. During the program's first three years, the city provided full-day education to nearly 135,000 additional children. And since the average New York family pays about $1,000 per month for private childcare, that means city parents were able to save an estimated $1.4 billion because of this one program.

How did de Blasio and his aides manage in such a short time to organize and implement this vast effort—obtaining the funds; selecting, inspecting, and equipping hundreds of sites across the city; hiring and training more than two thousand teachers and aides; marketing the new program to the public; and recruiting and registering the first 53,000 four-year-olds—and to do so without a major mishap?

"Everyone in the media thought, this is pie in the sky, never can happen, he's just feeding people nonsense," recalled de Blasio adviser Jonathan Rosen. "And to his enormous credit, he said, we're going to do this and we're going to do it right away, and that's going to show people."[15] After all, free pre-kindergarten for every four-year-old, along with new after-school programs for all middle-school pupils, was de Blasio's signature campaign pledge—and he had promised to launch both during his first year in office.

Most experts warned it couldn't be done so rapidly, especially since de Blasio planned to fund the $400 million he would need annually to run the program with a small .5 percent surcharge on the city income tax for the wealthiest residents—those making more than $500,000 annually.[16] Such a tax required approval from the state legislature in Albany, where it was sure to be blocked both by the Republican-controlled state senate and by Democratic governor Andrew Cuomo, given that Cuomo was determined to maintain his reputation as a fiscal conservative opposed to any higher taxes. Moreover, if funding from the state did somehow materialize, it wouldn't start flowing until Albany's annual budget was approved in April, and that would leave just five months until the new school year.

As expected, Cuomo refused to approve the tax increase, but he did consent in January 2014 to earmark up to $1.5 billion over five years from the state's annual budget for universal pre-K throughout the state, with most of that money going to New York City. He acknowledged, in effect, that de Blasio's plan had overwhelming public support. Furthermore, Cuomo also understood that the legislature had already approved a statewide universal pre-kindergarten program as far back as 1997 but had never fully funded it after the 2000 recession and the 9/11 terror forced major cutbacks in government services.[17] The governor nonetheless echoed those who predicted de Blasio couldn't deliver on his promise. "Pre-K has to be phased in—you don't have the capacity now," Cuomo said, adding: "If he [de Blasio] can phase it in faster than we think he can phase it in, God bless, we will pay."[18]

Cuomo and other skeptics did not realize, however, that de Blasio had been working out details of his pre-K initiative for months, or that he was determined to turn its launch into a grassroots advocacy campaign. Within days of his election victory, de Blasio recruited a group of seasoned early childhood experts to prepare a pre-K plan. Josh Wallack, an executive at the Children's Aid Society who once had served as policy director for de Blasio in the city council, headed the group. "We had something like six weeks to come up with that original plan," Wallack recalled. "One of the fortunate things for us is that we knew, and the mayor knew, there was already a strong experienced group of early childhood education providers that had been running community-based organizations with really high-quality programs."[19]

Wallack's group urged the mayor to build on the capacity of the existing network of providers, many of them nonprofit community organizations and churches, by creating uniform standards for all of them and offering technical assistance and support. On top of the 18,500 existing full-day pre-K slots, Wallack discovered, the city was already funding 38,500 half-day slots. So the massive effort included, among other things, turning a big portion of those half-day programs into high-quality full-day operations, finding sufficient space for them, recruiting and training more teachers, and supplying equipment and resources.

From April, when the state funding was approved, to the start of the school year in September, de Blasio oversaw the pre-K rollout as though it were an all-out political campaign. His aides established a war room on the fifth floor of 253 Broadway, an office building near city hall, and there they charted the daily progress of all aspects of the program.

"We brought in experts from the Department of Health, the Department of Buildings, Fire Department, Administration for Children's Services, Department of Education, Design and Construction," Wallack recalled, "to all work together to look case by case at each of the sites that were coming online, to figure out what they needed to get done and to work towards readiness for day one."[20]

The Department of Education scoured the country's education schools and solicited more than 6,700 job applicants. It created a first-ever database of all four-year-olds in the city, then launched a massive public relations campaign that included subway ads, mass mailings, and phone calls to every eligible family. At the same time, Wallack's team hired thirty-five community organizers—they were fluent in nine different languages among them—who fanned out into every neighborhood to hold community meetings and recruit pupils. "We had to figure out how to get the kids," said Deputy Mayor Buery. "We can create these seats, but unlike *Field of Dreams*, we didn't want to just believe that if we built it they would come. We were creating a big new program and we wanted to make sure it was a program that every family took advantage of."[21]

So intense and hurried were the last-minute preparations that the weekend before the opening of school, hundreds of new sites still had not been fully cleared for opening, and many were still lacking furniture. A chagrined Buery called the city's fire commissioner to ask for more help. "Over the weekend, I told the commissioner, we need the fire department to go visit approximately three hundred sites, to do a final walk-through to make sure they're okay. He simply said yes, and then got it done."

On the eve of the launch, Buery, Wallack, and a small team spent the entire night in the war room, confirming last-minute delivery of furniture, deciding to keep closed a handful of sites that were not ready. The next morning they waited for what they expected would be phone reports of dozens of snafus and screw-ups around the city. But the phones barely rang. The pre-K program the critics warned couldn't be done had launched with virtually no problems. At the same time, a parallel expansion of the city's after-school program for middle-school children also went off without a hitch, more than doubling the number of young people served from 55,000 to 115,000.[22]

The enormous success of the door-to-door outreach effort around the pre-K program convinced de Blasio's top aides to make neighborhood organizing an integral part of subsequent city hall initiatives, whether that was urging tenants facing eviction to seek out free legal services, or convincing homeless people found on the streets to enter a city shelter, or recruiting applicants for the new municipal ID card. "On a normal day, we might have hundreds of people out there, going out and pushing folks and talking to them," said Emma Wolfe, one of the mayor's top advisers. "It all depends on the given project."[23]

Reforming Police-Community Relations

"We're here today to turn the page on one of the most divisive problems in our city," Mayor de Blasio declared within a month of his inauguration. That problem was the controversy over stop-and-frisk. With his new police commissioner Bill Bratton at his side, de Blasio announced that he was reversing former mayor Bloomberg's decision to appeal a federal judge's August 2013 ruling that the city's stop-and-frisk tactics were unconstitutional. Instead, he was agreeing to reforms that U.S. district judge Shira Scheindlin had called for, including an independent monitor to oversee reform of stop-and-frisk. He thus fulfilled a promise that

had distinguished him from all other candidates during the mayoral campaign.[24]

Later that year, the mayor approved a separate $41 million set-
tlement in a racially charged case that had divided the city for
decades. In 1989, five African American and Latino teenagers had
been arrested and later convicted for the brutal rape and beat-
ing of a white female investment banker who had been jogging
in Manhattan's Central Park. Years later, those convictions were
overturned and the men, who by then were known as the Central
Park Five, were released, after another man, a career criminal,
confessed to the crime, and after DNA evidence proved he was
the actual assailant. The Central Park Five then sued the city, but
Mayor Bloomberg had repeatedly refused to settle the case, with
many veteran police officials and several of the city's major media
organizations continuing to claim the five were guilty, and with
many in the black community calling the case a modern-day version of the Scottsboro Boys frame-up. De Blasio agreed not only
to settle the lawsuit, but to award each of the five $1 million for
every year they had spent behind bars.[25]

By then, however, an unexpected tragedy had stunned the
city—the choking death of an unarmed black man, Eric Garner,
by a Staten Island cop. Garner's death, captured by a bystander
in a harrowing cell phone video that showed cops ignoring his
repeated plea of "I can't breathe," provoked massive protests across
the city. Barely two weeks later, the shooting death of Michael
Brown in Ferguson, Missouri, ignited national protests and turned
the cry of "Black lives matter" into a national movement. In New
York, Garner's death opened a rift between de Blasio and two
groups—Black Lives Matter advocates and the city's police unions.
The former assailed his continued defense of Commissioner Bratton's "broken windows" policing strategy, while the latter—leery
of de Blasio for his opposition to stop-and-frisk policies—accused
the new mayor of stoking anti-police sentiment. Then in November, a rookie cop on a vertical patrol in a Brooklyn public housing

project mistakenly fired his gun into a darkened stairwell, killing an unarmed African American man, Akai Gurley, who had entered the stairwell to walk downstairs. Gurley's death sparked numerous protests around the city from the Black Lives Matter movement. The new tension between police, the minority community, and city hall would turn before the end of 2014 into an open rebellion and a work slowdown by many cops against the new mayor.

Treating Workers with Respect

De Blasio moved rapidly during his first year to tackle other glaring examples of the economic Tale of Two Cities. Within days of his inauguration he announced an agreement with the new city council speaker, Melissa Mark-Viverito, to extend the paid sick leave bill that had passed the previous year so it would cover an additional 500,000 workers. The whole council then amended the law in rapid fashion and accelerated its implementation to April 1. As a result, 1.4 million people—nearly 50 percent of the city's workers—received for the first time a full week of employer-paid sick leave. The economic value of that single reform for those employees equals about $400 million annually, according to estimates of the city's Office of Management and Budget. But even if you just count the 500,000 who received the benefit from de Blasio's extension of the law, it still amounts to $165 million per year, or $495 million for the three years between April 2014 and April 2017.[26]

Exactly four months into his term, de Blasio made an even more striking announcement: his administration had reached a historic nine-year labor agreement with nearly 120,000 public school teachers and school employees represented by the United Federation of Teachers. In the months that followed, de Blasio's labor negotiators hammered out new long-term contracts with unions representing more than 90 percent of the 300,000 city employees. Those contracts provided small but steady annual wage increases of 1 percent to 3 percent, including retroactive pay, at a projected cost to the city of an astounding $15.8 billion by June 30, 2017, yet de Blasio accomplished that without any bitter labor conflict, and without creating any budget deficits or requiring any new taxes. Part of the solution was in getting the unions to wait until after 2018 for some $4.2 billion in retroactive lump sum wage payments. Another was getting their agreement to achieve more than $3.4 billion in health cost savings over the life of the new labor pacts.[27]

New York, of course, has always been a stronghold of labor unions. In 2014, nearly 900,000 of the city's private-sector and public employees were unionized, and they represented 25 percent of all wage earners, which was more than the double the nationwide unionization rate of 11.1 percent.[28] Despite a state law that forbids strikes by city employees, New York's municipal unions, with their ability to make big donations and supply hundreds of campaign volunteers to their favored candidates, remain a powerful force that every mayor must eventually confront. The UFT deal, however, was surprising for several reasons. First was its extraordinary length, far longer than the traditional three-year labor pacts of the past. Second was how swiftly it was reached after years of fierce antagonism between labor unions and Bloomberg's city hall. The teachers, after all, had gone nearly five years without a raise or a contract, while the pacts of virtually all city unions had gone expired for three years. During that time, Bloomberg had become such a foe of UFT president Michael Mulgrew that he even refused to grant the teachers the same 4 percent annual raise for the 2009–10 and 2010–11 fiscal years that all other municipal unions had received during a previous round of labor bargaining. That practice, known as "pattern bargaining," has long been accepted as the way city hall resolved labor relations given the prodigious and unwieldy size of its workforce. From sanitation truck drivers and librarians to crossing guards, park safety officers, and sewage plant workers, to architects and computer system managers, to cops, firefighters, and jail supervisors, to social workers and tax assessors, all belong to their own union—300,000 workers represented by 144 separate bargaining units, each with its own particular work rules and contracts. But the biggest unions—the UFT, along with District Council 37 (the umbrella group for non-uniformed city workers), and the police, fire, sanitation, and corrections department unions—traditionally set the "pattern" for wages. The first of the big unions to reach a wage agreement typically determines the percentage increase all city workers will receive in that round of bargaining.

In addition, the Municipal Labor Committee, the alliance of all city unions, collectively bargains with the city over health benefits for all employees. When de Blasio came into office, the MLC was headed by Harry Nespoli, the crusty, white-haired president of Teamsters Local 831, the sanitation workers union. Nespoli was a perfect choice to run the fractured labor alliance, given that he enjoyed good relations with the two biggest unions by far, D.C. 37 and the UFT, but also had strong ties with the scores of smaller unions that represented the police, fire, and New York City housing employees.

Bloomberg, however, had turned intransigent toward all the unions during his final term in office, not only demanding multiyear contracts with zero wage increases, but eliminating any reserves the city normally sets aside in the annual budget to fund future labor contracts. As a result, independent experts were predicting that if de Blasio attempted to pay the teachers the two years of 4 percent "pattern" increases due them from five years earlier, that alone would cost $3.5 billion, while any kind of wage increases for the other municipal unions could immediately throw the city into a massive $7 billion deficit.[29]

A fair resolution of those labor contracts, in other words, threatened financial disaster. Yet de Blasio also knew that the wages of a big portion of city workers—clerks in scores of government agencies, school aides, and parks employees—were barely above the poverty level. The average annual salary for more than 100,000 members of District Council 37, for example, was just $42,000, and the lower echelons desperately needed a raise. From the start, "the mayor put on the table that we will change the entire dynamic of how we deal with the workforce," budget director Fuleihan recalled.[30]

To underscore that, de Blasio chose as his chief labor negotiator someone well known to the municipal union leaders, Bob Linn. As a young man during the late 1970s, Linn had worked in Mayor Ed Koch's labor office, and in subsequent years he helped fashion labor agreements between Local 1199 and the private League of Voluntary Hospitals, all of which taught him that, when both management and labor wish to reach a labor deal, they almost always can.

Harry Nespoli warned Linn in January 2014 not to even start negotiations with other unions until city hall had reached a deal with the 150,000 workers who hadn't had a contract for five years, mostly the teachers and a handful of smaller unions. From then on, Linn met on an almost daily basis with UFT chief Michael Mulgrew. "Michael was pleased they were finally having a respectful conversation with the city over their concerns," Linn said. City hall's main requirement for any deal on higher wages, Linn told Mulgrew, was a comprehensive plan to achieve real savings in the skyrocketing cost of health insurance for city workers.[31]

"Nothing happened in this city for twenty years on health care savings," Fuleihan noted. "After two previous administrations known for management and other expertise, there was no office dedicated towards health care. It had been negotiated away in the contract and there was nothing anyone ever looked at."[32]

The union leaders clearly understood the need to cooperate with de Blasio, the first labor-friendly mayor in twenty years. And the teachers' contract represented the city's biggest and most expensive labor challenge. The UFT agreed to take the $3.5 billion due its members from the two years of 4 percent pattern bargaining raises that Bloomberg had so far denied them, and to stretch it out into a long-term "repayment plan" by the city to each UFT member. That back pay, however, would go only to teachers who were still employed, not to the thousands who had left the public school payroll since 2009. The UFT also agreed to modest but steady wage increases of 1 to 3 percent for the duration of what would be a second seven-year pact that would run until 2018. That second pact immediately became the new "pattern" for all the other unions. Finally, the Municipal Labor Committee approved a plan to achieve $3.4 billion in health care savings over four years, even taking the extraordinary step of helping finance the labor contracts by releasing $1 billion from a reserve fund that had accumulated in the city's coffers in a Health Stabilization Fund, but which could only be spent with the approval of both the city and the unions.[33] The results were long-overdue wage increases and back pay for virtually all city workers and a health savings plan that was guaranteed to save the city billions in future health care costs.[34]

Even the fiscally conservative Citizens Budget Commission immediately praised the teachers union settlement, noting that it "ensures some stability in labor relations with a major segment of the city workforce for the next five years."[35]

Those savings started to appear in short order. By merely conducting a first-ever audit of the city's health insurance rolls, officials eliminated thousands of people who were no longer eligible, thus reducing annual costs by $100 million. And by aggressively challenging rate increases from the main insurance providers, they saved hundreds of millions more. "That should have been happening all along," budget director Fuleihan said, "but it hadn't happened for twenty years."[36]

The independent budget commission would later caution that some of the city's health savings numbers were more imagined than real, but with de Blasio reporting healthy surpluses in the city's annual budget for each of his first three years in office, and with city workers pumping most of those increased wages back into the local economy, few people doubted that the new mayor, unlike Bloomberg, had managed to solve the city's biggest and most intractable financial problem with relative ease.[37]

The Burning Question of Housing

Most Americans continue to be astounded at the high cost of New York City housing. Not just by news accounts of sleek $50 million luxury condos that pierce the skyline, but by word-of-mouth tales of outlandish rents that tenants are charged for tiny rundown apartments in low-income neighborhoods. By the time Bill de Blasio entered city hall in 2014, one-half of the city's renter households were paying more than 33 percent of their income in rent (even higher than the 30 percent of income level defined as affordable by the federal government). An astonishing one-third of city rental households were paying *more than half their income for housing*.[38]

The new mayor vowed an all-out assault on the issue of affordable housing, both by preserving the city's dwindling stock and by launching an ambitious program to build tens of thousands of additional affordable units. In this area, however, de Blasio's record after three years can only be called mixed. Under his leadership, the city's rent guidelines board instituted a virtual freeze on legally permissible rent increases for nearly 1 million rent-regulated apartments, thus saving the residents of those units approximately $1.2 billion between 2014 and 2017 (see the introduction). In addition, annual evictions of tenants by landlords declined sharply, as more tenants gained access to expanded city-financed free legal assistance in housing court, and as the city council passed new anti-harassment laws geared at preventing unscrupulous landlords from forcing tenants to vacate their apartments. In September 2014, de Blasio

reinstituted a housing voucher program for families in danger
of becoming homeless. Called Living in Communities, the
program supplemented rents to landlords for poor tenants, and
by 2016 it had cost the city more than $195 million, according
to mayoral aides. Finally the New York City Housing Authority, which manages 185,000 units that are home to some of the
city's poorest residents, received major infusions of money from
de Blasio and the council to repair its dilapidated buildings.[39]

Yet those efforts have done little to stem the housing crisis,
given the city's growing population in recent years. In 2000, for
example, just before Bloomberg's election, the Census Bureau
counted 8,008,000 residents—a remarkable increase of 686,000
from 1990. The net gain then slowed to 167,000 between 2000
and 2010. But rapid growth resumed between 2010 and 2015,
as the city added more than 375,000 residents. That's more new
people added in five years than the total population of Norfolk,
Virginia, or Reno, Nevada.

Escalating rents and gentrification became the norm in many
low-income neighborhoods, as median apartment rents jumped
by 75 percent between 2000 and 2012, nearly twice the rate of
the rest of the country.[40] De Blasio thus faced two simultaneous trends—an influx of high-paid white professionals attracted
to the city's booming media, technology, and health industries,
and an even bigger growth of immigrant and nonwhite residents
who were drawn to the low-wage service sectors but who were
hard-pressed to pay skyrocketing housing costs. His answer, and
that of his deputy mayor for Housing and Community Development, Alicia Glen, was to somehow craft a synthesis between the
real estate industry's traditional "growth" model and the "use"
model of housing advocates. He proposed to preserve or build
200,000 units of affordable housing over ten years by rezoning
low-income neighborhoods such as Manhattan's East Harlem and
Inwood, Brooklyn's East New York, and a section of the South
Bronx, allowing developers to build higher structures, while

instituting mandatory percentages of up to 30 percent affordable housing. He sought, in other words, to trade the city's air rights for additional housing.

But community leaders criticized his affordable housing plan because more than two-thirds of all new housing would still be market rate, and because only a small percentage of the affordable units would be geared to the lowest-income families, where the greatest rent burdens exist. They were further dismayed by his choice of Alicia Glen, a former Wall Street executive who was unaccustomed to dealing with local communities, to head his housing reforms. Many had urged him instead to appoint as the city's top housing official Ismene Speliotis, who has headed for more than two decades the nonprofit Mutual Housing Association of New York, the group founded by ACORN to build and manage cooperative low-income housing during the Koch years.

"Ismene would have been the housing commissioner if Jon Kest had lived," a close political ally of de Blasio confided to me one day. Kest, who died of cancer less than a year before the mayoral election, had been one of de Blasio's most trusted advisers and had also worked closely with Speliotis for decades. Kest, Speliotis, and other housing activists wanted the next city administration to use its extensive powers of eminent domain, tax abatements, land zoning, and direct subsidies to incentivize the building of mostly low- and moderate-income, not market-rate, housing, as had been the norm in past administrations. But after Kest's death, the housing advocates say, de Blasio started to rely more on experts closely tied to the real estate industry. He became less willing to involve local neighborhood leaders and nonprofit groups in crafting housing policy. By late 2015, as Deputy Mayor Glen and the city's housing commissioner Vicki Been sought to win approval from the city council for a housing plan that guaranteed too few truly low-income units, protests erupted in numerous local neighborhoods against the plan. Under the mayor's proposal, they argued, gentrification would accelerate even in outlying areas such as East New York and the South Bronx. The council, however, eventually approved the plan by an overwhelming margin.[41] In doing so, de Blasio and council leaders initially ignored the reality that, even if their plans to build or preserve 200,000 affordable units succeeded, the city's sheer population growth, together with the real estate industry's drive for maximum profit, was likely to crush all hope of ending the city's affordable housing crisis, unless more drastic action was taken by local government.

Derailing the IT Gravy Train

De Blasio also moved within his first year to dismantle the vast shadow network of high-paid private information technology consultants who had become lodged inside every city agency during the Bloomberg era, and who kept devouring hundreds of millions of public dollars with terrible results. In May 2014, for example, First Deputy Mayor Anthony Shorris suspended all work on the controversial overhaul of the city's 911 system. The project had fallen years behind schedule under Bloomberg and was already $1 billion over budget, prompting de Blasio to order an independent investigation of what had gone wrong. "This problem could be out of control for both costs and delays," Shorris said at the time.[42]

A few months later, de Blasio canceled a $13 million contract that Bloomberg had awarded to consultants from National Aeronautics and Space Administration for work on the 911 overhaul. Under that contract, more than twenty NASA consultants had been paid average annual salaries of $250,000 just to monitor other private consultants assigned to the project. The city is "changing fundamentally" the 911 overhaul, a top de Blasio aide said, and would now directly supervise its own consultants. Shorris later ordered the dismissal of more than a hundred other consultants from defense giant Northrop Grumman, the project's main contractor, with city officials assuming its direct management. Each of those Northrop consultants, it should be noted, had been paid between $300,000 and $430,000 annually—more than either the mayor or the chancellor of the public schools.[43]

New York City's dramatic turn away from privatizing such a vital area as IT became complete in May 2015, when the mayor's aides reached a formal agreement with the main municipal union, District Council 37, to start in-sourcing hundreds of computer jobs at all city agencies and to give the work instead to municipal workers. "We want to get away from a reliance on outsourcing things that don't need to be outsourced," Shorris said in confirming the historic shift.[44]

The following year, the final portion of the city's long-delayed 911 overhaul—a $1 billion backup call center in the Bronx—was finally completed and opened, but under the supervision of city managers. "We fired the whole [private consultant] leadership team," First Deputy Mayor Shorris said, smiling. "Now the building is operational, the cops are taking the phone calls, and there is $100 million left in the budget." The same occurred with troubled IT projects at the Department of Education and other agencies, Shorris said. The vaunted efficiency and cost savings claimed by the private sector, in other words, turned out to be more sales pitch than fact.[45]

Two, Three, Many Reforms to Count

The sheer number of progressive changes in government policy launched by de Blasio and his allies in the council during their first three years in power can be difficult to grasp, but the impact of those reforms on the everyday lives of New Yorkers is undeniable. They signaled a stark reversal of the "growth machine" model that had reigned in the city for years. Here are just a few:

1. **More equitable funding for city parks**—Under former mayor Bloomberg, the privatizing of parkland for commercial ventures and huge investments in Manhattan parks such as the High Line, Randall's Island, and Hudson River Park became the norm. De Blasio launched instead in 2014 a community parks initiative that has now earmarked $285 million in capital funds to improve more than sixty neighborhood playgrounds and small parks, and another $150 million to build new soccer fields and hiking trails in five major parks in long-neglected neighborhoods such as Harlem, the South Bronx, Astoria, Queens, and Fresh Kills in Staten Island.[46]

2. **Municipal identification card**—In January 2014, de Blasio announced plans to issue a municipal photo identification card that could be used by any resident, citizen or noncitizen, who was older than fourteen for local identification purposes, including opening bank accounts, entering public buildings, and interacting with the police department. The card was officially issued the following year, and it mushroomed in use after Commissioner of Immigrant Affairs Nisha Agarwal convinced dozens of museums and cultural institutions to grant its holders a one-year free membership. By late 2016, nearly 1 million people had obtained the ID card, and de Blasio's aides estimated that New Yorkers using the card had saved $24 million in admissions fees as a result. After the election of Donald Trump, however, the city became embroiled in a court battle over its plans to discard the documents supplied by cardholders to prevent the incoming Trump administration from seizing the information to expedite deportation of undocumented immigrants.[47]

3. **Higher pay for the lowest-wage workers**—In September 2014, de Blasio issued an executive order extending the city's "living-wage" law to thousands of employees of

commercial tenants located on city-subsidized developments, and increasing the wage itself from $11.90 to $13.13
an hour. The combined action was projected to benefit
some eighteen thousand workers, with the lowest-paid
four thousand seeing their salaries increase by $10,000 a
year. A few months later, the city agreed to a $2-an-hour
hike in pay for some six thousand of its employees who had
been receiving less than the "living wage," and in January
2016 de Blasio announced that twenty thousand crossing
guards, seasonal, and other low-wage city workers would
receive a minimum of $15 an hour in pay. At the same
time, the mayor kept pressing Governor Cuomo and lawmakers in Albany to boost the state minimum wage.[48]

4. **Reducing water bills for home owners**—Throughout
the twelve years of the Bloomberg administration, water
rates for property owners skyrocketed, with annual increases averaging 8.5 percent. Those increases were not
only slashed in de Blasio's first three years—to an average of 2.8 percent—but in 2016 the mayor waived some
$563 million in rental payments the water board owed to
the city, then directed a part of the savings to be used to
provide credits of $183 to some 664,000 owners of one-
to three-story homes. The Rent Stabilization Association,
the lobbying group for landlords, immediately challenged
the credit in court because it did not apply to owners of
co-ops, condos, and rental buildings and the courts upheld the challenge. But by early 2017 de Blasio was still
seeking a water bill credit that could withstand a court
challenge.[49]

5. **Expansion of after-school and summer programs**
—A less publicized companion project that de Blasio vowed
to implement along with universal pre-K was a major expansion of after-school activities for middle schoolers. Between 2014 and 2016, the city enrolled 43,113 additional

children in after-school programs and 15,708 in summer programs, at an increased cost of $321 million.[50]

6. **Paid parental leave**—Through another executive order in December 2015, de Blasio granted six weeks of paid parental leave to some twenty thousand managerial employees in city government. His aides then announced the city was eager to negotiate with municipal union leaders a similar benefit for the rest of the 300,000 city workers, if some financial offsets to the cost could be negotiated. Four months later, Governor Cuomo and the state legislature, no doubt influenced by New York City's example, approved both a gradual increase in the state's minimum wage to $15 an hour and twelve weeks of paid parental leave for state employees, one of the strongest such policies in the nation.[51]

7. **Broadband for all**—With 22 percent of New Yorkers having no access to Internet service at home, de Blasio targeted elimination of the digital divide as a key part of his plan to reduce income inequality. He and his chief counsel, Maya Wiley, pursued that goal relentlessly. In June 2015, the city blasted telecomm giant Verizon after an audit revealed that the company's FiOS division was years behind in making high-speed broadband available throughout the city as required by its franchise contract, especially in low-income neighborhoods. De Blasio threatened to reject any discretionary city contracts to Verizon unless it dramatically improved its FiOS rollout. The following month the mayor announced that the city would spend $10 million to provide free wireless broadband to five public housing projects in the poorest neighborhoods, with total broadband infrastructure investment to jump to $70 million citywide. Wiley also fast-tracked a new franchise to turn old pay phone booths into new free wireless hot spots in all five boroughs, though that ambitious plan soon backfired

when the hot spots began attracting the city's homeless population.[52]

As the Crime Rate Falls, the Police Unions Rebel

In a bleak, Armageddon-like television ad released just before the 2013 mayoral election, Republican candidate Joe Lhota warned that "Bill de Blasio's recklessly dangerous agenda on crime" would thrust New York back to the 1980s when criminals over-ran the streets.[53] But something unexpected had happened by the third year of de Blasio's mayoralty: the city's murder and over-all crime rate, already at historic lows, kept dropping. Despite periodic alarmist tabloid headlines and concurrent social media memes reporting occasional spikes in shootings, the number of murders hovered at around the same 330 for each of those three years—far below the 2,000 annual homicides registered during the early 1990s. Meanwhile, the overall number of major crimes decreased from some 194,000 in 2013 to around 100,000 for 2016.[54]

Despite that drop in crime, and despite the popularity of Commissioner Bratton among ordinary cops, relations declined steadily between de Blasio and the leaders of several NYPD unions in the mayor's first year. This is nothing new for those familiar with New York history. Several mayors, from La Guardia to John Lindsay to David Dinkins to Rudy Giuliani, have had contentious relations with the city's police unions.[55] With de Blasio, however, all the police unions—the Patrolmen's Benevolent Association, as well as the smaller associations representing sergeants, detectives, lieutenants, and captains—were already unhappy over the labor agreements city hall had reached with the other municipal unions. Hoping for a better deal, they had refused to accept the "pattern" of modest wage increases those agreements established, with the PBA opting instead to go through a lengthy arbitration process. The union had tried arbitration once before under Bloomberg and secured a more generous wage package than the city's pattern settlement, but labor leaders typically refuse the arbitration option because it effectively relinquishes a union's power, and is considered a form of gambling with the fate of its members.

Then in December 2014, a chain of events began that led to de Blasio's first major crisis. On December 3, a Staten Island grand jury declined to indict Daniel Pantaleo, the officer who had choked Eric Garner to death. That same day, de Blasio, hoping to stave off an outbreak of the kind of violent protest that had occurred in Ferguson, appeared at a press conference in Staten Island alongside Eric Garner's family. "This is profoundly personal for me," the mayor said, as he sought to both console the family and calm the city. "I couldn't help but immediately think what it would mean to me to lose Dante. Life could never be the same thereafter." And while he did not directly criticize the grand jury's findings, de Blasio displayed empathy with the many New Yorkers who were outraged by the grand jury's decision. At one point, he even echoed the slogan of the protesters that "black lives matter." He mentioned how he and his wife had worried at times about the safety of their own biracial teenage son on the street, even instructing Dante "how to take special care" in encounters with police. He was affirming what most black and Latino residents—the majority of the city's population—had faced for decades, especially during the heyday of stop-and-frisk. But his words outraged the leaders and rank and file of the police unions.[56]

In the days that followed, peaceful protests erupted across the country over the Garner decision. At one point, more than thirty thousand people blocked traffic on the Brooklyn Bridge, and in an ensuing scuffle with some protesters at the bridge, two police lieutenants were assaulted. Pat Lynch, the fiery head of the Patrolmen's Benevolent Association, blamed de Blasio for an anti-police climate and began circulating a flyer that urged PBA members to ban the mayor and Council Speaker Melissa Mark-Viverito from any funeral for a dead police officer.[57]

"There was already this enormous tension," de Blasio's senior adviser Phil Walzak said in recalling the events. "Despite it all, the vast majority of protesters were acting very responsibly. The officers were acting very professionally, and it seemed to be going okay."[58]

In the charged atmosphere, Walzak said, "we felt the mayor needed to be a voice of compassion, of coming together in a time of tragedy and sorrow, so the city could begin to unify and heal as one." And that meant being "above the fray and not engaging in back and forth" with his most strident critics.

Then, on the afternoon of December 20, a crazed gunman fatally shot two young Brooklyn police officers, Rafael Ramos and Wenjian Liu, in an unprovoked attack as they sat in their patrol car. When de Blasio arrived that evening at Woodhull Hospital in Central Brooklyn, where Ramos and Liu had been taken, scores of police officers were already jammed in the hospital's hallways. "It was a very tense atmosphere," said Walzak, who accompanied the mayor. Everyone who was in the room was getting facts, preparing the press statement, getting information. We walked down the hallway and there were officers with their backs turned to us. It was a surreal and stunning moment."[59]

Outside the hospital, Lynch inflamed the situation even more by recklessly blaming de Blasio for the two officers' assassination. "That blood on the hands starts on the steps of city hall in the office of the mayor," Lynch said, with Ed Mullins, head of the Sergeants Benevolent Association, making a similar claim.[60]

In the days after the two officers were buried, a massive police slowdown occurred, with arrests and summonses by cops dropping more than 50 percent over the previous year. The wild charges by Lynch against the mayor and the worker slowdown, however, touched off even more public anger against the police unions, especially after major city leaders like Cardinal Timothy Dolan rebuked Lynch's actions.[61] By mid-January, the slowdown had fizzled and de Blasio had weathered his biggest crisis, though the PBA would remain a constant foe of his from that point on.

9

The Movement Spreads

[T]he people been suffering for a while, and fiery speeches are not going to do it. We've got to tell them how we're going to fix their streets; how we're going to feed them, how are they going to eat, where are they going to live. How are they going to avoid being in a neighborhood which goes unattended for so long that it becomes a target for urban renewal which is really just urban removal.

—Chokwe Lumumba, mayor of Jackson, Mississippi

The turning point for the new progressive revolt in urban America came in 2013. That May, Chokwe Lumumba, a veteran civil rights lawyer and former member of the radical Republic of New Africa, startled the political elite of the South when he won an election to the mayor's seat of Jackson, Mississippi—thus signaling that an unbowed black revolutionary was taking charge right in the heart of Dixie. Then in November, the same day that Bill de Blasio prevailed in New York, Bill Peduto, a maverick member of the Pittsburgh city council and persistent critic of the city's Democratic establishment, won election as mayor; in Minneapolis, Betsy Hodges, an experienced nonprofit executive and two-term member of the Minneapolis city council who had opposed public subsidies for a new Minnesota Vikings stadium, emerged from a crowded field of thirty-four candidates to capture that city's mayoralty; and in Boston, trade union leader Martin Walsh cobbled together an alliance of organized labor, white liberals, and key African American and Latino leaders to become the first labor official to be elected mayor in Boston's history. Out west, Ed Murray, a state legislator, won election as Seattle's mayor, in part by promising a $15-an-hour minimum wage, the same issue championed by a radical software engineer named Kshama Sawant, who became the first socialist elected to the Seattle city council since 1916.

More local victories by new grassroots movements ensued over the next two years. Ras J. Baraka, the son of the famed black poet and revolutionary Amiri Baraka, pulled off a surprise win in Newark's mayoral race in May 2014, while new progressives won city council races in Tempe, Arizona; Austin, Texas; and a half dozen other cities later in the year. Then in 2015, voters elevated another group of left-oriented newcomers to office in Denver, Seattle, Philadelphia, and other cities, while a durable anti-machine challenger nearly pulled off an upset in the race for mayor of Chicago. Cook County commissioner Jesús "Chuy" García forced incumbent Rahm Emanuel, a centrist Democrat who had been expected to coast to victory, into a run-off election before finally succumbing to him.

As their victories mounted, the new mayors and councilors started to fashion their own alliance of big-city politicians committed to attacking income inequality, and they even reached out to like-minded counterparts in other countries. As head of the nation's biggest city, de Blasio eagerly assumed a leading role in those efforts, though he soon came under fire from the established media and from more centrist politicians in the Democratic Party for daring to claim the mantle of spokesman for the progressive urban movement.

Governing as a progressive, however, proved a lot tougher than campaigning as one. In several cities, the new mayors did not have majority support for their program on their city council and they found many of their key initiatives there blocked by more conservative forces. In others, the alliance that secured the initial victory began to fracture over the sudden eruption of volatile incidents, such as police killings of African Americans. At other times, unresolved policy issues among them frayed the alliance: how to address the spread of charter schools, for example, or the rise of the so-called sharing economy, or how to create more affordable housing while also promoting economic development. In Pittsburgh, for example, Mayor Bill Peduto welcomed Uber's driverless cars, while in New York City, de Blasio sought to regulate the uncontrolled growth of Uber's existing model of ride sharing with actual drivers, though he soon encountered unexpected opposition from his close ally on the city council, Speaker Melissa Mark-Viverito.

Despite those fissures, the overall trend was becoming clear. By early 2016, America's major municipal governments had moved dramatically to the left. Of the country's seventy-five largest cities, 80 percent had Democratic mayors, many of whom were advocating a raft of liberal policies.[1] Later that year, after Republican Donald Trump pulled off his stunning victory against Hillary Clinton in the race for the White House, and after Republicans consolidated their control of Congress, the big cities emerged as the main resource and best hope for progressive change in the nation. But even as many of those cities prepared in early 2017 to challenge the Trump administration on issues like immigration clampdowns, on threats to withhold federal funds from so-called sanctuary cities, on education policy that favors private school vouchers and charter schools over public schools, on efforts to cut essential social service spending by the federal government, many of their mayors were facing personal tests of their own, with de Blasio, Murray, Hodges, Walsh, and several others all facing formidable challenges to their own reelection hopes.

Free the Land—A Revolution in Mississippi

No U.S. mayoral election in recent decades produced a more surprising result than the 2013 victory in Jackson, Mississippi, by
revolutionary activist and civil rights lawyer Chokwe Lumumba.
On May 21 of that year, Lumumba, a one-term city councilman
in Jackson, pulled off an upset win in a run-off against a rival
who had raised five times more money and who enjoyed more
than a ten-point margin in the polls only weeks before the vote.
Lumumba had been for decades one of the most prominent figures in the country's black liberation movement.

Born as Edwin Finley Taliaferro in Detroit in 1947 to parents
who had moved north during the Great Migration, he learned
early in his life about the civil rights movement from his mother,
who was active in the Student Nonviolent Coordinating Committee. In 1969, while a student at Wayne State University, he
changed his name to Chokwe Lumumba and participated in
campus protests there, then moved in 1970 to Mississippi, where
he soon became a vice president of the provisional Republic of
New Africa. Like the Black Panther Party, RNA members were
revolutionary nationalists, but unlike the Panthers, their goal
was to create an autonomous black republic in parts of the old
South where African Americans were a majority—an idea that
had been briefly espoused by Soviet leader Joseph Stalin and the
American Communist Party in the late 1920s, but subsequently
discarded by all but a few black Marxists and nationalists. Government repression decimated the RNA, and Lumumba returned
to Detroit, where he became a civil rights lawyer and represented
major black activists, including former Panthers Geronimo Pratt
and Assata Shakur, and rapper Tupac Shakur.

Lumumba moved back to Mississippi in 1990, however, where
he founded a successor group to the RNA called the Malcolm X
Grassroots Coalition. With coalition members, he created a net-

work of youth athletic and community service programs as part of a long-term project he called the Jackson–Kush plan. Its aim was to gradually win political power in eighteen contiguous black-majority counties of Mississippi, Louisiana, and Arkansas, where coalition leaders would institute a style of bottom-up governance based on people's assemblies, worker cooperatives, and, eventually, an independent black political party modeled on the 1960s Freedom Democratic Party of Fannie Lou Hamer. The Jackson–Kush plan hearkened in many ways to the nineteenth-century communities of utopian socialists. But in Jackson, the state capital and a city with a population that is more than 80 percent black, Lumumba's low-key, thoughtful approach to self-determination won him a loyal following in the black community. He was easily elected in 2009 to the city council, and he soon won new safeguards against racial profiling together with the Mississippi Immigrant Rights Alliance, with which he had often worked as an attorney. Even before his mayoral victory, he won grudging respect from the city's white economic and political elite for his willingness to work with residents on improved city services and equitable treatment for all. After the election, he won voter approval for a sales tax increase to fund infrastructure improvements and secured a new law that required all future city employees to reside in Jackson.

"We have formed like a people's assembly, that's key to what we've done here," he told me in an interview after his mayoral victory. "Every three months, the population can come out and participate in an open forum to say what's on their mind."

Lumumba seemed poised to defy all stereotypes that revolutionaries can't succeed in governing, but less than a year after his victory he rushed to a Jackson hospital emergency room complaining of chest pains. Several hours later, the country's most revolutionary mayor was pronounced dead of a heart attack. His followers then sought to keep the movement alive by backing Lumumba's son, Chokwe Antar Lumumba, in the race to fill the mayoral seat, but the son narrowly lost the contest to African American city councilman Tony Yarber, who racked up big vote totals in Jackson's white precincts.

The Year of the Maverick Mayors

After decades of watching its steel and manufacturing jobs shipped overseas, Pittsburgh was a typical Rust Belt metropolis in decline. In 1950, the Census Bureau counted nearly 677,000 city residents, but by 2006 the population had plummeted to less than half of that, just 312,000.[2] Meanwhile, its government was run by an entrenched Democratic Party leadership that was expert in patronage and corruption, and the city was so deeply in debt that it had spent more than a decade under state control of its finances. No one was more familiar with those problems than Bill Peduto, who had worked for nineteen years on the city council, first as a staff member and for three terms as an elected councilman. Peduto's grandfather Sam Zarroli had come to the United States from Italy in 1922 and been a part of the United Steelworkers organizing committee in its early years.[3] As the head of a rebel minority on the council, Peduto pioneered legislation to end nobid contracts and reform campaign finance laws, but he usually found himself on the losing side of most important votes, and had twice run unsuccessfully for mayor. But by 2013, following several years of the Great Recession housing crisis that ravaged cities like Pittsburgh, voters were in the mood for change. That year, the forty-nine-year-old Peduto put together a coalition of neighborhood groups, labor unions, and religious organizations that powered him to victory on his third try for mayor, and that even catapulted progressives into majority control of the city council.

Peduto surprised everyone with his innovative ideas on holding government accountable. He opened up all top city jobs to local residents and set up something called a Talent City initiative, run by a philanthropic foundation and a university, to vet applicants.

He invited any resident to volunteer for his transition team and offer policy recommendations. He created a series of open forums where he solicited public input, including Mayor's Night Out, town hall meetings in various neighborhoods along with his key officials; Mayor's Night, where he invited residents to city hall to meet with him one on one to discuss problems; and *Mayor's Night on the Air*, where he and his police commissioner joined a panel at a local radio station and responded to questions on police-community relations. Peduto even created a new Bureau of Neighborhood Empowerment to devise specific programs for long-neglected areas of the city.

As for more concrete policies, one of Peduto's first initiatives approved by the council in April 2014 was establishing a land bank to develop and dispose of more than 27,000 vacant properties. Two years later, however, the land bank came under criticism for taking too long to get up and running.[4] He also issued an executive order in November 2015 declaring $15 an hour minimum pay for all city workers by 2021, though, in practice, the order affected just three hundred of the city's more than three thousand municipal employees who were earning lower pay. An advocate of pre-K education, he won funding from the Obama administration for an expansion of the city's small pre-K program, which, while laudable, was still far short of a universal reform. And while he got the council to unanimously approve paid sick leave for all private-sector workers, the restaurant industry successfully sued to overturn the law in December 2015. Peduto has also drawn accolades nationally for dramatically expanding protected bicycle lanes, championing more mass transit improvements, making Pittsburgh a leader in sustainable development, and luring more young creative-class workers to the city by providing incentives to new tech and medical start-up firms. In short, Peduto's first three years yielded fewer concrete results than, say, Bill de Blasio's, yet by late 2016 he enjoyed a far greater favorability among Pittsburgh's residents than de Blasio did among his constituents.

Betsy Hodges, on the other hand, encountered greater difficulties in Minneapolis. Like de Blasio and Peduto, she had taken the city's business leaders by surprise, achieving victory thanks to the support of a vibrant new grassroots alliance, Minnesotans for a Fair Economy, which included the Service Employees International Union; TakeAction Minnesota, a group that boasted dozens of full-time organizers and a network of forty thousand supporters, and that had spearheaded the defeat in 2012 of a state referendum requiring photo identification for voters at the polls; the Centro de Trabajadores en Lucha, an immigrant workers' center; and Neighborhoods Organizing for Change, a largely African American activist group in North Minneapolis.[5] Her vow to create "One Minneapolis" by eradicating racial inequities in education, housing, and the criminal justice system resonated with the voters, and Hodges became part of a wave of victorious challengers in 2013, which included the first Latino, first Hmong, and first Somali members of the Minneapolis city council.

But the progressives fell short of securing a majority on the council, and since Minneapolis has a strong-council form of government, Mayor Hodges soon found key points of her platform—she often referred to them as her Working Families Agenda—blocked by that body's more conservative bloc. She damaged her own image by taking repeated trips out of town during her first two years, including to China and the Vatican, and to speak at several conferences by liberal groups. Then on November 15, 2015, the police killing of a twenty-four-year-old unarmed black man, Jamar Clark, touched off days of protests by Black Lives Matter activists that included the blocking of a major interstate highway and a tent encampment outside the North Minneapolis police headquarters. Marked by dozens of arrests, by the pepper spraying of protesters, and by the shooting of several protesters by a handful of white counter-demonstrators, those incidents sharply divided the city's residents. Even before Clark's death, Hodges, a champion of greater oversight of the police during her eight years on the council, had become a target of criticism over her response to police abuse. In an open letter to city residents in late 2014, she acknowledged continuing problems with some officers, noting: "If part of our community does not feel safe calling the police, if people do not report a crime or come forward as witnesses because they do not feel safe in relationship with the police, then nowhere in our city, and none of us, is safe."[6] Her remarks, however, angered the police union's leaders and confronted the new mayor with the quandary that inevitably haunts almost every left-oriented politician: how do you effectively reform the most powerful, most conservative, and least accountable department in any big city, the police department, without sparking outright rebellion in its ranks? Hodges sought a middle ground, calling for a federal justice department investigation of the incident yet allowing police to clear the Black Lives Matter encampment outside the police station. She thus came under criticism from both black leaders and the police union head, but also from some of her strongest allies, such as city council member Lisa Bender. "A few of us council members were out in the streets with those protesters," Bender said. "The mayor maintains that if she had positioned herself differently publicly or used different language to talk about what had happened, the police would have stopped listening to her, and it would have been harder to maintain that space for peaceful protest."[7] More protests erupted the following March, however, after prosecutors concluded that the two officers who shot Clark had been justified because he had reached for one of their guns as they struggled to restrain him. The continuing conflict over police-community relations dominated Hodges's first term, and while she did succeed in getting landmark paid sick leave legislation passed in May 2016, and she managed to change annual budget priorities to better fund underserved neighborhoods, much of her ambitious reform agenda stalled.[8]

Boston's Marty Walsh, like Hodges, found it difficult to achieve many of his initial campaign promises, yet he enjoyed widespread popularity during his first term in office. When Walsh became mayor in January 2014, Boston had the largest income inequality of any major American city—with 5 percent of its households earning $266,000 annually, while the bottom 20 percent were earning less than $15,000. As a large and growing hub for universities, hospitals, and technology companies, the city was booming, especially for young people with college degrees.[9]

Walsh was a construction worker who rose through the ranks of the city's labor movement, first as president of Local 223 of the Laborers' International Union and then as head of the powerful Building Trades Council, and who served a stint in the state legislature. In the race for mayor, he built an unusual alliance of labor unions with African American and Latino leaders. After all, the construction unions had for decades blocked the racial integration of their membership far more than any other unions. Sure, the laborers union, representing the least-skilled and lowest-paid sector in construction, had gradually become more black and Hispanic, but the skilled craft unions, plumbers, electricians, and operating engineers remained overwhelmingly white. Walsh not only preached racial unity, he vowed that his highest priority would be to attack poverty, which he called "the root of the underperformance and the achievement gap in our educational system." He garnered enormous financial support from trade unions nationwide and on election day fielded an army of four thousand union volunteers who turned out the vote, but even with that support he eked out a narrow victory of just five thousand votes in a field of twelve candidates for mayor.[10]

A survivor of childhood cancer and onetime alcoholic, Walsh endeared himself to the public with his easygoing personality, even as he accomplished few of his campaign promises. He did reach a labor contract with the city's teachers union that extended the school day, but his vow to sell Boston's city hall and use money from the sale to finance a universal pre-K program went nowhere, his promise to fix aging school buildings stalled in the face of continuing budget gaps, and his effort to bring the Olympic Games to Boston fizzled. Despite all that, more than two years into his term Walsh enjoyed high favorability ratings, even after two of his closest aides were arrested on federal extortion charges that they tried to strongarm a concert promoter into hiring union labor.[11]

A Socialist in Seattle

Seattle's municipal election of 2013 brought major changes in a city already known for its liberal politics. Veteran state legislator Ed Murray handily defeated incumbent Mike McGinn, to become the city's first openly gay mayor. But the Seattle story line that startled the nation was the victory of Kshama Sawant, a college instructor and member of the Trotskyist group Socialist Alternative, against a longtime Green Party member of the city council, Richard Conlin, who had originally been elected to office with fellow radical Nick Licata.

"Conlin always had a tin ear on social justice issues," Licata conceded. "Kshama beat him by running on the minimum wage. Her base became all of the young people who had been screwed out of decent housing and were working low-wage jobs. Nobody thought she could win, but people wanted to send a message that this was a serious problem."[12]

Sawant became the first socialist elected to a major public office in Seattle since 1916. The main planks of her campaign, a $15-an-hour minimum wage, a millionaire's tax, and imposition of rent control, sought to address the income inequality and skyrocketing housing costs that are common in all major cities.

But while Seattle is one of the country's fastest growing and most prosperous big cities, that growth has only deepened a vast wealth disparity. Between 2000 and 2012, 85,000 new households migrated to King County, with about half earning less than 50 percent of the median income and the other half more than

180 percent of the median.[13] Sawant's advocacy on the minimum-wage issue, in particular, garnered such widespread support that both McGinn and Murray ended up adopting it during their contest, and once Murray took office, he proposed and the new city council unanimously passed the first $15-an-hour minimum wage in a major city, to be phased in completely by 2021.[14]

When the measure passed, a jubilant Sawant hailed it as a major "reversal of fortune" that would affect 100,000 workers and that "signifies a transfer of income of $3 billion from the richest in the city to the bottom-most workers."[15]

Pushed by a more radical city council, Murray instituted reforms that mirrored de Blasio's successes in New York. He succeeded in getting a $58 million property tax hike passed to fund the phasing-in of up to two thousand new pre-K slots for low-income children, but not a universal program, and he passed paid parental leave and expanded mass transit routes.[16]

But housing policy proved to be for Murray, as it has been for de Blasio, a challenge to his progressive credentials. He opposed Sawant's push for rent control, loaded a committee he appointed to fashion his affordable housing plan with real estate developers, and sparked an uproar from community leaders when he proposed upzoning huge swaths of the city currently zoned for one-family homes.

Housing is "the number one issue," Licata said. "Minorities are being pushed out, there are visible homeless on the streets, young people in their thirties and forties that can't afford to buy a house," and so far Murray's affordable housing plan has not been enough.[17] Seattle's inability to address the affordable housing crisis was a harbinger of de Blasio's problems in New York, and of progressives' in San Francisco. In these luxury cities, where a square foot of land or air rights is so valuable, the real estate industry has been the most powerful of interest groups. As journalists Jack Newfield and Wayne Barrett once described it, the real estate moguls of New York City function as do oil barons in Houston.[18]

The People Take Back Newark

Located just fifteen miles west of New York City, Newark, New Jersey, has long been a metropolis in crisis. More than a third of its 280,000 residents are mired in poverty, it has one of the country's highest crime rates, and an astonishing 85 percent of the population is black and Hispanic, even as some of the nation's most prosperous white towns, like Short Hills, Ridgewood, and Glen Ridge, are only minutes away. Which is why the mayoral victory of Ras Baraka in 2014 was so momentous for the new urban progressive movement. A veteran public school teacher and a principal who turned around one of the city's most troubled high schools, Baraka was also a hard-nosed community organizer against police brutality, a member of the city council, and the son of Amiri Baraka, Newark's most famous African American poet, playwright, and revolutionary, but when he ran for mayor of the state's largest city, few of the political and economic elite expected him to win. After all, he had declared the race a referendum on the previous mayor, Cory Booker, who was a national celebrity in Democratic Party circles. Booker had vacated the mayoral post after winning a special election to replace deceased U.S. senator Frank Lautenberg. Charming and politically moderate, he had proved adept during two terms as mayor at garnering favorable press coverage, at using social media to advance his image as a technocrat and post-racial reformer, and at attracting a coterie of Wall Street executives and wealthy donors, many of whom envisioned him as the next Barack Obama. They included Facebook founder Mark Zuckerberg, who famously announced during a segment of the *Oprah* show in 2010, with Booker and New Jersey's Republican governor, Chris Christie, at his side, that he was donating $100 million to improve Newark's public schools.

Mayor Booker's record in office, however, was far less glamorous. The annual number of homicides and other serious crimes in Newark had increased by the time he left office even as they

declined in most other major cities, the public schools were in tat-
ters after nearly twenty years of state-imposed control, and while
Booker did foster new development in the city's business district,
those projects also spurred major gentrification.

"A lot of it [the Zuckerberg money] went to consultants,"
Baraka later said. "Eighty-something million dollars of it went
to a teacher contract, which fought to get rid of tenure, extend
the day, give teachers bonuses, all kinds of things like that. Not
much went towards pedagogy, went towards teacher training,
went towards teachers in classrooms to give them better resources
and opportunities for kids in the school."[19]

Zuckerberg's donation and the fate of the city's public schools
soon became a central issue in the mayoral race, with Baraka
heading a movement of parents who demanded an end to state
control of Newark schools and called for the resignation of Cami
Anderson, the education superintendent backed by Booker.
Anderson had infuriated public school parents by closing many
schools and eliminating the tradition of neighborhood schools—
initiating instead a centralized admission policy for all children
for both public and charter schools.[20]

And while Booker never formally endorsed anyone in the
hotly contested mayoral race, his equity and hedge fund backers
funneled more than $4.2 million to a pro–charter school group,
Newark First, to support Baraka's main opponent, Shavar Jeffries,
a former federal prosecutor and charter school founder. Newark First's biggest single donor, it would later be revealed, was
New York City mayor Michael Bloomberg, who personally gave
$400,000 to support Jeffries.[21]

The Baraka campaign raised considerably less money, but it
did manage to secure the backing of a handful of powerful labor
unions and the state's Working Families Organization. "They're
coming. From Wall Street. From Trenton. To sell us Shavar
Jeffries," warned one of the TV ads from Working Families.
"Chris Christie's allies and the Wall Street hedge fund types have

an agenda. Shut down Newark public schools. Shut out parents. And destroy our schools for their personal profit."[22]

Baraka framed the race as a contest between Newark residents seeking to reclaim control of their city and wealthy outsiders seeking to impose their own regime. That claim was burnished by his many years as an educator and community activist, and by his family's long history in Newark as advocates of black empowerment. Not only did the Baraka family trace its roots in the city back a hundred years, his father, Amiri Baraka (the former LeRoi Jones), while enjoying a worldwide reputation as a poet, playwright, novelist, and leading figure of the black liberation movement, took pride in Newark and promoted its black cultural institutions and community empowerment, and had helped elect the city's first black mayor, Kenneth Gibson, as well as Gibson's successor, Sharpe James. "My father would have large parties, whether it be revolutionaries from around the world, political prisoners, artists, jazz musicians—people from Max Roach to Nina Simone," Ras Baraka recalled after his father died in 2014.[23]

By then, however, the younger Baraka had spent two decades in the trenches of Newark's neighborhood activism and had carved out his own identity. There was the time in June 1997, for instance, when a Newark police officer fatally shot a thirty-one-year-old unarmed pregnant woman named Dannette "Strawberry" Daniels during a drug bust. The incident provoked outrage in the city's black community, and it prompted Baraka, who was only twenty-seven at the time, to spearhead a march by several hundred people to city hall, together with the Black Nia FORCE, a militant youth group he had founded while he was a student at Howard University. Newark's police responded with threats of outright rebellion, as hundreds of off-duty cops later staged a raucous counter-protest during which they shouted down Mayor Sharpe James and chanted, "No justice, no police."[24]

A decade later, Baraka was named principal of the city's failing Central High School. Before long, he eliminated the youth gangs that had plagued the school, extended the length of the school day, and sharply improved state test scores and graduation rates, all while serving as a member of the Newark city council.[25]

After defeating Jeffries in the 2014 mayoral race, Baraka surprised his critics with both his strength as a reformer and his ability to calm those in the business community and law enforcement who had been wary of his radical past. His biggest victory came in persuading Governor Christie to end two decades of state control of the Newark public schools. The transition, devised by a joint commission appointed by Baraka and Christie, was scheduled for completion by the 2017–18 school year, though some critics have suggested that Baraka conceded too much control in the process to a new board of education whose majority was composed of wealthy nonresidents of Newark.[26]

When it came to police-community relations, Baraka achieved what Newark's black community had been demanding for half a century—a citizen complaint review board. Only months after his election, a justice department investigation concluded that Newark police had engaged for years in "a pattern or practice of unconstitutional stops, searches, arrests, use of excessive force and theft by officers." The probe found that, out of hundreds of police abuse complaints filed by Newark residents between 2007 and 2012, only one had been substantiated by the department's own internal affairs division. The Newark police, in other words, enjoyed virtual impunity for any misconduct against the public during the Booker mayoralty. Baraka reached a consent decree with the justice department for an independent monitor. He also decreed by executive order in early 2015 a new civilian complaint board and granted it subpoena power. The American Civil Liberties Union hailed it as a model for police reform nationwide.[27] Then in May 2016, the city council unanimously made the complaint board permanent.

But with Newark's crime rate remaining stubbornly high, Baraka sought to rouse the public against street violence. He organized "Occupy the City" rallies to inspire residents to assist in crime prevention, he walked the streets with neighborhood leaders to diffuse tensions, and he launched "model neighborhood" initiatives in the poorest areas, directing more police there and city resources to clean up blight.[28]

"The police behavior has been completely different from the time Baraka became mayor, and we haven't seen a police killing in that time," Larry Hamm, head of Newark's People's Organization for Progress, said in July 2016.[29]

To ameliorate the city's poverty, Baraka got the council to pass an ordinance requiring developers who receive tax abatements and companies with city contracts to hire Newark residents for 51 percent of their jobs.

But he also proved adept at pleasing the city's traditional business elite. His first year in office, Baraka closed a $93 million gap he'd inherited in the city budget from Booker, without having to lay off any municipal workers. He pushed forward with ambitious plans to turn a twenty-four-acre parcel of downtown Newark into a park and retail, residential, and office space that will eventually connect Pennsylvania Station, the restaurants of the Ironbound section, and the Prudential Center entertainment and sports arena. "The progress that has been achieved in the last 90 days has been more than what was done in the last five years," Hugh Weber, the president of the Prudential Center, told the *New York Times* in August 2015.[30]

Changing City Councils

Gregorio Casar and Lauren Kuby symbolize the leftward shift in urban city councils that intensified throughout 2014. Casar captured a council seat in Austin, Texas, that year as part of a grassroots alliance against the traditional downtown business establishment, and so did Kuby in her own campaign for the council in Tempe, Arizona.

As a teenager, Casar had taken part in the immigrant rights protests that swept through his hometown of Houston, Texas, and across the nation in 2006. Two years later, as a student at the University of Virginia, he had volunteered for Barack Obama's presidential campaign.[31] After finishing school, he moved to Austin and became a leader of the Workers Defense Project, an advocacy group for low-wage workers that became an influential force in the city. Then at the age of just twenty-five, he won election to the city council, the first in Austin's history chosen by districts. Under the previous at-large system, the town's white liberal establishment had sewed up political control in the city even though Latinos comprised 35 percent of the population. But in 2014 this changed. Politically liberal newcomers, including Casar and two other Latinos, swept virtually all of the seats.[32]

Among the progressive reforms the new council approved was an ambitious effort to build more affordable housing by using revenue from the sale or lease of several city- and state-owned land parcels near downtown to private developers. These were sites of old decommissioned sewage treatment and coal-fired electric power plants (in Austin, the city owns the water and electric power company).

"The money that comes from any of that will go straight into the affordable housing fund," Casar said. "This policy alone is going to generate $70 to $80 million in just a few years into a fund that right now has just $1 or $2 million in it." And a big portion of that money, at least 40 percent, he added, will go to neighborhoods that are gentrifying to preserve affordable housing units and prevent further displacement of low-income families.[33]

Meanwhile in sun-drenched Tempe, which, much like Austin, is a fast-growing city dominated by a state university and technology firms, Lauren Kuby, a fifty-seven-year-old environmental activist, won an upset victory in the race for city council by promising to make Tempe a model of sustainable practices. Kuby, who has worked for years at Arizona State University's Julie Ann

Wrigley Global Institute of Sustainability, was surprised at how little attention the local government was paying to environmental policy, given that ASU was the heart of Tempe.

She knocked on fourteen thousand doors during her campaign. "I got elected on a sustainability platform and one of my goals was to really solarize the city, both in our government operations and to increase our renewable energy goal in commercial buildings and residences. In my thinking, every house that was capable of being solarized should be solarized."[34]

But once Kuby got elected, one of the big utility companies, the quasi-public Salt River Project, "decided to change the rules," she said. "They are now assessing a $50 minimum monthly fee on homes that install rooftop solar." Kuby fought back with a campaign to install two solar advocates on SRP's board of directors, whose members are elected by the rate payers. She further incurred the ire of the state's business groups when she began advocating the banning of single-use plastic bags and Styrofoam containers. Arizona's chamber of commerce and the retailers association then lobbied the state legislature to pass a law preempting such local bans. Undaunted, Kuby worked with public interest advocates to challenge the preemption law in court. "Our argument is that waste management is a matter of local, not statewide, interest," she said. "Historically, cities handle trash and recycling collection, and state encroachment defies Arizona's long-treasured value of local control."

Along with other progressives on the council, Kuby also backed earned sick leave and a raise in the minimum wage, but the council balked when the governor threatened to preempt any worker protections. So she joined a campaign by Arizona Healthy Working Families that collected more than 270,000 signatures to place both issues on the ballot before the voters. In November 2016, Proposition 206 was approved, mandating both earned sick leave throughout the state and an increase in Arizona's minimum wage from $8.05 an hour to $12 an hour by 2020. In one fell swoop on January 1, 2017, wages for over 800,000 Arizona residents jumped to $10 an hour. Less than three months later, the state's supreme court unanimously rejected a challenge to the new wage law by Arizona's chamber of commerce.[35]

Austin and Tempe, however, were not the only cities where progressives made major inroads. In Richmond, California, Gayle McLaughlin, who had been term-limited as that city's mayor, ran for a city council seat in 2014 and won, giving the Richmond Progressive Alliance a majority bloc on the council. They proceeded to pass a rent control law, the first reform of its kind in a California city in thirty years. But in the face of a campaign by the business community to repeal the law through a voter referendum, the council chose to rescind it, then correct some technical weaknesses in the original language, and sponsor its own pro–rent control referendum during the 2016 election year. That referendum, which passed with an overwhelming 66 percent of the vote, capped annual rent increases by landlords at no more than 3 percent.[36]

A Political Gale in the Windy City

Progressive candidates continued to battle for and win municipal seats around the country during 2015, but the contest that captured the most national attention that year was in Chicago, where Cook County commissioner Jesús "Chuy" García waged a fierce but unsuccessful challenge to incumbent mayor Rahm Emanuel, a centrist Democrat and former chief of staff to President Obama.

Among the success stories was Philadelphia, where community activist Helen Gym (see chapter 5) won election to the city council in her first race for political office, and Denver, where public interest lawyer Robin Kniech won a second term as an at-large member of the city council. Gym proceeded during her first year in office to win major increases in funding for community parks, recreation centers, and libraries, in large part by successfully championing a controversial bill that imposed taxes on big distributors of soda and sugary drinks. "The wealthy have made the center city their playground with some of the most generous tax subsidy programs in the country," Gym insisted. "But drive or walk five blocks outside of center city and we enter into neighborhoods that look like they haven't changed since [Mayor Frank] Rizzo's era. We've got a real need to rethink our approach."[37] Kniech, meanwhile, spearheaded the creation of a housing trust fund—financed by an increase in property taxes and a new fee on development—to build or preserve more than six thousand affordable housing units, and she secured the lifting of onerous local regulations on the city's growing recreational marijuana industry.[38]

It was the pivotal showdown in the nation's third-largest city, Chicago, however, that provided invaluable lessons for the growing urban reform movement. Historically controlled by Democratic Party bosses who were legendary for their corruption, for their hammerlock on municipal jobs and contracts, and for their manipulation of ethnic and racial divisions to maintain their power, Chicago has rarely been fertile soil for liberal reformers. Only the election in 1983 of Harold Washington, the city's first black mayor, briefly disrupted the machine's grip. But in 1987, only five months into his second term in office, Washington's sudden death from a heart attack dashed any hope of lasting reform. "Harold ran on an equity agenda, with neighborhoods being at the center of that agenda," García recalled years later. "But his death really demonstrated the danger of overreliance on an individual . . . and after he died the coalition shattered in so many pieces."[39]

García had been a crucial ally and disciple of Washington, who, during his first three years in office, repeatedly locked horns with Ed "Fast Eddie" Vrdolyak, the iron-fisted Cook County Democratic Party leader who controlled a slight majority of the fifty aldermen on the Chicago city council and who thus managed to block many of the mayor's initiatives. The phrase "corrupt backroom deal-making pol" would be a compliment for Vrdolyak, who was later convicted of a federal kickback scheme and sent to prison. After yet another indictment for corruption in 2016, he described his philosophy to a *Chicago Tribune* reporter saying: "They send business your way, so you get jobs for people. That's the way it's done. Me—it's the only place these people can go. I'm the committeeman, alderman, father confessor, cop, lawyer, employment agency. Me. I'm the man."[40]

Back in 1986, however, a civil rights lawsuit forced a redrawing of a handful of aldermanic districts, and García was elected to the council as part of a new group of aldermen, providing Mayor Harold Washington a progressive majority against Vrdolyak. After Washington's death, several leaders in his original coalition made their peace with the resurgent Democratic machine, but others, including García, continued to fight it.

More than twenty years would pass before a new neighborhood- and labor-based progressive movement began to emerge. In 2007, a handful of left-leaning insurgents won aldermanic elections; they included Scott Waguespack on Chicago's North Side and Toni Foulkes, a former national board member of ACORN, on the Southwest Side. Waguespack soon made a name for himself by exposing one of the biggest scandals of longtime mayor Richard Daley's administration. During his time in office from 1989 to 2011, Daley became a poster child of the big-city privatization mania. Among his initiatives was the $1.6 billion "Plan for Transformation," which involved tearing down public housing high-rises and redeveloping the land for mixed-income units with federal grants under Hope VI, the federal housing program launched by Bill Clinton and his first housing secretary, Henry Cisneros, as a way to placate the Republican majority in Congress. The project dragged on unfinished for years, with repeated horror stories of private developers making financial killings, while thousands of black residents were forced out of their homes.

But the biggest privatization scandal under Daley was the seventy-five-year deal his aides secretly negotiated in late 2008 with a consortium led by Wall Street giant Morgan Stanley and then gave city council members only two days to review before calling for a vote. Under the plan all parking meters would be privatized and switched from coin-operated to credit card, while the city, which was facing a major budget deficit, would be paid $1.1 billion over the lifetime of the agreement. But what Daley never revealed to the council was that meter rates would immediately jump as much as fourfold, and that meter hours would be extended until late at night and even on Sundays. News of these hidden arrangements sparked outrage throughout the city, even more so after Waguespack, one of only four aldermen who had voted against the deal, discovered internal records of the consortium that had been discarded in a trash dumpster and which showed that projected revenues from the meters were $5 billion! "They devalued the meters," Waguespack later said. "Morgan Stanley and these other firms said, it's not really worth anything, so give it to us to run." Those parking meters are operated today by LAZ Inc., with a major shareholder being the Abu Dhabi Investment Agency.[41]

The parking meter debacle was only the first of several privatization efforts that Daley resorted to during his final years in office. They included selling the skyway over the city's South Side and parking garages downtown, and they turned him into a national leader in the movement to privatize government services. But most of those deals were desperate measures by Daley to plug massive deficits his administration had piled up, the largest deficits in Chicago's history. "Daley was strategically selling off chunks because he'd been running the city on borrowed money and the chickens were coming home to roost," said John Arena, another progressive alderman elected in 2011.[42]

That year, with Daley opting not to run for reelection, Rahm Emanuel, the hard-nosed former congressman and Obama aide, ran for mayor instead and cruised to victory. But it did not take long for Emanuel, who is widely known for his take-no-prisoners style of governing, to incur the wrath of one of the city's most powerful labor organizations, the Chicago Teachers Union, and its feisty president, Karen Lewis. A veteran teacher, Lewis had been elected its president in 2010 with the support of a militant rank-and-file caucus, and her victory had unnerved the more moderate leaders of the American Federation of Teachers, including its president Randi Weingarten. Lewis was determined to have her union spearhead a new progressive political alliance in Chicago modeled on that of the Harold Washington era. Called the Grassroots Collaborative, it brought together labor unions like the teachers and SEIU's health care division with Action Now, the Chicago spin-off of the defunct ACORN, and nearly a dozen other neighborhood and immigrant rights groups. Many of the same organizations then created a unified political arm that they called United Working Families.[43]

In September 2012, the Chicago Teachers Union launched its first school strike in a quarter century after its contract expired and Mayor Emanuel insisted, per his "educational reform," on major concessions from the union, including the use of student test scores to evaluate teachers and the weakening of teacher seniority provisions. The strike, which lasted for seven days, garnered considerable support from the public and represented Emanuel's first major defeat, with the union managing to rebuff many of the mayor's proposals.[44] The next spring Emanuel announced that fifty public schools would be shuttered, a number unparalleled in the history of American cities, and all those to be closed would be in predominantly African American and Latino neighborhoods. The announcement triggered protests and parent sit-ins at many of the targeted schools.[45]

At the time, education expert Diane Ravitch pointed to Chicago as reflecting a national trend:

In city after city, the civic and business elite . . . has taken the position that they'll close schools. And what they're mostly doing is privatizing them. I mean, you have to understand that the closing schools argument is not simply about public schools getting better, which obviously they don't . . . it is part of a larger scheme to advance privatization, to create privately managed charter schools that are non-union schools. And Chicago now has about 75,000 children in non-union charter schools.[46]

By 2014, Emanuel's war against teachers and public schools, along with the rising number of murders and gun violence in Chicago, had made him hugely unpopular. That year, public opinion polls showed teachers union leader Karen Lewis leading him in a hypothetical race for mayor. Lewis was definitely planning to run, but later that year she abandoned her plans after she was diagnosed with a brain tumor. The progressive alliance backing her then rushed to find a suitable replacement; its members eventually chose former Harold Washington ally Chuy García.

In the first round of the February 2015 mayoral race, Emanuel failed to get a majority of the vote to win outright, so he was forced into a run-off against García. The mayor's campaign then poured millions of dollars into television ads that sought to depict García as a candidate who would favor the city's Latino community and ignore the black community. The campaign worked. Emanuel won a large enough slice of votes from African Americans to ensure his victory.

Only weeks later, however, the public learned that city hall and the police department had refused to release a shocking video of the killing of an unarmed black youth, Laquan McDonald, who had been shot sixteen times by a Chicago police officer back in

October 2014. The city negotiated a $5 million settlement with the dead youth's family during the run-off election, one that required the video to be kept secret until all legal proceedings in the case were concluded. But public pressure forced release of the video, and the officer who killed McDonald was later indicted for first-degree murder. Many in Chicago came to believe that if the Laquan McDonald video had been released before the election, Emanuel would have lost his reelection bid.

Despite Chuy García's defeat, the number of progressive aldermen on the Chicago city council had climbed to eleven by 2015, and their ability to influence legislation was growing. One of the big achievements of the newly formed progressive caucus is a "Privatization, Transparency and Accountability Ordinance" that passed in November 2015. "It mandates that bills can't pass in less 48 hours, and [requires] independent assessments of their feasibility," said Alderman John Arena.

Thus progressives continued to make significant inroads in political power across urban America in recent years, increasing their numbers and influence in city council chambers and capturing control of more and more mayoralties.

10

Fierce Resistance and Major Missteps

It was never my intention to nibble around the edges with policies of timid maintenance; I ran to take dead aim at the crisis of our time.

—Mayor Bill de Blasio, Manchester, England, 2014

During Bill de Blasio's first three years in office the city's financial and real estate elite launched an extraordinary effort to turn him into a one-term mayor. Throughout that time, a daily stream of attack ads appeared on New York television and radio stations, virtually all of them sponsored by a small band of powerful lobbying groups, which included hedge fund backers of charter schools, the city's main landlord association, and the ride-sharing company Uber. Those groups spent nearly $20 million on media ads targeting the mayor between 2014 and 2016—nearly twice as much as it cost de Blasio to run for mayor in 2013.[1] Meanwhile, a former campaign manager for ex-mayor Bloomberg launched a "New York Deserves Better" website in June 2016 and sought to recruit potential challengers against de Blasio. A few months later, wealthy residents of Manhattan's Upper East Side joined with the county Republican Party in an almost comical effort to create a "Stop de Blasio" ballot line for three assembly district races that garnered just 1 percent of the vote. And in the surrounding suburbs, Republicans in the state senate managed in

2016 to hold on to their party's slim majority in Albany by producing commercials and campaign literature that tied their Democratic challengers to de Blasio and his policies.[2] Throughout it
all, Governor Andrew Cuomo publicly feuded with the mayor,
repeatedly blocked key de Blasio initiatives, and even intervened unilaterally in city affairs during major crises, declaring,
for example, a mandatory quarantine at New York City airports
in October 2014 for health professionals returning from West
Africa's Ebola outbreak, and even ordering the city's roads and
subways shut down in January 2015 on the eve of a major snow
blizzard—all without consulting de Blasio. And then there were
the media attacks. Several major news outlets, including the *New
York Post*, the *Daily News*, and WCBS-TV, routinely produced
stories that depicted the mayor as incompetent, hypocritical, even
corrupt, and that ridiculed him as fixated on traveling around
the country to promote himself as a "progressive" leader while
quality of life in the city plummeted. Never in the city's modern
history had so many of its powerful forces been so aligned against
its chief executive.

As time passed, that narrative began to gain real traction among
the public even though the hard facts and data of de Blasio's record
directly contradicted the claims of a city spiraling downward.
Take street crime, for example. By 2016, the city's overall crime
rate had dropped to its lowest level since the start of the modern
Compstat tracking system in 1993—despite dire predictions by
the mayor's opponents that it would skyrocket, and despite brief
month-to-month spikes in violence that the tabloid press turned
into screaming front-page headlines—with both shootings and
murders at record lows.[3]

Then there was the economy. Not only did tourism continue to
boom, with a record 58.5 million visitors in 2015, so did the real
estate industry, as city tax revenues from commercial property
jumped by an astounding 20 percent between 2013 and 2016.[4]
More important, the city's middle- and working-class residents

saw significant boosts to their pockets from de Blasio's policies targeting economic inequality. Wealth transfers and cost savings from those policies, as previously noted, amounted to at least $21 billion during the mayor's first few years in office (see chapter 8). At the same time, the city added 500,000 jobs between 2010 and 2015, the largest five-year gain in its history, almost equal to the total number of private-sector jobs in a city as large San Francisco. Half of those gains occurred during de Blasio's first two years in office, with median household income jumping by 5.1 percent during 2015 alone. And that figure was expected to rise even higher in 2017, as the phase-in of the state's new $15-an-hour minimum wage began to kick in. That wage increase alone was expected to lift more than 300,000 city residents out of poverty by 2018.[5]

De Blasio's remarkable successes, however, were tarnished by questionable personal actions, both large and small. During his first year, for example, the mayor showed up late so often to public events that his tardiness became a running joke in press accounts and a source of exasperation even for his supporters.[6] Then there was the horse debacle. De Blasio had vowed to end the use of horse carriages in Central Park, an issue vital to animal rights groups that had backed him for mayor but of little importance to most New Yorkers. Editors at the *Daily News* launched an "imaginary civic crusade," as author Eric Alterman aptly named it, against the carriage ban. In Alterman's words:

> Story after story portrayed de Blasio as a horse-hating job killer, and in July the *Daily News* sent its own employees to City Hall with sacks carrying 40,000 signatures it allegedly collected in opposition to the planned changes. The paper published no fewer than 129 stories about the horse carriages following the mayor's inauguration. Fifty-three of these came during just sixteen days in April; nine of them were on

the front page, and an amazing seventeen stories were
published on three days alone.[7]

Meanwhile, the *Post* hammered the mayor repeatedly, and with
arguably a better case, about his penchant for late-morning work-
outs on weekdays at his old neighborhood gymnasium in Park
Slope, when he would normally be expected to be handling city
business.[8] But far more significant than the deliberate magnifi-
cation of the mayor's personal flaws into big issues was a string
of criminal investigations by both federal and state authorities
of possible pay-to-play corruption between close advisers to the
mayor and real estate developers and wealthy donors who did
business with the city. While none of those probes had resulted
in criminal charges by early 2017, their existence had cast a cloud
over the administration and became fodder for daily questions
from the press, thus threatening serious damage to the mayor's
reelection hopes.

Finally, several key groups of progressive activists who had been
instrumental in the original de Blasio coalition grew increasingly
disillusioned with city hall policies that appeared dismissive of
neighborhood concerns. Those disillusioned included advocates
for low-income housing, parent groups fighting to improve public education, and activists against police misconduct.

Spinning a Tale of Two de Blasios

Anyone watching local television in New York City from 2014 to
2016 was sure to come across almost daily commercials attacking
Mayor de Blasio, even though there was no mayoral race in those
years. They seemed to be everywhere and they invariably spoofed
de Blasio's popular "Tale of Two Cities" slogan. The estimated
total spent on such ads during those years approached $20 mil-
lion. There were, for example, those sponsored by the Rent Stabilization Association, the lobbying group for 25,000 landlords in

the city. The most ubiquitous of them began: "Mayor de Blasio says New Yorkers pay too much rent; landlord de Blasio pockets over $100,000 a year from his tenants," before adding, "Mayor de Blasio denies the revenues landlords need for repairs and property taxes; landlord de Blasio raises the rents of his tenants for operating costs. It's the Tale of Two Blasio's [sic] . . . politics and hypocrisy." The reference to "landlord de Blasio" was to a small home with two apartments in Brooklyn's gentrified Park Slope neighborhood where the mayor's mother, Maria de Blasio Wilhelm, had lived until her death in 2007, and which her son subsequently rented out. The ad never mentioned what any reasonable review of the facts showed: that such small properties have never been subject to city rent stabilization laws, that de Blasio's financial disclosure forms showed that his income from the property failed to cover its operating expenses and mortgage costs, and that his actual tenants referred to him in press accounts as a model landlord who responded punctually to their maintenance requests and often shoveled snow from the rental property's sidewalk himself.[9] Still, the ad's constant repetition—during 2016, the RSA shelled out some $2.3 million for such commercials—created an indelible image of a politician who said one thing in public while practicing the opposite in private. As one recent study of political commercials noted: "If there is anything close to an iron law in advertising, it is this: repetition works; the more exposure to a brand's advertising, the better. . . . People are more inclined to believe what they have heard before."[10]

Likewise the Patrolmen's Benevolent Association depicted the mayor as shafting hardworking police officers on pay increases: "Mayor de Blasio promised to end income inequality, but he's refusing to protect the families of the men and women who protect their city," a narrator warned as images of cops and their families flashed on the screen. "Tell the Mayor: Police officers have families too. Pay them fairly."[11]

But the biggest and most consistent ad blitz against de Blasio came from charter school proponents. In 2014, two pro-charter groups, Families for Excellent Schools and the Coalition for Opportunity in Education (also known as the Invest in Education Coalition), spent an astounding $13 million for lobbying and advertising in New York State. The bulk of that money, nearly $10 million, came from Families for Excellent Schools, a group bankrolled largely by Wall Street hedge fund executives. FES used most of that money to finance large public rallies in which charter school operators closed their schools and bused their students, parents, and teachers to rallies in New York City and Albany to protest de Blasio's policies. Such blatant use of young schoolchildren by a government-funded institution to influence lawmakers signaled a new, some would say bizarre, escalation in the war over public education. Not surprisingly, FES also spent some $3.5 million that year on television ads specifically targeting de Blasio, and, according to its federal tax filings, the group even paid former Bloomberg spokesman Stu Loeser $395,000 as its media consultant.[12]

A key participant in most FES rallies is Eva Moskowitz, the CEO of the largest charter school operation in New York City, the Success Charter Network. An abrasive former city councilwoman with admitted mayoral ambitions of her own, Moskowitz became de Blasio's most implacable nemesis. Under Mayor Bloomberg, she enjoyed virtual carte blanche to rapidly expand her network of schools. Bloomberg and his various education chancellors often praised Moskowitz for producing some of the highest standardized test scores in the city, and they kept ordering traditional neighborhood public schools to share space in their buildings with her Success Academy schools, even when parents, educators, and political leaders in the affected communities vehemently opposed the practice, commonly known as "co-location." The city provided such spaces for free to charter schools, one of the few cities in the country to adopt such a policy. Moskowitz and her wealthy backers have always argued that charter schools, although privately managed, are simply another version of public schools, since they receive most of their funds in annual per-pupil payments from local school districts and are open to all students through a public lottery system, so they should therefore have the same free access to public school buildings as do traditional public schools. But critics rightfully point out that charter school management groups are private entities and that their unbridled growth represents the steady dismantling of public education. Furthermore, there is growing evidence that charter schools push the most vulnerable students (those with learning disabilities, behavioral problems, non–English speakers, and those from homeless families) back into the public school system in order to ensure a student body with superior test scores. Many of the private conservative investors who bankroll them do so with an eye on future vendor opportunities for online learning, curriculum, and tracking of student performance, and, most of all, with the hope of breaking teachers unions and lowering professional requirements and pay for classroom teachers—all to ensure future super-profits from a deregulated education market.[13]

Under Bloomberg, a series of co-location school wars erupted in neighborhoods across New York City. Moskowitz was at the center of many of those wars, inevitably demanding more space as her schools grew, with the Success Academy section of any building then routinely remodeled with new furniture, paint, bathrooms, and computers, while the traditional public school remained dingy and run-down, their students and teachers feeling like second-class citizens in their own building. In a series of *Daily News* columns from 2009 to 2016, I documented the combative style of Success Academy toward traditional public schools, as well as the network's far higher rate of suspending children with behavioral problems, and its pushing out of special needs children. But Success Academy has repeatedly defended its "zero tolerance" approach for students who misbehave, with Moskowitz claiming her schools use "an appropriate disciplinary and restorative

approach to reinforce our behavioral expectations."[14] Nonetheless, Moskowitz continued to receive tens of millions of dollars from the nation's financial elite while spending exorbitant
amounts of money on a massive campaign to market and solicit
applications to her schools to, in her own words, increase market
share, all while paying herself a hefty salary that in 2015 exceeded
$600,000 annually.[15]

Many grassroots parents' organizations backed de Blasio's run
for mayor after he promised to end such blanket co-locations of
charter schools inside public schools, and they were buoyed when,
on the campaign trail, he singled out Moskowitz's Success Academy as the prime example of abuse of co-location. Even Leonie
Haimson, leader of the nonprofit parent group Class Size Matters, had high hopes for change under a Mayor de Blasio at first.
Haimson, who produces the NYC Public School Parents blog and
is one of the most knowledgeable education advocates in the city,
spearheaded several successful lawsuits over city and state educational policy. But she soon became critical of de Blasio and
Schools Chancellor Fariña for what she saw as their failure to heed
parent concerns in city hall's school reform efforts.

Once in office, de Blasio was hit by a barrage of television ads
from Moskowitz and her Wall Street backers, who circumvented him by pouring money into the coffers of Albany lawmakers
and winning the backing of Governor Cuomo at a major charter
school rally for the continued rapid expansion of charter schools.
If de Blasio refused to provide free space for charter operators
inside public school buildings, the legislature then ordained, the
city would have to pay for them to utilize private facilities. The
charter school co-location fight thus became the first major defeat
of de Blasio's administration.[16]

So, even as de Blasio achieved some real victories in the fight
against income inequality, the relentless ad campaign against
him by the charter school lobby, combined with those of the real

estate industry and the police union, created an image of him as fomenting such inequality.

One figure emerged to gather the anti–de Blasio movement into a big tent. In June 2016, Bradley Tusk, the former manager of Michael Bloomberg's successful 2009 mayoral campaign, established a new website, NYC Deserves Better, with the sole goal of encouraging challengers to de Blasio in the 2017 mayoral race. Tusk, who runs a half dozen businesses and communications firms, claimed he was financing the anti–de Blasio effort with his own money, while he also garnered as clients two powerful entities that were then waging their own public relations war against the mayor: the Patrolmen's Benevolent Association and Uber, whose uncontrolled wild-west-type expansion de Blasio was determined to limit in New York City.[17]

Tusk had once served as a deputy to former Illinois governor Rod Blagojevich. Most Americans remember Blagojevich as the governor who was arrested by federal agents in 2008 and eventually convicted on corruption charges that included trying to sell an appointment to the Senate seat vacated by Barack Obama. During his stint with Blagojevich, Tusk had pressed to make Illinois the first state to privatize management of its lottery. He then went to work at Lehman Brothers to pursue that bank's efforts to arrange sell-offs of state lotteries nationwide—at least until the subprime mortgage crisis led to Lehman's own collapse. The privatizing of the Illinois lottery, which only took place after Tusk left the state, turned out to be a colossal failure. It began in 2011, when a firm called Northstar Lottery Group assumed day-to-day management of the lottery. Northstar not only produced less in annual payouts to the state than it had promised, it often failed to deliver many payouts to ticket buyers who had won cash prizes, claiming that they had to wait until state budgetary problems were resolved. The revelations finally prompted Illinois governor Bruce Rauner to fire the company in January 2017.[18]

Daring to Look Beyond New York

From the start of his mayoralty, de Blasio believed no single city, not even New York, could successfully reduce income inequality on its own. He envisioned himself part of a broader progressive movement that must first win control of city halls across America, achieve concrete improvements in the lives of local residents in each of those cities, and eventually gather the strength to transform federal urban policies. He also saw that new movement as worldwide in scope, as more and more left-oriented mayors won election in key cities abroad, thus opening up the possibilities of cross-border urban alliances. To the urban elite, many of them accustomed to cynically viewing the pronouncements of all politicians as self-serving, these were wild-eyed dreams from a novice mayor with an inflated sense of his own importance, grandiose notions not heard since the days of John Lindsay. How dare de Blasio think so big? How dare he continue to insist that ending income inequality was the "moral imperative" of our time? Better that he concentrate on picking up the garbage, filling potholes, and keeping the city prosperous, they warned. And, most of all, stay close to home.

De Blasio refused to heed them. His first year in office he traveled to a British Labour Party conference in Manchester, England, where he drove home the worldwide nature of the growing wealth divide, proclaiming: "It was never my intention to nibble around the edges with policies of timid maintenance; I ran to take dead aim at the crisis of our time. And I became Mayor because everyday New Yorkers, too, were hungry for a clean break from the status quo."[19]

Two months later he gave the keynote speech in Washington, D.C., at the annual conference of Local Progress, the fledgling alliance of city officials that advocates more liberal policies than the U.S. Conference of Mayors (see chapter 5), and the following year he hosted the group's annual meeting in New York.

In April 2015, he astonished the Democratic Party's political establishment by refusing to immediately endorse Hillary Clinton's presidential campaign, even though he had managed her Senate campaign back in 2000. "I think she's one of the most qualified people to ever run for this office and, by the way, thoroughly vetted," de Blasio said in a televised interview on *Face the Nation*, while adding that he wanted "to see the substance" of Clinton's platform, her "vision" for the country. There was little doubt at the time that insurgent Democratic presidential candidate Bernie Sanders was far closer in viewpoint to de Blasio than Clinton was, so by refusing for several months to endorse her, de Blasio put unexpected pressure on Clinton to align herself more with Sanders's program. The following month, de Blasio announced in Washington, D.C., the founding of a new left-of-center political alliance, the Progressive Agenda. Surrounded by mayors and members of Congress from around the country, he unveiled a new thirteen-point program for the group, one he compared to the Republican Party's 1994 Contract with America. Many of the points, in fact, reflected the very issues de Blasio was championing in New York: universal pre-K, paid sick leave, paid family leave, comprehensive immigration reform, higher taxes for the wealthy. The group even began planning a presidential forum on urban problems for December 2015.

Then in July, de Blasio joined more than sixty of the world's mayors in a special two-day summit in Rome on climate change convened by Pope Francis, part of an effort to ramp up pressure on world governments to reach a climate accord at the world climate talks in Paris that December.

De Blasio's Progressive Agenda, however, encountered unexpected headwinds. First, he faced increased criticism from the city's press for his out-of-town trips and time spent on pursuing his national goals. Then several of the original signatories, including Pittsburgh mayor Bill Peduto, sought to distance themselves from the group when top national Democratic Party officials dismissed it. Finally, when none of the presidential candidates agreed to attend the forum the agenda had planned, de Blasio was forced to cancel it. Progressive Agenda thus became an embarrassing bust.[20]

The conservative *New York Post*, not surprisingly, soon took to calling de Blasio "King of the Road," for his many out-of-town trips. "During his 22 months in office, de Blasio has spent 33 weekdays taking nonofficial trips as far away as Italy and California." By comparison, the *Post* noted, former mayor Bloomberg had "spent just 19 weekdays on the road for anything other than official business."[21] The *Post*, of course, was skillfully rewriting history when it came to Bloomberg. The reality is that few mayors in the city's modern history spent more time out of New York City than Bloomberg, who routinely flew out of the city by midday on Fridays on his private plane to escape to his palatial mansion in Bermuda for long weekends, and who always refused to divulge his whereabouts to the press when he was gone.

As the *New York Times* noted in one of the few articles that ever examined this unusual practice:

> New York City mayors have historically prided themselves on working seven days a week and racing to the scene of an emergency even on the weekends.
>
> Mr. Bloomberg does not. His aides know better than to schedule public events after Friday mornings, allowing the mayor to make his getaways to Bermuda on Friday afternoon and be back in New York by Sunday evening. (Of the 17 Fridays since Dec. 31, the mayor had no public events scheduled after 10 a.m. on 13 of them.)[22]

But given the constant crises that erupt in a city like New York, Bloomberg was found at times to be inexplicably absent. In 2011, for example, when a massive blizzard paralyzed the city around

Christmas weekend, neither Bloomberg nor several of his top aides were seen in public for two days, and his spokesmen, when asked, refused to say where he'd been. It was later reported that his plane had been spotted at a Bermuda airport. And when a Metro-North commuter train derailed in early December 2013 in the Bronx, killing four people and injuring more than sixty, Bloomberg never appeared at the scene. Photos later surfaced of him golfing in Bermuda hours after the accident had occurred.[23] None of these secretive out-of-town absences by Bloomberg, however, attracted the kind of tabloid headlines that de Blasio's very public travels did. One was just a billionaire master of the universe, calmly and repeatedly jetting away to his island mansion for relaxation and declaring his travel off-limits to the public, with most of the press dutifully accepting his ground rules. The other was depicted by that same local press as a bumbling dreamer, stumping across the land for an end to income inequality—a modern-day Don Quixote who refused to accept that his job was filling potholes and balancing budgets, not changing society.

Where to House the People?

By the end of his third year in office, Mayor de Blasio had devoted enormous time and resources to his signature promise of tackling the city's affordable housing crisis, and while he could point to some real success in that area, his efforts had not significantly improved the availability of housing for New York's lowest-income families, nor had he ameliorated the city's homeless population, as the number of homeless residents in city shelters reached a record sixty thousand in 2016 and homelessness turned into the mayor's most visible and intractable problem.

Among de Blasio's unprecedented achievements, as previously noted, were the virtual freezing of rents for regulated apartments, major physical improvements in buildings managed by the New York City Housing Authority, and sharp reductions in annual housing evictions through increased funding for legal services for tenants and new anti-harassment laws (see chapter 8). But would his ambitious ten-year, $8 billion plan to build or preserve 200,000 affordable housing units, the largest municipal housing effort of its kind in the country's history, sufficiently increase the city's affordable housing stock to meet the needs of a fast-growing population? Sixty years of urban history, along with the basic laws of capitalism, offer ample evidence that the real estate industry will recoil from building low-income housing when there is so much profit to be made from luxury housing.

In January 2017, however, city hall announced that 62,506 units had been financed for poor and working-class New Yorkers during the administration's first three years. That included 21,963 started during 2016—the most affordable units launched in a single year since the end of the Ed Koch era—with the city having spent $788 million that year on those units, nearly twice the $400 million allocated in de Blasio's first year.[24]

But the glowing numbers obscured a fundamental weakness in the original housing plan: the bulk of those "affordable" units remained out of reach for the city's poorest residents. Only 40,000 apartments (20 percent of those to be produced) were to be targeted for the nearly 380,000 city households with incomes under $41,950 that were classified as being "severely rent-burdened"— or already paying more than 50 percent of their income for rent. Meanwhile, 80 percent of the planned units (160,000) would go to families with higher incomes, categories in which only 72,000 households were severely rent-burdened. A whopping 22,000 of those units would be earmarked for households making between $100,681 and $138,435. And while it is no doubt true that even families with such incomes (a two-parent household of a transit worker and a teacher, for example) are squeezed by the high cost of New York City housing, de Blasio's plan sparked widespread criticism from low-income housing advocates. Those advocates claimed it granted developers the chance to construct bigger buildings in which 75 percent of units would still be market rate, but where even the 25 percent of permanently affordable units barely addressed tenants with the greatest need. "We still have to attract development to the city," de Blasio told me in late 2015. "If we don't create a viable financial offer, then they [developers] will just walk away." His plan, known as mandatory inclusionary housing (MIH), the mayor insisted, gave the city the tools "to lean even heavier [on developers] to have more low-income housing."[25]

His argument cannot be dismissed easily, given how private developers have historically refused to build low-income housing and given the federal government's abandonment of new public housing construction more than forty years ago. "De Blasio is at least the first mayor in this city's history to require developers by law to build 25 percent affordable units," Ydanis Rodriguez, a city councilman from Washington Heights and Inwood, said.[26] But veteran low-income housing advocates insist the city could do better. Ismene Speliotis, for instance, has been building and managing low-income housing for decades as director of the nonprofit Mutual Housing Association of New York. She faults de Blasio for largely shunning nonprofit housing groups while offering more public subsidies to for-profit developers. In low-income areas like Brooklyn's East New York, for example, which city hall targeted early on for rezoning to spur more housing construction, Speliotis warned that de Blasio's "affordability" levels were so much higher than the neighborhood's existing median income that the rezoning will only spur gentrification. "It docs nothing for the residents," Speliotis said. "You pass that and you feel good about yourself, but it does nothing."[27]

De Blasio steadfastly rejected criticism from housing advocates that the top aides he chose to spearhead his housing plan—including former Wall Street executive Alicia Glen, his deputy mayor for housing and economic development; Vicki Been, his housing commissioner; and Carl Weisbrod, the chair of the city

planning commission—were ignoring concerns of local neighborhoods and were too cozy with the real estate industry, that
they were, in effect, a more liberal version of the old "growth
machine" proponents. By 2016, however, the administration
appeared to heed such criticisms. That year, for all new residential projects that received city financing, city hall increased
the percentage of affordable units targeted to very-low-income
families—those making less than $24,500 annually—to 20 per-
cent. That was a much higher figure than the 8 percent goal
de Blasio's original plan had projected for very-low-income families. Then, in January 2017, both Weisbrod and Been suddenly
announced their resignations. By then, de Blasio could rightfully claim that he was not only moving full steam ahead with
his promised housing plan, but he had heeded the outcry from
neighborhood leaders and made some improvements to it along
the way.[28]

The same could not be said of the crisis of homelessness, which
has clearly risen steadily under de Blasio, with a record population
of nearly sixty thousand people residing in homeless shelters by the
end of 2016—eight thousand more than when he took office—and
with the city forced to rent up to four thousand hotel and motel
rooms per night because of lack of sufficient shelter space and periodic stories in press outlets like the *New York Post* about the decline
in the city's quality of life.[29] Such stories, however, conveniently
ignore the reality that New York is one of the few cities in the
nation that is legally required by court decree to provide shelter
to homeless residents or that the homeless population skyrocketed
during the Bloomberg era, yet received very little press attention.

When Bloomberg took office in 2002, there were 31,000 people in city homeless shelters. By the time he left, the population
had shot up by 69 percent to more than 52,000. The reasons for
that were clear for anyone who bothered to investigate. In 2005,
the mayor ordered a halt to granting Section 8 housing vouchers
or priority for public housing to homeless families, a policy that

had existed for years and that had provided permanent housing that was less expensive than shelters. Then in 2011, Bloomberg refused, following a cutoff in state funding of the Advantage Program, which subsidized housing for the homeless, to continue the city's funding for that program. Housing advocates warned both times that those policies would cause the homeless population to mushroom, and that's exactly what happened. By the time de Blasio was sworn in he was faced with the perfect storm: not only had the city and state withdrawn permanent housing alternatives for the homeless, but the spiraling costs of the private rental market made it even harder for the working poor to afford an apartment. From 2011 to 2014, the city's homeless shelter population zoomed by five thousand annually. "First of all, there was no longer an exit from the shelter system, so the numbers were just piling up," said Steven Banks, the Human Resources Administration commissioner. "Second of all, people were coming back into the shelters because they couldn't maintain their housing" once the Advantage Program ended.[30]

Governor Frenemy

From the start of de Blasio's mayoral tenure, his most formidable foe turned out to be not the Republican Party establishment, not Wall Street executives, nor landlords, nor the police unions, but another fellow Democratic heavyweight and his onetime boss, Andrew Cuomo. As we have seen, Governor Cuomo, who had cultivated an image as a centrist Democrat, refused in early 2014 to back de Blasio's plan to permanently fund the city's universal pre-K program through a small tax increase on the wealthiest New Yorkers. He was also among the biggest skeptics who publicly questioned whether the new administration could even launch such an ambitious program in such a short time, though he did eventually agree to earmark money from the regular state budget for the pre-K program.

In March 2014, only weeks after de Blasio took office, Cuomo made clear that he was prepared to block key parts of de Blasio's agenda. Appearing in Albany at a public rally of the charter school movement to pressure state lawmakers for more funding, Cuomo declared: "We are here today to tell you that we stand with you. You are not alone. We will save charter schools." That event occurred on the same day that de Blasio was speaking at a separate Albany rally of public school parents and the teachers unions seeking pre-K funding.[31]

Everyone knew that de Blasio had vowed to limit the growth of charter schools in the city and to end the mass closings of public schools that had occurred annually under Bloomberg. So Cuomo was thus serving notice that he was replacing Bloomberg as the main champion of charter school growth. For a man known to harbor future presidential aspirations, it certainly helped that charter school backers on Wall Street were showering Cuomo with campaign contributions. One 2015 study found that 570 hedge fund managers gave more than $40 million in campaign contributions to Albany politicians since 2000, with the biggest beneficiary of those donations, at $4.8 million, being Cuomo. More than $600,000 came from the directors or family members of just one charter network, the Success Academy schools run by Eva Moskowitz.[32]

Not surprisingly, Cuomo and the Albany lawmakers handed charter school operators a big victory by amending state education law to require New York City to provide free space for charters in public school buildings or pay for much of their space in private buildings.

The governor's animosity toward de Blasio, however, went far beyond school policy differences. After all, the mayor later risked alienating his left-wing base to help Cuomo when he publicly lobbied the Working Families Party against endorsing a strong third-party challenge to Cuomo's reelection from Zephyr Teachout, a charismatic Fordham University professor. De Blasio personally negotiated a compromise between the Working Families Party and Cuomo in which the governor promised, if elected, to back a $13-an-hour minimum wage for New York City workers and the so-called DREAM Act for undocumented college students. But the following year, Cuomo proposed a far lower minimum-wage hike, only $11.50 for workers in the city and $10.50 for the rest of the state, and did nothing to win passage of the DREAM Act.[33] In an interview back then, Cuomo insisted to me: "Thirteen dollars an hour minimum doesn't have a chance to pass in this state." De Blasio and the Working Families Party, he warned, were unrealistic in their demands.

One year later, as city after city across the country passed higher minimum-wage laws, as the Bernie Sanders campaign mushroomed, with its attack on income inequality and its call for a $15-an-hour federal wage hike, the centrist Cuomo started to shift more to the left politically. Suddenly, he became the champion not just of $13 but of $15 an hour. He even instituted paid family leave for state workers. He started to out–de Blasio the mayor.

But even as he shifted closer to de Blasio's agenda on economic issues, Cuomo became more combative toward the mayor. Some of this is simply part of the historic dynamic between New York governors and the city's mayors. Whether it was Rockefeller and John Lindsay, Mario Cuomo and Ed Koch, or George Pataki and Rudy Giuliani, mayors and governors, even when they are from same party, have always feuded. Part of it is the frustration of all governors that they are stuck in Albany with few real powers and virtually no media attention, while New York City mayors have a much larger bureaucracy to run and are constantly in the news.

"The actual state government is basically the Department of Transportation and mental health institutions, and the tax department," one top de Blasio aide who has also worked in state government described it. "The mayors have all the toys as far as governors are concerned. They're in the media center, they are with all the money people, they control 350,000 employees, they have bonding capacity."

There is, in addition, a psychological dimension to the feud between Cuomo and de Blasio, according to several people who have worked closely with both men. The deep rift that developed between them has been a complete surprise to de Blasio, who had always defended and supported Cuomo in arguments with more left-wing Democrats. Back in 2002, for instance, when Democratic Party leaders, including Harlem congressman Charlie Rangel and even Bill Clinton, pressured Cuomo to agree to a humiliating withdrawal from a Democratic primary for governor against State Comptroller Carl McCall, de Blasio loyally backed Cuomo to the end, then helped mediate his withdrawal.

"Ever since 2002, Andrew decided that there are no Democrats who can have power in this town beside him," said one person who worked as a close aide to both men.

The losers in this deep political rift, however, have been New York City residents, who are periodically faced with battles between two leaders who should be working together.

A New People's Government or Old-Time Pay-to-Play?

As Bill de Blasio prepared in January 2017 to launch his campaign for reelection, the big question among his supporters was: will the mayor end up in handcuffs first? By then, state and federal agencies had launched at least five separate investigations into possible pay-to-play corruption schemes involving some of de Blasio's top aides and closest advisers, though none had actually been accused of a crime. But as the various probes dragged on, and as de Blasio continued to be dogged with questions about them from the press, the mayor became more defensive and hostile, and a dark cloud seemed to envelop city hall. It brought to mind for some political observers the infamous last days of the Ed

Koch era, days captured so vividly by journalists Jack Newfield and Wayne Barrett in *City for Sale*, their classic account of how Democratic political bosses Meade Esposito, Stanley Friedman, and Donald Manes turned New York City government during the 1980s into a racketeering enterprise, yet Koch, who gladly welcomed their political support, somehow never noticed their thievery.

Was it possible that de Blasio, the politician who had vowed to end the Tale of Two Cities, had instead brought back the corrupt government of old? Or were these criminal probes all part of a false narrative engineered by the city's 1 percent to divide and weaken public support for de Blasio and his progressive movement?

Reality is always more complex. No doubt, many powerful figures in the city were determined to end this radical experiment in government. But the emergence of so many criminal probes also reflected a deep flaw in de Blasio's political rise. That flaw was his belief that he could fight the system while also depending on key figures within the system; that he could seamlessly combine grassroots neighborhood activists and labor leaders of all political stripes with a major wing of the Democratic Party's neoliberal "growth" machine of consultants, lobbyists, and wealthy donors, many of whom typically regard proximity to political power as a way to make money, no matter who was in charge.

This unwieldy alliance, of course, had its roots in de Blasio's forays into managing campaigns for Al Gore and Hillary Clinton while organizing at the same time for the independent Working Families Party. And it was reflected most in the mayor's effort to fashion an outside lobbying force to push through and publicize his major reforms. They included the Campaign for One New York (initially titled UPK NYC), which helped win public support for universal pre-K and also spearheaded an effort by de Blasio in 2014 to win a Democratic majority in the state senate, and United for Affordable NYC, a group that promoted the

mayor's housing initiatives. Such groups have flourished in politics since the Supreme Court's *Citizens United* decision because
they can solicit unlimited donations to indirectly support a candidate's policies and thus avoid individual restrictions on campaign
contributions. Before it was closed down in March 2016, Campaign for One New York raised more than $4 million, much of
it from wealthy donors and unions with business before the city.
In de Blasio's defense, his aides at least voluntarily disclosed the
names of those donors, which the law did not require him to do.
Still, the stench of old-style pay-to-play politics was unmistakable. An FBI probe of Campaign for One New York, for instance,
questioned Joseph Dussich, the owner of a company that sells rat-
repellent trash bags, about his conversations with de Blasio and
the mayor's chief fund-raiser, Ross Offinger. Dussich happened
to have donated $100,000 to the Campaign for One New York
and subsequently received a Parks Department contract to supply the agency his company's trash bags. Agents also subpoenaed
documents from a transportation executive who gave $100,000
to de Blasio's effort to win a Democratic majority in the state
senate, and then received funding from a wage subsidy program
created by de Blasio. And they obtained documents from Two
Trees Management, a real estate firm that gave $100,000 to the
Campaign for One New York. A year before it gave the donation, the firm negotiated a deal with de Blasio to win development rights for a large residential building at the old Domino
factory along the Brooklyn waterfront by agreeing to increase the
percentage of affordable housing units. The mayor later unveiled
plans for a new tram line along the waterfront that Two Trees had
championed.[34]

Often, these same companies hired friends and unpaid advisers
to the mayor as their consultants. Two Trees, for example, hired
Jonathan Rosen of the BerlinRosen public relations firm. Rosen,
as we have seen, is one of de Blasio's closest friends and was a key
campaign strategist for the mayor. BerlinRosen, along with Hill-

top Public Solutions, another company run by top de Blasio advisers Nick Baldick and Bill Hyers, and AKPD, headed by another mayoral strategist, John Del Cecato, were collectively paid more than $2 million by One New York to promote the universal pre-K program. Rosen also represented some of the city's biggest real estate companies, all of which have major business interactions with city government. Yet he listed himself as a public relations representative instead of a lobbyist. He thus skirted legal regulations that require lobbyists to register with the city and file annual reports disclosing who their clients are and which city agencies they appear before.

When some agencies and reporters sought documents and emails between these outside consultants and city hall, de Blasio's aides took the unusual position that the emails of Rosen, Baldick, Hyers, Del Cecato, and even from U.S. ambassador to South Africa Patrick Gaspard, the mayor's closest friend, would not be released because they were "agents of the city." In other words, they were part of city government even though they were not on the public payroll, and their correspondence with city hall was an internal deliberation of city agencies, thus exempt from disclosure under freedom of information laws. So here was de Blasio, who had promised the most transparent government in the city's history, suddenly making the bizarre claim that he had a "shadow cabinet" whose deliberation could not be revealed to the public. "He is blinded about hack behavior, and the influence of people who get paid a lot of money to influence him," a close friend of de Blasio told me.

By the end of 2016, however, the mayor could no longer justify his "shadow cabinet" claim. Just before Thanksgiving, he started releasing hundreds of such emails to the press, and promised to reveal such correspondence from outside advisers in the future. By then, however, the damage had been done to his image of running a transparent government.

Investigations continued into other areas. There was the issue, for example, of unusual donations to NYCLASS, the animal rights group seeking to ban horse carriages in Central Park. Press reports revealed that the national hospitality labor union UNITE HERE gave $175,000 on June 1, 2013, to NYCLASS, only three months after de Blasio's cousin, John Wilhelm, retired as the union's president. Why a labor union would donate so much money to an obscure animal rights group is worthy of questioning all by itself, certainly by the union's members. But two days after receiving that donation, NYCLASS passed the exact same amount of money to a political action committee that was running TV ads attacking mayoral hopeful and then–city council speaker Christine Quinn, an ad campaign that seriously damaged Quinn's favorability among the voters. A big beneficiary was de Blasio, who had vowed to ban the horse carriages once he was elected. Federal agents subsequently launched a probe into whether the donation violated campaign finance laws that forbid the coordination of spending between a candidate and nonprofit advocacy groups and was, in effect, the laundering of money to benefit de Blasio's candidacy.

Despite the remarkable achievement of de Blasio's first three years and the city's continued economic revival, any one of those inquiries could have resulted in criminal indictments of his top aides or advisers, thus posing a threat to his reelection chances and an enormous setback for the new progressive movement. But on March 16, 2017, the mayor received a surprising reprieve. That day, both federal and state prosecutors announced separately that their lengthy and extensive probes had ended with no criminal charges being lodged against him or anyone connected to him. The U.S. attorney's office for the Southern District of New York noted in a statement that its investigators did find evidence that de Blasio or those close to him had contacted city agencies on behalf of businesses seeking city contracts, businesses from which de Blasio had also solicited donations. But there was "no evidence of personal profit" to the mayor, the statement added, and, given "the high burden of proof" and "the clarity of existing law," the office had decided not to bring charges. In a more detailed statement, Manhattan District Attorney Cyrus Vance Jr. concluded the actions of de Blasio and his aides in funneling large sums of money during 2014 through local upstate Democratic Party organizations, part of an effort to end Republican domination of the state senate, appeared to "violate the spirit and intent" of state campaign finance law. But those actions, Vance concluded, were not criminal, since the mayor and his aides were repeatedly assured at the time by an attorney that the fund-raising tactics were legal (see afterword).[35]

Having dodged any criminal charges, de Blasio saw his prospects for reelection suddenly brightened. The likelihood that a major Democratic office holder might decide to challenge him in the September primary dropped dramatically. Still, his image as a progressive reformer had been damaged. More importantly, key grassroots organizations in housing, education, and criminal justice reform, groups that backed him for mayor in 2013, were becoming more critical of his policies. If de Blasio hoped to cruise to a second term, he faced having to reconnect with those groups and address their concerns. As for the advocates, they confronted critical choices of their own, the kind of choices that every left-wing or progressive social movement has always faced. Criticizing those who hold political power, after all, is easy; actually exercising power, running a progressive government, is far more difficult. Those who attain high positions in government will inevitably disappoint a portion of their supporters, will inevitably exhibit human weaknesses and flaws, and some are bound to betray their followers altogether.

So whether it was Bill de Blasio in New York, Bill Peduto in Pittsburgh, Betsy Hodges in Minneapolis, or Martin Walsh in Boston—all of them up for reelection in 2017—or Ras Baraka in Newark in 2018, liberals and radicals in each city faced deciding how important it was to maintain power in these crucial pockets of urban resistance in the age of Donald Trump and of Republican domination of Washington and most state capitals.

At a time when urban America is both a sanctuary for undocumented immigrants and an engine of enormous prosperity, when our cities remain centers of inclusion and diversity in a nation gripped by intolerance and ultranationalism, how important would it be to rally around progressive local leaders, with all their flaws and failures, in the long and winding fight to reclaim Gotham for its people?

Afterword

To chronicle the story of a new and diffuse social movement is a daunting task for any writer, whether you are a daily journalist rushing to report some specific event in that movement's life, a long-form narrator striving to interpret the growing movement's broader impact, or an academic scholar who comes along years later to situate the movement within the grand arc of history. Each method has its limitations. Long-form narration in real time, the approach chosen here, has its own particular risks and perils. No one can predict, after all, how things will end. Popular revolts have a habit of starting one way and suddenly veering in a totally different direction. Political leaders often jettison their early ideals and "adapt" to new realities, or they are toppled by personal demons, or they succumb to the aphrodisiacs of power or money, or they simply decide to betray their original supporters.

Moreover, given the many months that typically elapse between completing a book of this kind and its release to the general public, major incidents sometimes transpire that eclipse or even contradict portions of the original account. As I was completing my final edits to this manuscript in March and April of 2017, for instance, unexpected developments took place that had the potential to alter the reelection prospects of two protagonists of this story, New York's Bill de Blasio and Seattle's Ed Murray, and the election results in Jackson, Mississippi.

On March 16, after massive yearlong investigations into possible pay-to-play corruption in New York's city hall and allegations of campaign finance law violations, federal and state prosecutors announced they would not file criminal charges against Mayor de Blasio or any of his top aides and advisers. Given the months of public attention to their probes, both the U.S. Attorney for the Southern District of New York and the Manhattan District Attorney took the unusual step of publicly revealing their conclusions. In a one-page statement, federal investigators said they found the mayor and his aides had "solicited donations from individuals who sought official favors from the city," and that de Blasio had subsequently intervened with city agencies on behalf of some of those same donors, but their probe found "no evidence of personal profit" by the mayor, and they thus concluded there was little likelihood of proving a crime had been committed.[1]

On the same day, Manhattan District Attorney Cyrus Vance produced a more extensive ten-page summary of his inquiry into allegations by the state board of elections that de Blasio had violated campaign fundraising limits during the summer of 2014, when he raised millions of dollars from a few dozen wealthy donors and labor unions in a failed effort to help Democrats regain control of the New York state senate.

After reviewing more than one million documents, emails, and bank records, many of them obtained through subpoenas and search warrants, and after directly interviewing more than fifty people, Vance blasted de Blasio's 2014 fundraising scheme as "contrary to the intent and the spirit of the laws that impose campaign contribution limits," but he concluded that the mayor and his aides could not be charged with a crime, since they had consulted at every step with an attorney who was an expert in campaign finance law, and since that attorney had repeatedly advised them their actions were legal.

Vance's letter, however, offered startling details of how de Blasio and those around him had resorted to the same kind of dark money fundraising and skirting of campaign spending limits that Democrats often accuse Republicans of employing. It also revealed that Governor Andrew Cuomo was initially involved along with de Blasio in approving the strategy, which top state Democrats dubbed the "Coordinated Campaign."

The Putnam County Democratic Committee, for example, received more than $671,000 from a few wealthy donors that summer—twenty times more money than it had ever received during a statewide election. Within days, the committee trans-ferred $640,000 to the senate campaigns of two Democrats in the county, thus evading state law that limited individual dona-tions of money to a political candidate to $10,300. Even more startling, the two Democratic senate candidates, according to Vance, then "immediately expended virtually all of the funds on political consultants such as BerlinRosen, AKPD, and Red Horse Strategies"—firms whose executives were close friends or advisers of de Blasio.

In other words, the mayor and his aides raised the money, and then used the state committees as virtual pass through to the Democratic senate candidates, with those candidates spending the money on the very consultants who also happened to work for the mayor. New York campaign finance limits are so porous, Vance concluded, that this kind of "end around" did not rise to the level of a crime, though it certainly violated the "spirit" of the law.[2]

The simultaneous decision of two law enforcement agencies to close their probes without a single indictment marked a major victory for de Blasio, who had always insisted he and his aides had broken no laws. It was a costly victory, however. The mayor was hounded for more than a year by press accounts that often depicted him as corrupt, and during that time he was unable to enact the kind of bold reforms that marked his first two years in office. The damage to his reputation among some voters was likely to endure. On top of that, he and his closest aides incurred tens of millions of dollars in legal fees responding to subpoenas for

documents and sitting through lengthy interviews with investigators from two separate probes.

"You can't imagine what it's like to have the FBI knock at
your door twice at seven o'clock in the morning and slap you
with a subpoena," said one mid-level Democrat who told me he
incurred more than $250,000 in legal bills and who character-
ized the overzealous agents assigned to the probe as "part of a
witch-hunt."

Once prosecutors concluded their investigations, the cloud
surrounding the de Blasio administration quickly dissipated. So
did the likelihood of a primary challenge to his reelection by a
fellow major Democrat such as city comptroller Scott Stringer,
public advocate Letitia James, or Brooklyn congressman Hakeem
Jeffries, though the mayor was still sure to face a handful of minor
challengers. "I'm not interested in tilting at windmills," acknowledged former Bloomberg adviser Bradley Tusk, who had been
actively seeking opponents to de Blasio. "It all came down to
indictments and there were no indictments, so there's not much
else to do." Even Republican leaders saw little likelihood of
defeating de Blasio in the November election.[3]

Two weeks later came the first sign that the de Blasio coalition
was preparing to launch a new series of progressive reforms. On
April 2, a blue ribbon commission created by the city council to
investigate conditions at Rikers Island, the city's main jail system,
issued its report.

"Should New York City continue to employ a penal colony
model that needlessly confines thousands of local residents on an
isolated Island where they, and their guards, are exposed to inhu-
mane treatment that leaves a lifetime of damage?" asked the commission, which was chaired by Jonathan Lippman, New York's
former chief judge. "Our answer is unequivocal: 'No.'"

It urged "without hesitation or equivocation, permanently
ending the use of Rikers Island as a jail facility in any form or
function," further noting:

> Closing Rikers Island is far more than a symbolic gesture. It is an essential step toward a more effective and more humane criminal justice system. We must replace our current model of mass incarceration with something that is more effective *and* more humane.

Council Speaker Melissa Mark-Viverito, not de Blasio, originally envisioned the commission and first raised the idea, one long advocated by opponents of mass incarceration, of closing the notorious Rikers complex. De Blasio declared the notion unfeasible initially, but a few days before the commission released its report, he suddenly changed his stance and announced his own plans to close Rikers within ten years, if the inmate population continued its years of decline. The future of Rikers thus emerged as the clearest example of Mark-Viverito and the council pushing de Blasio to adopt more radical positions, especially in criminal justice reform.

But even as an embattled Mayor de Blasio found new life after his scandal saga, at the other end of the country, Seattle mayor Ed Murray suddenly found himself accused in a civil lawsuit of child sexual abuse. His accuser, a forty-six-year-old man, claimed Murray repeatedly "raped and molested" him in the 1980s, starting when the man was a fifteen-year-old high school dropout. The story broke in the *Seattle Times* on April 6, at a point when Murray was enjoying more than 60 percent popularity in voter polls and appeared to be cruising toward victory in his reelection campaign. Separate from the lawsuit, the *Times* story also revealed allegations from two other men who claimed Murray sexually abused them decades ago, when he worked at a Portland home for troubled youths and they were residents there. One of the men had raised his allegations to authorities in 1984, but they filed no criminal charges against Murray back then.[4]

Murray immediately denied all the claims. Within days he produced a doctor's report that directly contradicted a description of his genitals his accuser had included in the law-suit. Still, the stunning allegations severely damaged his reelection chances. Many grassroots leaders were already critical of the mayor's cozy relationship with city's political establishment. In early March, Nikkita Oliver, a thirty-one-year-old attorney and community organizer who had been active with the city's Black Lives Matter movement, announced she was running against Murray as the standard-bearer of a new Peoples Party of Seattle. A featured speaker at Oliver's campaign launch was the city's popular socialist councilmember Kshama Sawant. Then, less than two weeks after the *Seattle Times* story broke, former mayor Mike McGinn, the man Murray had defeated in a close election in 2013, announced he was entering the August 1 non-partisan primary to regain the seat. It quickly became apparent the sixty-two-year-old Murray could not survive. On May 2, he acknowledged that by announcing he would not run for a second term.

The same day Murray ended his political career, a thirty-four-year-old progressive lawyer and human rights activist won a resounding victory in the Democratic mayoral primary in Jackson, Mississippi. Chokwe Antar Lumumba, the son of Chokwe Lumumba, that city's radical former mayor, won 55 percent of the vote against incumbent mayor Tony Yarber and several other candidates, virtually assuring he would be that city's next mayor. As mentioned previously, following the death of the elder Lumumba from a heart attack in 2014 after only eight months in office, Yarber defeated his son in a special election to fill the seat. But the junior Lumumba, who had been a top aide to his father, continued to work with the Malcolm X Grassroots Movement, backed local auto plant workers in their struggle for labor rights, and co-founded the Mississippi Human Rights Collective, which spearheaded efforts to remove the Confederate insignia from the state's flag. Those efforts won him a broader following among Jackson's voters and enabled him to emerge victorious in his second effort, thus making it possible for city's experiment in radical government to continue.

Such twists and turns in local politics are all too commonplace, but when it comes to the cities examined in this book we would be mistaken to allow a particular upheaval or setback in one or another locale, or the failures of one or another leader, to obscure for us the bigger picture of a political and social movement that has been steadily gathering strength in urban America for more than a decade. That movement's finest moments are yet to come.

—May 2017

Acknowledgments

I am indebted to Carl Bromley at The New Press for shepherding this book to publication. Carl's meticulous editing, incisive questions, and frequent suggestions for additional sources all dramatically improved the final product. Many thanks as well to Ellen Adler for taking a big risk in publishing a book on a subject that kept changing before our eyes, to Liana Krissoff for her wonderful copyediting, and to Emily Albarillo for her willingness to rearrange the schedule whenever I missed a deadline, and to Lissette Flores, as well, for her research assistance and transcribing of all interviews.

My gratitude to the score of grassroots activists, union leaders, and government officials in New York and a dozen other cities who graciously consented to be interviewed for this book. Thanks as well to all my colleagues at the New York *Daily News*, from which I retired in 2016. Most of the reporting on urban affairs reflected here took place during my twenty-nine years as a columnist at that paper, where many terrific colleagues routinely shared with me their own insights on the city, among them Jerry Capeci, Greg Smith, Barbara Ross, Ying Chan, Kirsten Danis, Jack Newfield, Tom Robbins, Bill Farrell, Michael Daly, and, of course, the legendary Pete Hamill.

I would also like to acknowledge the pioneering work of Charles Abrams, Roger Biles, Julian Brash, Robert Caro, Manuel

Castells, Peter Dreier, Steve Early, Amy Hillier, Adrienne Hollo-
way, Kenneth Jackson, Jane Jacobs, John Logan, Harvey Molotch,
John Mollenkopf, James Parrott, Marsha Ritzdorf, Thomas Sugrue, and June Manning Thomas, all of whose scholarship shaped
my understanding of urban governance and the central role of
race and class in conflicts over land, space and place in the modern
city.

Special thanks to Tom Robbins, one of New York City's finest journalists and a good friend, for reading portions of the
manuscript and providing valuable feedback. And finally, thanks
to Lilia Fernández, whose brilliance, devotion, and love have
brightened my life in ways I never imagined.

Notes

Introduction

1. Jane Jacobs, *The Death and Life of Great American Cities* (New York: Random House, 1961), p. 317.

2. James Parrot, "Briefing on Mayor de Blasio's Preliminary FY 2016 NYC Budget: Addressing Needs and Budgeting Cautiously as the Recovery Progresses," New York Fiscal Policy Institute, March 2015, p. 24. Accessed at: http://fiscalpolicy.org/wp-content/uploads/2015/03/Budget-Briefing -NYC-FY-2016.pdf.

3. Sam Roberts, "Gap Between Manhattan's Rich and Poor Is Greatest in U.S., Census Finds," *New York Times*, September 17, 2014.

4. "What Is the Greatest Threat to the World? Depends on Where You Live," Pew Research Center, October 16, 2014. Accessed at: http://www .pewresearch.org/fact-tank/2014/10/16/what-is-the-greatest-threat-to -the-world-depends-on-where-you-live.

5. In 1978, just one-tenth of 1 percent of U.S. families—a mere 160,000 households—owned 7 percent of the nation's wealth, but by 2012 their share of total wealth had zoomed to 22 percent. That year, 1 percent of families—those with net assets above $4 million—held 42 percent of all wealth. Meanwhile, the bottom 90 percent of American families saw their share of the nation's wealth plummet from a high of 35 percent in the mid-1980s to just 23 percent in 2012. See Emanuel Saez and Gabriel Zucman, "Wealth Inequality in the United States Since 1913: Evidence from Capitalized Income Tax Data," National Bureau of Economic Research, Working Paper 2065. Accessed at: http://www.nber.org/papers/w20625.

6. Richard Dobbs et al., "Urban World: Mapping the Economic Power of Cities," McKinsey Global Institute, March 2011. Accessed at: http:// www.mckinsey.com/global-themes/urbanization/urban-world-mapping -the-economic-power-of-cities.

7. Joel Rogers and Satya Rhodes-Conway, "Cities at Work: Progressive Local Policies to Rebuild the Middle Class," Center for American Progress Action Fund, February 2014, p. 5.

8. Will Wilkinson, "Why Does Donald Trump Demonize Cities?" *Washington Post,* March 17, 2017.

9. Jim Tankersley and Ana Swanson, "Donald Trump Is Assembling the Richest Administration in Modern American History," *Washington Post,* November 30, 2016.

10. Based on author's interviews and correspondence with top city officials. For pre-K figures, those officials based their estimate on 134,578 net new pre-K seats that were filled during the first three years of universal pre-K, with each family saving $1,000 per month in private pre-K costs, or $10,000 per year for a ten-month school year. For paid sick leave, the Office of Management and Budget estimates that approximately 500,000 to 580,000 employees who reside in New York City were covered by the expanded sick leave law passed in early 2014, and that those employees averaged slightly less than three paid sick days per year, at a total cost to employers of $165 million annually.

11. New York City Rent Guidelines Board, *2016 Housing Supply Report,* May 26, 2016, pp. 3–4. Accessed at: http://www.nycrgb.org/downloads /research/pdf_reports/16HSR.pdf. Also, New York City Rent Guidelines Board, *2015 Income and Expense Study,* March 12, 2015, pp. 4, 6. Accessed at: http://www.nycrgb.org/downloads/research/pdf_reports/ie15.pdf. Estimated savings to tenants is from author correspondence with city officials at the Office of Management and Budget, who compared past average annual increases that landlords received of 3.2 percent with average increase they were granted from 2014 to 2017 of 0.3 percent.

12. John R. Logan and Harvey Molotch, *Urban Fortunes: The Political Economy of Place* (Berkeley: University of California Press, 1987), p. 178. Among other invaluable studies, see: Thomas Sugrue, *The Origins of the Urban Crisis: Race and Inequality in Postwar Detroit* (Princeton, NJ: Princeton University Press, 1996); Kenneth Jackson, *Crabgrass Frontier: The Suburbanization of the United States* (New York: Oxford University Press, 1983); June Manning Thomas and Marsha Ritzdorf, eds., *Urban Planning and the African American Community: In the Shadows* (Thousand Oaks, CA: Sage Publications, 1997); and, most recently, Roger Biles, *The Fate of Cities: Urban America and the Federal Government, 1945–2000* (Lawrence: University of Kansas Press, 2011).

13. *Building the American City,* Report of the National Commission on Urban Problems to the Congress and to the President of the United States (Washington, D.C.: U.S. Government Printing Office, 1698), pp. 67, 85.

14. A useful summary of that debate can be found in Julian Brash, *Bloomberg's New York: Class and Governance in the Luxury City* (Athens: University of Georgia Press, 2011), pp. 4–16. For an eloquent argument against the

ravages of neoliberalism, see journalist and environmental activist George Monbiot's "Neoliberalism—the Ideology at the Root of All Our Problems," *The Guardian*, April 15, 2016.

15. "14 Cities and States Approved $15 Minimum Wage in 2015," National Employment Law Project press release, December 21, 2015. Accessed at: http://www.nelp.org/content/uploads/PR-Minimum-Wage-Year-End-15 .pdf.

16. "Mayor de Blasio Announces Guaranteed $15 Minimum Wage for All City Government Employees, Benefitting 50,000 Additional New Yorkers." Accessed at: http://www1.nyc.gov/office-of-the-mayor/news/019-16 /mayor-de-blasio-guaranteed-15-minimum-wage-all-city-government -employees--#/0.

17. For an early account of the Peduto and Hodges elections, see Harold Meyerson, "The Revolt of the Cities," *American Prospect*, April 22, 2014. Accessed at: http://prospect.org/article/revolt-cities; also Gabriel Thompson, "Minneapolis Has Long Been Fractured by Racial Inequity. Can a New Mayor Change That?," *The Nation*, September 3, 2014. Accessed at: https://www.thenation.com/article/one-minneapolis-possible.

1. Family Ghosts: The Making of Bill de Blasio

1. Author's interview with John Wilhelm, July 29, 2016.

2. For the best account of the various official steps by de Blasio to change his name, see Greg Smith, "Mayoral Hopeful Bill de Blasio Has Had Three Different Legal Names, Court Records Show," *New York Daily News*, September 22, 2013.

3. Jennifer Fermino, "Bill de Blasio Mayoral Campaign Ad Tells of Demons of an Alcoholic Father," *New York Daily News*, June 10, 2013. Also Javier C. Hernandez, "From His Father's Decline, de Blasio 'Learned What Not to Do,'" *New York Times*, October 13, 2013.

4. Ibid. Also author's interview with John Wilhelm, op. cit.

5. See FBI "Warren Wilhelm File" for Loyalty Oath Board, January 6, 1953, US AID. Accessed at: https://archive.org/stream/WarrenWilhelm /Wilhelm,%20Warren_djvu.txt.

6. Ibid.

7. Landon R.Y. Storrs, "Bill de Blasio Is Not Afraid of Red Scare Ghosts," *The Nation*, October 30, 2013.

8. FBI, "Warren Wilhelm File," op. cit.

9. Hernandez, "From His Father's Decline," op. cit.

10. Tom Robbins and Anna Sale, "Between World War II and His Suicide, De Blasio's Father a Cold Warrior," WNYC, October 14, 2013. Accessed

at: http://www.wnyc.org/story/between-wwii-and-his-suicide-de-blasios
-father-cold-warrior.

11. Hernandez, "From His Father's Decline," op. cit.

12. Robbins and Sale, "Between World War II and His Suicide," op. cit.

13. Author's interview with John Wilhelm, op. cit.

14. Andrew Friedman, *Covert Capital: Landscapes of Denial and the Making of U.S. Empire in the Suburbs of Northern Virginia* (Berkeley: University of California Press, 2013), pp. 83–84, 257.

15. Author's interview with John Wilhelm, op. cit.

16. Robbins and Sale, "Between World War II and His Suicide," op. cit.

17. Author's interview with Maureen Fiedler, August 23, 2016.

18. Javier C. Hernandez, "A Mayoral Hopeful Now, de Blasio Was Once a Young Leftist," *New York Times*, September 22, 2013.

19. Ibid.

20. Author's interview with Ken Sunshine, June 16, 2016.

21. Ibid.

22. Author's interview with First Deputy Mayor Anthony Shorris, husband of Maria Laurino, September 23, 2016.

2. Race, Class, and the Urban Growth Machine

1. Logan and Molotch, *Urban Fortunes*, op. cit., p. 1.

2. Ibid., p. 2.

3. Nathaniel S. Keith, *Politics and the Housing Crisis Since 1930* (New York: Universe Books, 1973), p. 11.

4. For housing during the First World War, see Biles, *The Fate of Cities*, op. cit., pp. 1–2. For black migration, see Chicago Commission on Race Relations, *The Negro in Chicago: A Study of Race Relations and a Race Riot* (Chicago: University of Chicago Press, 1922), pp. 79, 106; Charles Abrams, *Forbidden Neighbors: A Study of Prejudice in Housing* (New York: Harper & Brothers, 1955), pp. 81–85; and Sugrue, *The Origins of the Urban Crisis*, op. cit., pp. 19–31.

5. For the Supreme Court decision, see *Buchanan v. Warley*, 245 U.S. 60 (1917); for the spread of zoning, see Jackson, *Crabgrass Frontier*, op. cit., pp. 241–42; for racially exclusive zoning, an excellent summary is Christopher Silver, "The Racial Origins of Zoning," in Thomas and Ritzdorf, *Urban Planning and the African American Community*, op. cit., pp. 23–42; for Chicago housing discrimination, see *The Negro in Chicago*, op. cit., p. 215; for class bias in zoning, see *Building the American City*, op. cit., pp. 7–8.

6. Keith, *Politics and the Housing Crisis Since 1930*, op. cit., p. 22.

7. Biles, *The Fate of Cities*, op. cit., pp. 2–9, 11; C. Lowell Harriss, *History and Policies of the Home Owners' Loan Corporation* (Washington, D.C.: National Bureau of Economic Research, 1951), p. 1. Accessed at: http:// www.nber.org/chapters/c3205.pdf; also white paper of Federal Reserve Bank staff member Jonathan D. Rose, "The Incredible HOLC? Mortgage Relief During the Great Depression," January 15, 2010. Accessed at: http: //iga.ucdavis.edu/events/Research/All-UC/conferences/santa-clara-10 /Rose%20paper.PDF; also *Building the American City*, op. cit., pp. 108–10; also Alexander von Hoffman, "A Study in Contradictions: The Origins and Legacy of the Housing Act of 1949," *Housing Policy Debate* 11, no. 2, Fannie Mae Foundation (2000): 302–3.

8. Amy E. Hillier, "Residential Security Maps and Neighborhood Appraisals: The Home Owners' Loan Corporation and the Case of Philadelphia," *Social Science History* 29, no. 3 (Summer 2005): 207–33.

9. Frederick Babcock, *The Valuation of Real Estate* (New York: McGraw-Hill, 1932), pp. 86, 91; Ernest M. Fisher, *Principles of Real Estate* (New York: Macmillan, 1923), p. 116; Homer Hoyt, *One Hundred Years of Land Values in Chicago* (Chicago: University of Chicago Press, 1933), p. 114.

10. Biles, *The Fate of Cities,* op. cit., pp. 9–10.

11. Abrams, *Forbidden Neighbors,* op. cit., p. 172. For a summary of city-by-city segregation policies in public housing, see Richard Rothstein, "Race and Public Housing: Revisiting the Federal Role," *Poverty and Race Research Action Council* 21, no. 6 (November/December 2012).

12. Biles, *The Fate of Cities*, op. cit., p. 101.

13. Abrams, *Forbidden Neighbors*, op. cit., pp. 229–30.

14. John P. Dean, "Only Caucasian: A Study of Race Covenants," *Journal of Land and Public Utility Economics* 23, no. 4 (November 1947): 428–32. For Levittown, see Jackson, *Crabgrass Frontier*, op. cit., pp. 234–41; also Bruce Lambert, "At 50, Levittown Contends with Its Legacy of Bias," *New York Times*, December 28, 1997.

15. Charles Bagli, "A New Light on a Fight to Integrate Stuyvesant Town," *New York Times*, November 21, 2010. For a more detailed view of displacement from Stuyvesant Town, see Abrams, *Forbidden Neighbors*, op. cit., pp. 251–59. For Stuyvesant Town as urban redevelopment precursor, see von Hoffman, "A Study in Contradictions," op. cit., pp. 304–5; Biles, *The Fate of Cities*, op. cit., p. 35; for Board of Estimate hearing, see "Stuyvesant Town Approved by Board," *New York Times*, June 4, 1943.

16. Abrams, *Forbidden Neighbors*, op. cit., pp. 174–75.

17. U.S. Census Bureau, "Tracking the American Dream: Fifty Years of Housing Changes," Statistical Brief, April 1994. Accessed at: https://www .census.gov/prod/1/statbrief/sb94_8.pdf. See also Von Hoffman, "A Study in Contradictions," op. cit., pp. 303–9.

18. Keith, *Politics and the Housing Crisis Since 1930*, op. cit., pp. 105–7, 131–33.

19. Abrams, *Forbidden Neighbors*, op. cit., pp. 245–46.

20. Robert A. Caro, *The Power Broker: Robert Moses and the Fall of New York* (New York: Vintage Books, 1975), pp. 1013–14.

21. Ibid., p. 20.

22. Abrams, *Forbidden Neighbors*, op. cit., p. 249.

23. Biles, *The Fate of Cities*, op. cit., pp. 162–63. Logan and Molotch, *Urban Fortunes*, op. cit., p. 168.

24. Clarence N. Stone, *Economic Growth and Neighborhood Discontent: System Bias in the Urban Renewal Program of Atlanta* (Chapel Hill: University of North Carolina Press, 1976), pp. 49, 79; Biles, *The Fate of Cities,* op. cit., p. 36.

25. Jacobs, *The Life and Death of Great American Cities*, op. cit., p. 4.

26. Abrams, *Forbidden Neighbors*, op. cit., pp. 82–83.

27. Ibid., pp. 93–96, 103; also Sugrue, *Origins of the Urban Crisis*, op. cit., pp. 72–75; also Louis E. Martin, "The Truth About Sojourner Truth," *The Crisis*, April 1942, pp. 112–13.

28. Raymond Mohl, "The Second Ghetto and the 'Infiltration Theory' in Urban Real Estate, 1940–1960," in Thomas and Ritzdorf, eds., *Urban Planning and the African American Community*, op. cit., p. 63.

29. For Chicago, see Abrams, *Forbidden Neighbors*, p. 103; for Detroit, see interview with Sugrue, "Auto Industry Decline, Racial Tension at the Root of Detroit's Collapse," *Associated Press*, July 21, 2013. Accessed at: http://www.pennlive.com/midstate/index.ssf/2013/07/auto_industry_troubles_racial.html.

30. Raymond Mohl, "The Second Ghetto," op. cit., pp. 60–64; for a chilling account of the widespread racial terror around housing during the 1950s, see Abrams, *Forbidden Neighbors*, op. cit., pp. 81–90, 122–32.

31. Report of the National Advisory Committee on Civil Disorders, *The Kerner Report* (New York: Pantheon Books, 1968), p. xviii.

32. Biles, *The Fate of Cities*, op. cit., pp. 38, 62–111.

33. *The Kerner Report*, op. cit., p. 2.

34. National Commission on Urban Problems, *Building the American City*, op. cit., pp. 84–87.

35. On Douglas Commission, ibid., pp. 10–11. On Housing Act of 1968, see Biles, *The Fate of Cities*, op cit., pp. 153–154. For public-private partnerships, see Alexander von Hoffman, "Calling upon the Genius of Private Enterprise: The Housing and Urban Development Act of 1968 and the Liberal Turn to Public-Private Partnerships," *Studies in American Political Development* 27 (October 2013): 165–94.

36. Biles, *The Fate of Cities*, op. cit., pp. 158–59.

37. Ibid., pp. 178–81; John T. Metzger, "Planned Abandonment: The Neighborhood Life-Cycle Theory and National Urban Policy," *Housing Policy Debate* 11, no. 1 (2000), Fannie Mae Foundation: 16–17.

38. Housing and Community Development Act of 1974. Accessed at: https://www.hudexchange.info/resources/documents/Housing-and -Community-Development-Act-1974.pdf. See also Biles, *The Fate of Cities*, op. cit., pp. 190–91.

39. For a James Downs profile, see John Metzger, "Planned Abandonment," op. cit., pp. 10–13. For the role of Downs in Near West Side development, see Lilia Fernández, *Brown in the Windy City* (Chicago: University of Chicago Press, 2012), pp. 107–20.

40. Peter Applebome, "After the Riots: From Riots of 60's to Riots of the 90's, a Frustrating Search to Heal a Nation," *New York Times*, May 8, 1992; also Metzger, "Planned Abandonment," op. cit., pp. 8–14.

41. In 1974, a federal judge ruled that Chicago's Public Housing Authority had systematically denied blacks admission to public housing in white neighborhoods and he ordered the city to build integrated new projects. The Ford administration promptly blasted the decision and supported Chicago's appeal to the Supreme Court, claiming that moving poor people into the suburbs would have a "chilling effect" on those communities. Nonetheless, the high court upheld the order in a unanimous decision. See Biles, *The Fate of Cities*, op. cit., pp. 215–16.

42. Ibid., p. 248.

43. Ibid., p. 283.

44. Ibid., pp. 250–86.

45. Ibid., pp. 284–316.

46. Ibid., pp. 318–47. Center on Budget Policy Priorities report, accessed at: http://www.cbpp.org/sites/default/files/atoms/files/2-24-09hous-sec2.pdf.

3. Radical Outsider or Political Insider?

1. Jennifer Kingson Bloom, "Filling the Del Toro Seat: Litmus of District's Priorities," *New York Times*, March 5, 1995; Juan Gonzalez, "Del Toro Gang's Time Up," *New York Daily News*, March 8, 1995.

2. Author's interview with Francisco Diaz, November 3, 2016.

3. Author's interview with Dan Cantor, national director of Working Families Party, November 3, 2016.

4. Jack Newfield and Wayne Barrett provide a gripping account of Koch's deal with the bosses in *City for Sale: Ed Koch and the Betrayal of New York* (New York: Harper & Row, 1988), pp. 130–40.

5. Frank Lombardi, "Election Stampede Shocks Diaz and Pals," *New York Daily News*, March 16, 1995.

6. Author's interview with Ken Sunshine, June 16, 2016.

7. Author's interview with Bertha Lewis, July 6, 2016.

8. John Atlas, *Seeds of Change: The Story of ACORN, America's Most Controversial Antipoverty Community Organizing Group* (Nashville: Vanderbilt University Press, 2010), pp. 9–26. Atlas provides a richly sourced and sympathetic account of the group's rise. For a conservative critique that is far more polemical than fact-based, see Matthew Vadum, *Subversion, Inc.: How Obama's ACORN Red Shirts Are Still Terrorizing and Ripping off American Taxpayers* (Washington, D.C.: WND Books, 2011).

9. Steven Greenhouse, "Child Care Workers in New York City Vote to Unionize," *New York Times* October 24, 2007; also author's interview with Fran Streich, August 22, 2016.

10. Author's interview with Bertha Lewis.

11. Kenneth R. McGrail, "New York City School Decentralization: The Respective Powers of the City Board of Education and the Community School Boards," *Fordham Urban Law Journal* 5, no. 2 (1976).

12. On WFP support for de Blasio's school board race, author's interview with Bill Lipton, New York state director of Working Families Party, May 26, 2016; on Fariña's influence, Eliza Shapiro, "The Woman Who Shaped de Blasio on Schools," *Politico*, December 12, 2013.

13. Peter Meyer, "Will Mayor de Blasio Turn Back the School Reform Clock?" *Education Next* 14, no. 2 (Spring 2014); also author's interview with John Wilhelm, July 29, 2016.

14. Author's interview with Ken Sunshine.

15. James Bradley, "Park Slope Scramble," *Village Voice*, August 28, 2001.

16. Author's interview with Steve Kest, former national ACORN leader, June 15, 2016.

17. Author's interview with John Wilhelm.

18. Diane Cardwell, "Racial Politics of 2001; Unhealed Wounds in 2005," *New York Times*, May 8, 2005; Juan Gonzalez, "Mark Must Take the Blame," *New York Daily News*, November 8, 2011; also Atlas, *Seeds of Change*, op. cit., pp. 135–37.

19. Author's interview with Steven Banks, October 6, 2016.

20. Author's interview with Jonathan Rosen, of BerlinRosen, July 6, 2016.

21. Charles Bagli, "In New Sale, Starrett City Would Stay Affordable," *New York Times*, June 2, 2008; also author's interview with Jonathan Rosen.

22. Author's interview with Jonathan Rosen.

4. The High Cost of Michael Bloomberg's New York

1. Brash, *Bloomberg's New York*, op. cit., p. 17.

2. In his seminal study of the information technology revolution, sociologist Manuel Castells argues that "without new information technology global capitalism would have been a much-limited reality. . . . Thus, informationalism is linked to the expansion and rejuvenation of capitalism, as industrialism was linked to its constitution as a mode of production." Manuel Castells, *The Rise of the Network Society*, 2nd edition (Oxford, UK: Blackwell Publishing, 2000), p. 19.

3. Ruth Ford and Adrienne Day, "Beyond CityTime," *City Limits*, November 14, 2011. Accessed at: http://www.theinvestigativefund.org/investigations/politicsandgovernment/1581/beyond_citytime. That report, however, appears to have only contracts from the city's annual expense budget, thus missing hundreds of millions of dollars annually that are spent for professional consultants and other contractors through the separate capital budget.

4. Benjamin Lesser and Greg Smith, "Firms That Got Big Tax Breaks Gave Bundle to Rudy Giuliani's Campaigns," *New York Daily News*, December 23, 2007.

5. For hospitals, see Alan Finder, "Court Deals Blow to Giuliani's Hospital Privatization Plan," *New York Times,* March 31, 1999; for Edison Schools vote, see Abby Goodnough, "Scope of Loss for Privatizing by Edison Stuns Officials," *New York Times*, April 3, 2001; for Maximus, see Tom Robbins, "A Maximus Postscript," *Village Voice*, June 17, 2003.

6. See Julian Brash's excellent description in *Bloomberg's New York*, op. cit., pp. 10–21; also see Richard Florida, *The Rise of the Creative Class: And How It's Transforming Work, Leisure, Community, and Everyday Life* (New York: Basic, Books, 2002).

7. Dan Steinberg, "The Monumental Myths of Michael Bloomberg," *Progressive Planning* no. 198 (Winter 2014).

8. NYU Furman Center, "State of New York City's Housing and Neighborhoods in 2015," pp. 5–6. Accessed at: http://furmancenter.org/research/sonychan.

9. New York City Rent Guidelines Board, "2016 Income and Affordability Study," April 15, 2016, p. 9. Accessed at: http://www.nycrgb.org/downloads/research/pdf_reports/ia16.pdf.

10. Bridget Fisher, "The Myth of Self-Financing: The Trade-offs Behind the Hudson Yards Redevelopment Project," Schwartz Center for Economic Policy Analysis and Department of Economics, New School for Social Research, Working Paper #14, July 2015, p. 12.

11. George Lefcoe and Charles Swenson, "Redevelopment in California: The Demise of TIF-Funded Redevelopment in California and its Aftermath," *National Tax Journal* 67, September 2014; also Fisher, "The Myth of Self-Financing," op. cit., pp. 3–7.

12. "On the Far West Side: City's Hudson Yards Interest Subsidies Reduced in Near Term, yet Future Subsidies Remain," New York City Independent Budget Office, May 2016. Accessed at: http://www.ibo.nyc.ny.us/iboreports/on-the-far-west-side-citys-hudson-yards-interest-subsidies-reduced-in-near-term-yet-future-subsidies-remain-may-2016.pdf.

13. Juan Gonzalez, "Unfinished West Side Commercial Development Cost Taxpayers $650 m," *New York Daily News*, November 19, 2014.

14. When the city offered a twenty-year tax abatement worth $328 million to Related Companies in 2013 for one of Hudson Yards' first office towers and mall, the IBO noted: "Providing a property tax abatement for the mall means the city will need to pump more money than previously expected into Hudson Yards to meet the development's debt service obligations." See "Next Phase of Hudson Yards May Come with Increasing Costs for the City," New York City Independent Budget Office, October 3, 2013. Accessed at: http://ibo.nyc.ny.us/cgi-park/?p=757.

15. James Parrott "New York City Taxes: Trends, Impact, and Priorities for Reform," New York Fiscal Policy Institute, January 13, 2015, p. 5. Accessed at: http://fiscalpolicy.org/wp-content/uploads/2015/01/NYC-Tax-Report-Jan-13-2015.pdf.

16. Fisher, "The Myth of Self-Financing," op. cit., p. 20.

17. Juan Gonzalez, "Stadium Lawyers Suit Up," *New York Daily News*, May 3, 2005.

18. A January 2009 calculation by the city's Independent Budget Office pegged the total of city, state, and federal subsidies for the stadium at $528 million, while a separate report by a state assembly committee in 2008 estimated the cash and tax breaks at $850 million. A separate calculation by Neil deMause, of the *Field of Schemes* website, pegged the subsidies in 2009 at $1.1 billion. The main factor driving deMause's higher calculation was the $234 million value of the city-owned land where the stadium sits. None of those reports, however, took into account massive lost revenues from the parking garage system that was part of the stadium project. The Bronx Parking Development Company, which operates the system, defaulted on its separate $237 million in tax-exempt bonds soon after those garages opened. See more below. See Charles Bagli, "Yankees Deal May Have Violated the Law," *New York Times,* September 16, 2008; also Eliot Brown, "IBO: New Yankee Stadium Costing City, State $528 M," *New York Observer*, January 14, 2009; also http://www.fieldofschemes.com/documents/Yanks-Mets-costs.pdf.

19. New York City Independent Budget Office, "Costs Climb for Replacing Parks Displaced by New Yankee Stadium," Fiscal Brief, January 2009.

Accessed at: http://www.ibo.nyc.ny.us/iboreports/Yankeeparks12709.pdf. See also Charles Bagli, "Yankees' Stadium Plan Stepping up to the Plate," *New York Times*, June 15, 2015.

20. Bettina Damiani, "Insider Baseball: How Current and Former Public Officials Pitched a Community Shutout for the New York Yankees," *Good Jobs New York*, July 2007, p. 4. Accessed at: http://www.goodjobsfirst .org/sites/default/files/docs/pdf/insider_baseball_report.pdf. For change in number of parking spaces, see "Official Statement of New York City Industrial Development Agency, Civic Facility Revenue Bonds" (Bronx Parking Development Company, LLC Project), Series 2007, p. 1. Accessed at: http://emma.msrb.org/MS266667-MS241975-MD472350.pdf. For pollution concerns, see Bettina Damiani, "Loot, Loot, Loot for the Home Team: How the Proposal to Subsidize a New Yankee Stadium Would Leave Residents and Taxpayers Behind," report from Good Jobs New York, p. 16, February 2006. Accessed at: http://www.goodjobsfirst.org/sites/default /files/docs/pdf/lootfinal3.pdf. For Joyce Hoigi, see Juan Gonzalez, "Loot for the Home Team," *New York Daily News*, March 23, 2006.

21. In addition, the MirRam Group, a lobbying firm cofounded by Roberto Ramirez, a former assemblyman and Bronx Democratic Party chair and close friend of Carrion, received $301,900 from the Yankees in the first quarter of 2006 to line up support from Bronx politicians, and the team doled out $83,000 to Stanley Schlein, a longtime behind-the-scenes power broker in Bronx politics, to lobby the city council for the stadium. See Damiani, "Insider Baseball," op. cit., pp. 11–13.

22. Timothy Williams, "Bronx Board Is Shuffled After Rejecting New Stadium," *New York Times*, June 19, 2006.

23. Juan Gonzalez, "Congress Probing Whether City Wildly Inflated Value of Land for New Stadium," *New York Daily News*, July 27, 2008; also Juan Gonzalez, "E-mails Reveal How City Went to Bat for Yankees to Inflate Value of Stadium Land," *New York Daily News*, December 16, 2008.

24. Ibid.

25. Richard Sandomir, "Yankees Slash the Price of Top Tickets," *New York Times*, April 28, 2009.

26. During the 2015 season, ticket and skybox revenues dropped to $276 million—*just $10 million more than the old Yankee Stadium produced in its last season of 2008.* For 2015 revenues, the most recent that is publicly available, see "Yankee Stadium LLC, 2015 Company Annual Financial Information," accessed at: http://emma.msrb.org/ES799763-ES628477-ES1023975.pdf; for 2008 stadium revenues, see "$258,999,944.60 New York City Industrial Development Agency Pilot Revenue Bonds, Series 2009A (Yankee Stadium Project)," p. 62, accessed at: http://emma.msrb.org/MS278144-MS276487 -MD560920.pdf.

27. Juan Gonzalez, "Bronx Kids Still Waiting for New Fields," *New York Daily News*, April 10, 2009.

28. Dan Steinberg, "The Monumental Myths of Michael Bloomberg," *Progressive Planning* no. 198 (Winter 2014): 7.

29. Juan Gonzalez, "Taxpayers Will Fund Yankees VIP Parking, Taxpayers Will Get Less Money," *New York Daily News*, January 1, 2008.

30. A top city official involved in planning the garage project revealed to the author in 2012 that his agency knew the garages would be money losers, but "we were ordered by city hall to make the numbers work."

31. Greg B. Smith, "Taxpayers' Running Tab: Cost for Parkland at Yankee Stadium up 67%," *New York Daily News*, January 28, 2009.

32. Juan Gonzalez, "Pricey Yankee Stadium Parking Garages Hardly Used and Owner Heading for a Default on $237 Million in Bonds," *New York Daily News*, February 3, 2012.

33. See "Notice of Event of Default," accessed at: http://emma.msrb.org/EP750872-EP582979-EP984570.pdf; also "Yankee Stadium LLC, 2015 Company Annual Financial Information," accessed at: http://emma.msrb.org/ES799763-ES628477-ES1023975.pdf.

34. Juan Gonzalez, "Mike Shift on Park: Open to Changes in Deal on Use of Randalls Island," *New York Daily News*, November 3, 2006; also Timothy Williams, "On Randalls Island, New Ball Fields via Deal with Elite Schools," *New York Times*, February 10, 2007; also Juan Gonzalez, "Unfair Play for Pricey Park," *New York Daily News*, May 25, 2007.

35. Juan Gonzalez, "City Hall Tunes Out Judge's Ruling on Randalls Island Pay-to-Play Ballfield," *New York Daily News*, February 12, 2008.

36. For water park, see Juan Gonzalez, "Water Park Boondoggle Builder Misses Deadline," *New York Daily News*, September 21, 2007; for tennis center, see Juan Gonzalez, "Bloomberg Funds Randalls Island Playpen for Rich on City's Dime While Nearby East Harlem Goes Begging," *New York Daily News*, January 4, 2012.

37. Juan Gonzalez, "Mayor Bloomberg's Union Square Park Restaurant Deal Tasteless," *New York Daily News*, April 30, 2008.

38. Juan Gonzalez, "Donald Trump's New Golf Course at Ferry Point Park in Bronx Has Become $230 Million Sand Trap for Taxpayers, but a Big Bonanza for Real Estate Mogul," *New York Daily News*, April 3, 2015.

39. Juan Gonzalez, "High-Tech Computerized Payroll System for City Employees Costs Taxpayers Big," *New York Daily News*, December 3, 2009. See also Juan Gonzalez, "City Council to Probe CityTime; Timekeeping and Payroll System Costing City $700 Million," *New York Daily News*, December 17, 2009.

40. Juan Gonzalez, "Consultants Getting $722 m from City for Doomed CityTime Computer Project," *New York Daily News*, March 25, 2010. See also "Witness Testifies That Top City Official Gave CityTime Consul-

tant Fre Rein," *New York Daily News*, October 18, 2013. See also "Three Leaders of Citytime Fraud Each Sentenced in Manhattan Federal Court to 20 Years in Prison," Department of Justice Press Release, April 28, 2014. Accessed at: https://www.justice.gov/usao-sdny/pr/three-leaders-citytime -fraud-scheme-each-sentenced-manhattan-federal-court-20-years.

41. City of New York Department of Investigation, "Investigation into the City's Program to Overhaul the 911 System Reveals Significant Mismanagement at the Root of Cost Overruns and Delays," February 6, 2015. Accessed at: http://www1.nyc.gov/assets/doi/downloads/pdf /ectp_report_and_press_release_20150206.pdf.

42. Robert Gearty, "Cougar's Ex-husband, Willard 'Ross' Lanham, Who Stole $1.7 Million from the DOE, Sentenced to Three Years in Prison," *New York Daily News*, September 18, 2012. See also Juan Gonzalez, "Ross Lanham Case: New Form of Racketeering Inside City Agencies Is Unleashed," *New York Daily News*, April 29, 2011; also Juan Gonzalez, "Crooked Adviser Costs NYC $123M by Cheating Federal School-Tech Program," *New York Daily News*, March 10, 2016.

43. Juan Gonzalez, "Web of Questions Arises About DOE Contractors Charging Taxpayers for Outsourced Programmers," *New York Daily News*, April 13, 2011. See also Juan Gonzalez, "Alleged Fraud by Future Technology Associates Was Like Taking Millions from a Baby," *New York Daily News*, September 29, 2011.

44. Juan Gonzalez, "NYCHA's New $36M Computer System Is a Cyber-Monster for Tenants and Landlords," *New York Daily News*, November 11, 2011.

45. Juan Gonzalez, "City to Contractor: Pretty Please, Could You Take Back This $549 Million Wireless Network?," *New York Daily News*, February 15, 2012. Also, Juan Gonzalez, "City Wants to Sell Its $500 Million Underused WiFi Network to Improve Service at Lower Cost," *New York Daily News*, March 4, 2015.

5. Urban Neighborhoods in Revolt: The First Wave

1. Peter Dreier, "Radicals in City Hall: An American Tradition," *Dissent*, December 19, 2013. See also Russel B. Nye, *Midwestern Progressive Politics: A Historical Study of Its Origins and Development, 1870–1950* (East Lansing, MI: Michigan State University Press, 1959), pp. 169–242, provides an excellent account the movement's high tide.

2. Author's interview with Nick Licata, July 7, 2016.

3. Bob Young, "Nick Licata, City Council: Political Maverick Emerges as Mover," *Seattle Times*, September 12, 2004.

4. Nick Licata testimony to Committee on Oversight and Government Reform, House of Representatives, March 29, 2007. Accessed at: http://slog.thestranger.com/files/2007/03/Licata.Testimony.Narrative.pdf.

5. Author's interview with Nick Licata.

6. Young, "Nick Licata, City Council," op. cit.

7. Josh Feit, "Key Amendments: Council Member Nick Licata Challenges Sonics Subsidy," *The Stranger*, February 23, 2006.

8. "Is Seattle's Ban on Plastic Bags Working?" KIRO-TV, July 12, 2016. Accessed at: http://www.kiro7.com/news/local/is-seattles-ban-on-plastic-bags-working/398584499.

9. Joel Rogers and Satya Rhodes-Conway, "Cities at Work: Progressive Local Policies to Rebuild the Middle Class," Center for American Progress Action Fund, February 2014, p. 201; also Mark Stiles, "Under Sweeping Change, Seattle Builders Must Pay Affordable Housing Fee," *Puget Sound Business Journal*, November 10, 2015. Accessed at: http://www.bizjournals.com/seattle/morning_call/2015/11/under-sweeping-change-seattle-builders-must-pay.html.

10. Mike Parker, "Communities Fight for Community Control over Corporate Power," *Social Policy* 43, no. 2 (Summer 2013): 5–6; also Steve Early, *Refinery Town: Big Oil, Big Money, and the Remaking of an American City* (Boston: Beacon Press, 2017), pp. 20–27. Early's study provides the most comprehensive account to date of the origin and evolution of the Richmond Progressive Alliance.

11. Author's interview with Gayle McLaughlin, July 8, 2016.

12. Heather Smith, "How a Cop's Blows Turned Richmond's Andres Soto into a Climate Activist," *Grist*, April 25, 2014. Accessed at: http://grist.org/climate-energy/how-a-cops-blows-turned-richmonds-andres-soto-into-a-climate-activist.

13. Juan Reardon, "How Did RPA Get Started," date unknown. Accessed at: http://richmondprogressivealliance.net/docs/RPA_Origins.pdf. See also Parker, "Communities Fight," op. cit., pp. 6–7.

14. Wayne Brash and Tawanda Scott Sambu, "Paying Kids Not to Kill," CNN, May 20, 2016. Accessed at: http://www.cnn.com/2016/05/19/health/cash-for-criminals-richmond-california. Also author's interview with Gayle McLaughlin; also Early, *Refinery Town*, op. cit., pp. 100–2.

15. "Richmond License Tax, Measure T (November 2008)," Ballotpedia. Accessed at: https://ballotpedia.org/Richmond_Business_License_Tax,_Measure_T_(November_2008); author's interview with Gayle McLaughlin.

16. Resolution No. 020522 of the Philadelphia City Council, April 25, 2003. Accessed at: http://legislation.phila.gov/attachments/8243.pdf .

17. Author's interview with Wilson Goode Jr., July 8, 2016.

18. Ibid.

19. Author's interview with Helen Gym, July 8, 2016.

20. Kathryn E. Wilson, "'Same Struggle, Same Fight': Yellow Seeds and the Asian American Movement in Philadelphia's Chinatown," *Pennsylvania Magazine of History and Biography* 140, no. 3 (2016): 423–25.

21. Tommy Rowan, "What if the Phillies Ballpark Had Been Built in Central Philly?," *Philly.com*, April 28, 2016. See also Mike Liu, "Philadelphia Chinatown Fights Stadium Development," *Azine*, December 15, 2000; also "Nutter on 2nd Philly Casino: 'We Need to Move Forward,'" *Philly.com*, November 18, 2014.

22. Jacques Steinberg, "In Largest Schools Takeover, State Will Run Philadelphia's," *New York Times*, December 22, 2001.

23. Author's interview with Helen Gym.

24. Susan Snyder, "Plan Would Bolster Troubled City Schools," *Philadelphia Inquirer*, February 15, 2008.

25. Rachel Gordon, "SF Supervisors Shift to the Left/Mayor's Moderate Allies on Board Lost in Runoff Elections," *San Francisco Chronicle*, December 14, 2000.

26. Author's interview with John Avalos, July 9, 2016.

27. Ibid.; see also "Mayor Lee, Supervisors, and SFMTA Announce $6.8 Million Gift from Google to Fund Free Muni for Low Income Youth," Office of San Francisco Mayor, February 27, 2014. Accessed at: http://sfmayor.org/article/mayor-lee-supervisors-sfmta-announce-68-million-gift-google-fund-free-muni-low-income-youth. See also "San Francisco on Tuesday Became the Second U.S. City to Raise Its Minimum Wage to $15 an Hour," *CNN Money*, November 5, 2014. Accessed at: http://money.cnn.com/2014/11/05/news/san-francisco-increased-minimum-wage.

28. Author's interview with John Avalos.

29. Author's interview with Letitia James, September 6, 2016. For Vann, see Kareem Fahim, "Once a Young Turk, Now Challenged by One," *New York Times*, November 1, 2009.

30. Author's interview with Letitia James.

31. Juan Gonzalez, "Build Admits Ratner Funding," *New York Daily News*, October 18, 2005.

32. Author's interview with Letitia James.

6. The Wall Street Crash and the 99 Percent

1. Juan Gonzalez, "We Wuz Robbed!," *New York Daily News*, March 21, 2007.

2. Nick Mathiason, "Three Weeks That Changed the World," *The Guardian*, December 27, 2008.

3. Juan Gonzalez, "We Wuz Robbed!," op. cit.

4. For New York City, see: Juan Gonzalez, "Set Up for a Fall," *New York Daily News*, March 28, 2007. For racial, ethnic disparities nationwide, see Debbie Gruenstein Bocian, Wei Li, and Keith S. Ernst, "Foreclosures by Race and Ethnicity: The Demographics of a Crisis," Center for Responsible Learning Research Report, June 18, 2010, p. 10. Accessed at: http://www.responsiblelending.org/mortgage-lending/research-analysis/foreclosures-by-race-and-ethnicity.pdf.

5. Michael Barbaro and Tim Arango, "Bloomberg Said to Test a Term-Limit Reversal," *New York Times*, August 22, 2008.

6. Michael Barbaro and David W. Chen, "Bloomberg Expected to Seek Third Term as Mayor," *New York Times,* September 30, 2008.

7. Jonathan Hicks, "Councilman Balks at Procedure to Change Term Limits," *New York Times*, October 6, 2008; "For Mayor of New York City," *New York Times*, October 23, 2009; Editorial, "Make It Mike—Again: Voters Should Cast Their Mayoral Ballot for Bloomberg," *New York Daily News*, October 25, 2009; Editorial, "Bloomberg for Mayor," *New York Post*, October 23, 2009; Sewell Chan and Jonathan Hicks, "Council Votes, 29 to 22, to Extend Term Limits," *New York Times*, October 23, 2008.

8. "In Campaign Ad Race, Bloomberg and Corzine Dominate Opponents," *Nielsen Wire*, October 8, 2009. Accessed at: http://www.nielsen.com/us/en/insights/news/2009/in-campaign-ad-race-bloomberg-and-corzine-dominate-opponents.html. See also "Mayor Bloomberg Spends Close to $1M a Day in Re-election Push: At This Pace $95M by Election Day," *New York Daily News*, October 23, 2009.

9. "New Yorkers Make Their Voices Heard: A Report on the 2009 Elections," New York City Campaign Finance Board, September 1, 2010, p. 8; also Gred David, "Mayoral Poll Fault," *Crain's*, August 23, 2013.

10. David Chen and Michael Barbaro, "Bloomberg Wins 3rd Term as Mayor in Unexpectedly Close Race," *New York Times*, November 3, 2009.

11. Juan Gonzalez, "Once Enemies, Now They March Together: Organized Labor Expected to Join Wall Street Protest," *New York Daily News*, October 5, 2011.

12. Juan Gonzalez, "Mayor Bloomberg, Gov. Cuomo Deaf to Suffering Masses as Occupy Wall Street Movement Grows," *New York Daily News*, November 4, 2011.

13. Ibid.

14. Rich Lamb, "Occupy Wall Street Protesters Target JPMorgan Chase CEO Jamie Dimon—Who Is Overseas," CBS New York, October 12, 2011. Accessed at: http://newyork.cbslocal.com/2011/10/12/occupy-wall-street-protesters-plan-to-demonstrate-outside-jpmorganchase-hq.

15. Juan Gonzalez, "One-Day Strike by Fast-Food Workers at McDonald's, Burger King, and Other Restaurants Is Just the Beginning," *New York Daily News*, November 29, 2012.

16. Author's interview with Steve Kest, June 15, 2016. See also David Rolf, *The Fight for $15: The Right Wage for a Working America* (New York: The New Press, 2016), pp. 90–96.

17. Juan Gonzalez, "Immigrant Business Owners Get Little Help from the City," *New York Daily News*, February 16, 2012.

18. Juan Gonzalez, "Secret Consumer Affairs Quota System for Violations Slaps Business Owners with Sky-High Fines: 'It's Shameful,'" *New York Daily News*, June 17, 2013. See also Juan Gonzalez, "Sign, Sign, Everywhere a Sign—but the Wrong One Earns NYC Stores $8K Fines," *New York Daily News*, June 18, 2013.

7. Insurgents Capture City Hall

1. David W. Chen, "De Blasio, Announcing Mayoral Bid, Pledges to Help People City Hall Forgot," *New York Times*, January 27, 2013. See also Helen Klein, "Public Advocate De Blasio Officially Enters the Race for Mayor," *Brooklyn Reporter*, January 28, 2013.

2. Juan Gonzalez, "Is Christine in Like Quinn? Not Quite Yet, Despite Poll Predictions," *New York Daily News*, November 8, 2012; Tina Moore, "Bloomberg Still Warm to Quinn for Mayor but Is Keeping His Choice to Himself," *New York Daily News*, March 27, 2013.

3. Author's interview with Ken Sunshine, June 16, 2016.

4. David W. Chen, Larry Buchanan, and Ford Fessenden, "Bill de Blasio's Circle of Power," *New York Times*, November 8, 2013. See also author's interview with Jonathan Rosen, July 6, 2016.

5. Author's interview with Phil Walzak, September 29, 2016.

6. Sam Roberts, "Mayor Making It No Secret: He'll Endorse Quinn in 2013," *New York Times*, August 28, 2011. See also Eric Alterman, *Inequality and One City: Bill de Blasio and the New York Experiment, Year One*, The Nation Co. LP (Kindle Locations 377–79).

7. Juan Gonzalez, "It's Time for City Council Speaker Christine Quinn to Stop Stalling a Vote on Mandatory Sick Pay for Workers," *New York Daily News*, March 19, 2013.

8. Margaret Hartmann, "Quinn Folds, Makes Deal to Give New Yorkers Paid Sick Leave," *New York Magazine*, March 29, 2013.

9. Author's interview with Bill Lipton, May 26, 2016.

10. Greg Smith, "FBI Investigating Claim Christine Quinn Was Threatened for Refusing to Support Carriage Horse Ban During the Mayoral Race," *New York Daily News*, April 25, 2014.

11. UNITE HERE, the national hotel and garment workers union, for instance, donated $175,000 to NYCLASS in June 2013, shortly after John Wilhelm retired as president, and a few days later NYCLASS donated the same amount to New York City Is Not for Sale. See Greg Smith, "FBI Investigating Donations to NYCLASS from Men Close to Mayor de Blasio That May Have Been Used Toward Anti-Christine Quinn Campaigners," *New York Daily News*, May 4, 2014. Levenson's Advance Group was subsequently fined $15,000 in October 2015 by the city's Campaign Finance Board for illegally helping NYCLASS avoid campaign finance limits while backing candidates for the city council. See Greg Smith, "Advance Group Fined for Helping Anti-Horse Carriage Group NYCLASS Avoid Contribution Limits for City Council," *New York Daily News*, October 8, 2015. Lobbyist Levenson has in the past also been a spokesman for ACORN when the group was accused of voter registration fraud, and one of Levenson's partners at the Advance Group is Michael Gaspard, brother of de Blasio's close friend and adviser Ambassador Patrick Gaspard.

12. Celeste Katz and Jonathan Lemire, "Anthony Weiner Makes It Official: He's Running for Mayor," *New York Daily News*, May 22, 2013. See also David W. Chen, "City's Largest Union Says It Will Endorse de Blasio," *New York Times*, May 23, 2016.

13. "Stop and Frisk Facts," New York Civil Liberties Union. Accessed at: https://www.nyclu.org/en/stop-and-frisk-facts.

14. Editorial, "Injustices of Stop and Frisk," *New York Times*, May 13, 2012.

15. Josh Margolin, "Christine's Ray of Hope," *New York Post*, January 2, 2013.

16. Author's interview with Jonathan Rosen, July 6, 2016.

17. That May, Liu's campaign treasurer and one of his main fund-raisers were convicted of attempted fraud and other federal charges for accepting illegal campaign contributions in a straw donor scheme.

18. Michael Barbaro, "Thompson Sees No Need to Ban a Police Tactic," *New York Times*, May 29, 2013. See also Alisa Chang, "Council Speaker Quinn Demands Greater Oversight of NYPD's Stop-and-Frisks," WNYC, February 8, 2012; also Dennis Slattery and Jonathan Lemire, "Anthony Weiner Says Stop-and-Frisk Should Be Reformed at Al Sharpton Event," *New York Daily News*, June 8, 2013.

19. For the Community Safety Act, see J. David Goodman, "City Council Votes to Increase Oversight of New York Police," *New York Times*, June 27, 2013. For the Bloomberg campaign against Judge Scheindlin, see Ginger Adams Otis and Greg Smith, "Federal Judge to Rule on Stop-and-Frisk Case Biased Against Cops: Report," *New York Daily News*, May 22, 2013.

20. David Freedlander, "Dante de Blasio's Killer Ad May Have Won the NYC Primary for His Dad," *Daily Beast,* September 14, 2013.

21. *Floyd vs. City of New York,* 08 Civ 1034 (SAS), pp. 12–13. Accessed at: http://ccrjustice.org/sites/default/files/assets/Floyd-Liability-Opinion -8-12-13.pdf.

22. "NYC 2013: The Mayoral Primaries," *New York Times,* September 16, 2013. Accessed at: http://www.nytimes.com/projects/elections/2013/nyc -primary/mayor/map.html; Also *Times* tally of general election, November 6, 2013. Accessed at: http://www.nytimes.com/projects/elections /2013/general/nyc-mayor/map.html.

23. Michael M. Grynbaum and Kate Taylor, "Mayoral Ally Elected Speaker, Furthering City's Liberal Shift," *New York Times,* January 8, 2014.

8. New Day in Gotham

1. Author's interview with New York City Office of Management and Budget Director Dean Fuleihan, October 6, 2016.

2. Author's interview with New York City Commissioner of Health and Human Services Steve Banks, October 6, 2016.

3. Melanie Grayce West and Michael Howard Saul, "De Blasios Are Largely No-Shows at New York City's High-Profile Society Affairs," *Wall Street Journal,* May 4, 2015.

4. Lis Miller, "Chirlane McCray's City," *New York Magazine,* May 8, 2014.

5. Author's interview with First Deputy Mayor Anthony Shorris, September 23, 2016.

6. See Nat Hentoff and Nick Hentoff, "Rudy's Racist Rants: An NYPD History Lesson," Cato Institute, July 14, 2016. Accessed at: https://www .cato.org/publications/commentary/rudys-racist-rants-nypd-history -lesson. See also Catherine S. Manegold, "Rally Puts Police Under New Scrutiny," *New York Times,* September 27, 1992.

7. Report of the Commission to Investigate Allegations of Police Corruption and the Anti-Corruption Procedures of the Police Department, July 7, 1994, Appendix 8. Accessed at: https://www.scribd.com/document /248581606/1994-07-07-Mollen-Commission-NYPD-Report.

8. Ibid., p. 1

9. Ibid., p. 53.

10. Eli Rosenberg, "How NYC's Decade of Rezoning Changed the City of Industry," *Curbed New York,* January 16, 2014. See also Kareem Fahim, "Despite Much Rezoning, Scant Change in Residential Capacity," *New York Times,* March 21, 2010.

11. Author's interview with Dean Fuleihan.

12. Author's interview with Steven Banks.

13. Author's interview with Deputy Mayor for Strategic Policy Richard Buery, September 21, 2016.

14. Author's interview with Jonathan Rosen.

15. Ibid.

16. Marc Tracy, "De Blasio Should Just Admit It: He Wants to Tax the Rich," *New Republic*, January 27, 2014.

17. As the *New York Times* noted in 2008, "More than 10 years after New York's political and education leaders promised to work toward providing access to pre-kindergarten classes to every 4-year-old across the state, more than a third of the 677 local school districts have no such programs." See Winnie Hu, "A Promise of Pre-K for All Is Still Far off in New York," *New York Times*, August 22, 2008.

18. Kenneth Lovett, "Cuomo Skeptical of de Blasio's Pre-K for New York City but Still Vows Support," *New York Daily News*, January 23, 2014.

19. Author's interview with Josh Wallack, September 21, 2016.

20. Ibid.

21. Author's interview with Richard Buery.

22. Editorial, "Universal Pre-K Takes Off," *New York Times*, September 1, 2014.

23. Author's interview with Emma Wolfe, director of intergovernmental affairs, September 29, 2016.

24. Benjamin Weiser and Joseph Goldstein, "Mayor Says New York City Will Settle Lawsuits on Stop-and-Frisk Tactics," *New York Times*, January 30, 2014.

25. Benjamin Weiser, "Settlement Is Approved in Central Park Jogger Case, but New York Deflects Blame," *New York Times*, September 5, 2014.

26. Author's interviews and correspondence with city officials.

27. Author's interviews and correspondence with city labor relations and budget officials and with the heads of key municipal unions.

28. Ruth Milkman and Stephanie Luce, "The State of the Unions 2015: A Profile of Organized Labor in New York City, New York State, and the United States," Joseph S. Murphy Institute for Worker Education and Labor Studies, September 2015. Accessed at: https://www.gc.cuny.edu/CUNY_GC/media/CUNY-Graduate-Center/PDF/Communications/1509_Union_Density2015_RGB.pdf.

29. Citizens Budget Commission, "7 Things New Yorkers Should Know About Municipal Labor Contracts in New York City," May

2013. Accessed at: http://www.cbcny.org/sites/default/files/REPORT
_7ThingsUnions_05202013.pdf.

30. Author's interview with Dean Fuleihan. For average salary of District Council 37 members, see Diane Williams, "Contract Covers 100,000, Pact Raises Pay, Adds Funds for Units," *Public Employee Press*, 2014. Accessed at: http://www.dc37.net/news/PEP/7_2014/contract.html.

31. Author's interview with New York City Director of Labor Relations Bob Linn, September 29, 2016.

32. Author's interview with Dean Fuleihan.

33. Juan Gonzalez, "A Little Respect Was All That Was Needed for De Blasio, Teachers' Union to Make Agreement," *New York Daily News*, May 1, 2014. See also Juan Gonzalez, Corinne Letsch, and Jennifer Fermino, "Leadership of Municipal Labor Committee Approves Proposal to Save $3.4 Billion in Health Savings in City Labor Contracts," *New York Daily News*, May 8, 2014.

34. Under the plan, if $3.4 billion in savings is not achieved during the first four years, an independent arbitrator will order new reforms, including the requirement that city workers pay premiums for part of their health insurance; but if the plan achieves more than the targeted goal, the first $365 million in additional savings would be turned into a bonus rebate for city employees. See testimony of Commissioner of the Office of Labor Relations Bob Linn to city council, April 2, 2015. Accessed at: https://www1.nyc.gov/assets/olr/downloads/pdf/collectivebargaining/testimony-city-council-with-exhibits.pdf.

35. Maria Doulis, director of the Citizens Budget Commission, in *New York Daily News*, May 1, 2014.

36. Author's interview with Dean Fuleihan.

37. See "Giving Credit Where Credit Is Due? New York's $1.3 Billion in Health Insurance Savings," Citizens Budget Commission, December 29, 2014. Accessed at: http://www.cbcny.org/cbc-blogs/blogs/giving-credit-where-it's-due-new-york-city's-13-billion-health-insurance-savings.

38. New York City Rent Guidelines Board, "2016 Income and Affordability Study," April 15, 2016, p. 9. Accessed at: http://www.nycrgb.org/downloads/research/pdf_reports/ia16.pdf.

39. See Mireya Navarro, "Evictions Are Down by 18%; New York Cites Increased Legal Services," *New York Times*, February 29, 2016. See also "Mayor de Blasio Signs Three New Laws Protecting Tenants from Harassment," New York City press release, September 3, 2015. Accessed at: http://www1.nyc.gov/office-of-the-mayor/news/590-15/mayor-de-blasio-signs-three-new-laws-protecting-tenants-harassment. Also, "Linc Program Paying Landlords Big Bucks," by Citywide Housing Services. Accessed at: http://www.citywidehousingservices.com/advice/living-in-communities

-linc-housing-program-paying-landlords-big-bucks; and Jennifer Fermino and Greg Smith, "Mayor de Blasio, City Council Commit $210 Million to Improve Conditions in NYCHA Developments," *New York Daily News*, July 8, 2014.

40. "The Growing Gap: New York City's Housing Affordability Challenge," report by New York City comptroller Scott Stringer, April 2014, p. 1. Accessed at: http://comptroller.nyc.gov/wp-content/uploads /documents/Growing_Gap.pdf.

41. See Juan Gonzalez, "Growing Citywide Revolt Against de Blasio's Affordable Housing Plan," *New York Daily News*, November 24, 2015. See also Sally Goldenberg and Gloria Pazmino, "Council's Support for Mayor's Housing Plan Tested as Key Members Balk," *Politico*, August 12, 2016.

42. Juan Gonzalez, "Mayor de Blasio Puts Troubled 911 Upgrade on Hold for Probe of Budget, Schedule Delays," *New York Daily News*, May 19, 2014.

43. Juan Gonzalez, "Mayor de Blasio Ditches NASA Contract for Overhaul of 911 System After Costs Skyrocket," *New York Daily News*, September 5, 2014. See also Juan Gonzalez, "City Takes Control of Flawed 911 System Overhaul from Private Consultants," *New York Daily News*, December 3, 2014.

44. Juan Gonzalez, "City Officials to 'In-source' IT Consultants, Expect to Save $3.6 Million a Year Through This Plan," *New York Daily News*, June 5, 2015.

45. Author's interview with Anthony Shorris, September 23, 2016.

46. "Mayor de Blasio Doubles Community Parks Initiative to $285 Million," City Hall press release, October 6, 2015. Accessed at: http://www1 .nyc.gov/office-of-the-mayor/news/692-15/mayor-de-blasio-doubles -community-parks-initiative-285-million. See also "New York City Announces $150 Million in Funding for 5 City Parks," CBS Radio, August 18, 2016. Accessed at: http://newyork.cbslocal.com/2016/08/18 /city-park-funding.

47. Jen Kirby, "New York City Will Stop Saving Personal Data for Municipal ID Holders," *New York Magazine*, December 8, 2016.

48. Matt Flegenheimer, "De Blasio's Order Will Expand Living Wage Law to Thousands More," *New York Times*, September 29, 2014. See also Sally Goldenberg, "City Hall-D.C. 37 Re-negotiate Raises for Lowest-Paid Workers," *Politico*, May 15, 2015.

49. See "FY 17 Water Rate Proposal to the New York City Water Board," by the New York City Department of Environmental Protection, April 8, 2016, p. 40. Accessed at: http://www.nyc.gov/html/nycwaterboard/pdf /public_notices/fy17_dep_water_rate_proposal_web.pdf; also Erin Durkin, "New York City Homeowners Will Get $183 Giveback on Water Bills," *New York Daily News*, April 25, 2016; also, Marcia Kramer, "After 2

Failures in Court, De Blasio Tries Again to Give Homeowners Water Bill Credit," CBS NewYork, February 17, 2017.

50. Interviews and correspondence between author and city officials.

51. Rebecca Traister, "New York Just Created a Revolutionary New Family Leave Policy," *New York Magazine*, April 1, 2016.

52. Matthew Flamm and Erik Engquist, "De Blasio Administration Goes After Verizon for Failing to Deliver FiOS," *Crain's*, July 13, 2015. See also Associated Press, "City Will Provide Free Broadband to More Than 16,000 Public Housing Residents," July 16, 2015. See also Maya Wiley, "Broadband City: How New York Is Bridging Its Digital Divide," *The Nation*, January 8, 2016; and "New York's Wi-Fi Kiosks Disabled After Complaints of People Watching Porn," *The Guardian*, September 14, 2016.

53. Mara Gay, "Joe Lhota Ad: 'Bill de Blasio's Recklessly Dangerous Agenda on Crime Will Take Us Back,'" *New York Daily News*, October 16, 2013.

54. See "Major Crime in New York City, 2009–2015," *Newsday*. Accessed at: http://data.newsday.com/long-island/data/crime/new-york-city-crime-rate. See also New York City Police Department, Compstat Report, accessed at: http://www.nyc.gov/html/nypd/downloads/pdf/crime_statistics/cs-en-us-city.pdf.

55. See John Nichols, "Bill de Blasio Is Not the First New York City Mayor to Clash with Police Unions," *The Nation*, December 28, 2014.

56. Michael M. Grynbaum and Nikita Stewart, "De Blasio Reacts as Mayor and a Father," *New York Times*, December 3, 2014.

57. "NYC Police Union Wants de Blasio Banned from Funerals," *Fox News*, December 14, 2014. Accessed at: http://www.foxnews.com/us/2014/12/14/nyc-police-officers-want-deblasio-banned-from-funerals.html.

58. Author's interview with Phil Walzak.

59. Ibid.

60. Rocco Parascandola, Jennifer Fermino, and Bill Hutchinson, "NYPD Cops Furious with Bill de Blasio Turn Their Backs on the Mayor as He Enters Hospital Where Officers Died," *New York Daily News*, December 21, 2014.

61. Editorial, "Pat Lynch, Who's the Enemy in Your NYPD Union Wars?" *New York Daily News*, December 19, 2014.

9. The Movement Spreads

1. Ryan Deto, "Can Cities like Pittsburgh Continue Their Progressive Ways in Republican-Controlled Waters?," *Pittsburgh City Paper*, November 23, 2016.

2. "Pittsburgh's Population Halved Since 1950," *Pittsburgh Business Times*, June 28, 2007.

3. Harold Meyerson, "The Revolt of the Cities," *American Prospect*, April 22, 2014.

4. Moriah Balingit, "Pittsburgh Council Passes Land Bank Idea," *Pittsburgh Post-Gazette*, April 14, 2014; also Natasha Khan "Is Pittsburgh's Land Bank Operational? City Says Yes. Residents Disagree," PublicSource, September 7, 2016. Accessed at: http://publicsource.org/is-pittsburghs-land -bank-operational-city-says-yes-residents-disagree.

5. Gabriel Thompson, "Minneapolis Has Long Been Fractured by Racial Inequality. Can a New Mayor Change That?" *The Nation*, September 3, 2014. Accessed at: https://www.thenation.com/article/one-minneapolis -possible. See Mark Zdechlik, "TakeAction Minnesota Draws Attention for Political Victories," Minnesota Public Radio, November 25, 2013. Accessed at: https://www.mprnews.org/story/2013/11/25/politics /takeaction-minnesota.

6. "An Open Letter from Mayor Betsy Hodges to the Communities of Minneapolis," October 8, 2014. Accessed at: https://mayorhodges .com/2014/10/08/an-open-letter-from-mayor-betsy-hodges-to-the -communities-of-minneapolis.

7. Author's interview with Lisa Bender, July 9, 2016.

8. "Minneapolis Approves 'Landmark' Paid Sick Leave Law," *Minneapolis Post*, May 27, 2016. See also Erin Golden, "Turbulent Year Challenges Mayor Hodges' Path Toward 'One Minneapolis,'" *Minneapolis Star-Tribune*, January 2, 2016.

9. "City and Metropolitan Inequality on the Rise, Driven by Declining Incomes," Brookings Institution. Accessed at: https://www.brookings .edu/research/city-and-metropolitan-inequality-on-the-rise-driven-by -declining-incomes.

10. "Boston's New Labor Mayor: Could His Win Be a Progressive Blueprint for America?" *Alternet*. Accessed at: http://www.alternet.org/labor /bostons-new-labor-mayor-could-his-win-be-progressive-blueprint -america. See also Brian Wright O'Connor, "The Personal Story of Mayor Martin J. Walsh," *Boston Common Magazine*, June 23, 2014.

11. Eric Levenson, "Here's Where Mayor Walsh's State of the City Promises Stand Today," *Boston Globe*, January 19, 2016.

12. Author's interview with Nick Licata.

13. Chris Kardish, "Ed Murray: One of America's Most Progressive Mayors," *Governing the States and Localities*, August 2015. Accessed at: http:// www.governing.com/topics/politics/gov-seattle-ed-murray.html.

14. Gregory Wallace, "Seattle Approves $15 Minimum Wage," *CNN Money*, June 3, 2014. Accessed at: http://money.cnn.com/2014/06/02 /news/economy/seattle-minimum-wage.

15. Author's interview with Kshama Sawant on *Democracy Now!*, June 5, 2014.

16. KPLU News Staff, "Seattle Mayor Murray Declares Victory for Proposition 1B's Pre-K Pilot Program," November 4, 2014. Accessed at: http://knkx.org/post/seattle-mayor-murray-declares-victory-proposition-1bs -pre-k-pilot-program; also http://www.governing.com/topics/politics /gov-seattle-ed-murray.html.

17. Author's interview with Nick Licata.

18. Newfield and Barrett, *City for Sale*, op. cit., p. 151.

19. Author's interview with Ras Baraka on *Democracy Now!*, November 23, 2015.

20. Naomi Nix, "Baraka Asks for Newark Superintendent's Resignation Again," NJ.com, January 15, 2015.

21. "Spending by Outside Groups on Newark Mayor's Race Topped $5 Million," NJ.com, July 28, 2014.

22. John Celock, "Hedge Fund Attack Part of New Newark Ad," *Celock Report*, May 5, 2014. Accessed at: http://johncelock.com/hedge-fund -attack-part-new-newark-ad.

23. David Giambusso, "Ras Baraka Reflects on the Loss of His Father and His Ongoing Legacy," NJ.com, January 13, 2014. Accessed at: http://www.nj.com/essex/index.ssf/2014/01/ras_baraka_reflects _on_the_loss_of_his_father_and_his_ongoing_legacy.html.

24. "Police Anger Unsettles Already Edgy City," *New York Times*, June 19, 1997.

25. Newark's Central High School Sees Success with High Graduation Rate Despite Challenges," NJ.com, June 28, 2011. Accessed at: http:// www.nj.com/news/index.ssf/2011/06/newarks_central_high_school_se .html.

26. "After 21 Years, Local Control Poised to Return to Newark Schools Next Fall," NJ.com, August 22, 2016. Accessed at: http://www.nj.com/essex /index.ssf/2016/08/newark_likely_to_regain_local_control_of_district .html. See also "Cami Anderson Was Right," Bob Braun's Ledger, October 19, 2015. Accessed at: http://www.bobbraunsledger.com/cami -anderson-was-right.

27. "Newark's New Cop Watch Board Should Be a National Model for Police Accountability," ACLU, May 8, 2015. Accessed at: https://www .aclu.org/blog/speak-freely/newarks-new-cop-watch-board-should-be -national-model-police-accountability.

28. "Defying Expectations, Mayor Ras Baraka Is Praised in All Corners of Newark," *New York Times*, August 31, 2015.

29. Author's interview with Larry Hamm. July 23, 2016.

30. Kate Zernicke, "Defying Expectations," op. cit.

31. Author's interview with Austin City Councilman Gregorio Casar, July 10, 2016.

32. "What's Left? For Nearly Four Decades, White Liberals Have Dominated Austin Politics. Now the City May Finally Embrace True Progressivism," *Texas Observer*, December 2, 2013.

33. Author's interview with Gregorio Casar.

34. Author's interview with Tempe Councilmember Lauren Kuby, July 8, 2016.

35. Mary Joe Pitzi, "Court: Arizona's new minimum wage takes effect Sunday," *Arizona Republic*, December 29. 2016; also, Mary Jo Pitzi, "Arizona Supreme Court Rejects Minimum-Wage Challenge," *Arizona Republic*, March 14, 2017.

36. Bay Area News Group, "Richmond Rent Ordinance Formally Repealed," *East Bay Times*, November 4, 2015. Accessed at: http://www.eastbaytimes.com/2015/11/04/richmond-rent-control-ordinance-formally-repealed; also Gilliane Edevane, "After Long Battle, Rent Control Comes to Richmond," NBC Bay Areas, November 9, 2016. Accessed at: http://www.nbcbayarea.com/news/local/After-hard-fought-battle-Rent-Control-Comes-To-Richmond-400503751.html.

37. Author's interview with Helen Gym, July 8, 2016.

38. "Robin Kniech Pushes for Compromise," *Denver Business Journal*, September 23, 2016. Accessed at http://www.bizjournals.com/denver/news/2016/09/23/robin-kniech-pushes-for-compromise.html.

39. Author's interview with Cook County Commissioner Jesús "Chuy" García, June 18, 2016.

40. "Ex-Ald. Ed Vrdolyak Indicted on Tax Charge in Tobacco Settlement," *Chicago Tribune*, November 15, 2016.

41. Ben Joravsky and Mick Dumke, "Fail: Part Two: One Billion Dollars," *Chicago Reader*, May 21, 2009. See also author's interview with Chicago alderman Scott Waguespack, July 8, 2016.

42. Author's interview with Chicago alderman John Arena, July 8, 2016.

43. BobboSphere, "The Chicago Election: The Electoral Revolution That Didn't Happen," *Daily Kos*, April 20, 2015.

44. Michael Pearson, "Wins, Losses and Draws in Chicago School Strike," CNN.com, September 19, 2012. Accessed at: http://www.cnn.com/2012/09/19/us/illinois-chicago-teachers-strike.

45. Author's interview with Jitu Brown of Chicago's Journey for Justice Alliance, on *Democracy Now!*, September 4, 2015.

46. "Chicago to Shutter 50 Public Schools: Is Historic Mass Closure an

Experiment in Privatization?," *Democracy Now!*, May 28, 2013. Accessed at: https://www.democracynow.org/2013/5/28/chicago_to_shutter_50 _public_schools.

10. Fierce Resistance and Major Missteps

1. According to one ad tracking study, the largest anti–de Blasio spender was Uber ($7.6 million), followed by the pro–charter schools group Families for Excellent Schools ($6.6 million); a pro-charter and pro–school voucher group, New Yorkers for a Balanced Albany ($2.6 million); the main landlord lobby group, the Rent Stabilization Association ($2.4 million); and the Patrolmen's Benevolent Association ($620,000). Meanwhile, de Blasio spent $13.5 million on his 2013 campaign. See http://www.nyccfb.info/PDF/per/2013_PER/2013_PER.pdf.

2. Brendan Cheney, "'Stop de Blasio' Line Gets Little Traction on Upper East Side," *Politico*, November 9, 2016.

3. The 101,606 major crimes recorded in 2016 was a drop of more than 4 percent from the previous year. The number of murders, 335, was the second lowest in the city's history, surpassed only by the 333 achieved during de Blasio's first year as mayor, and representing only a fraction of the 2,262 murders recorded back in the high-crime year of 1990, while incidents of shootings dropped below 1,000 for the first time since such statistics were tracked. See Benjamin Mueller and Al Baker, "Drop in Gang Violence Drove New York City Shootings Below 1,000 in 2016," *New York Times*, January 3, 2017; also Graham Rayman, Rocco Parascandola, and Larry McShane "Here's How the NYPD Brought City Crime Rate to a Record Low in 2016," *New York Daily News*, January 5, 2017.

4. For tourism, see http://www.nycandcompany.org/research/nyc -statistics-page; for real estate taxes, see https://www.rebny.com/content /rebny/en/newsroom/press-releases/2017_Press_Releases /NYC_Real_Estate_Industry_Tax_Revenue_Increased_2016.html.

5. For jobs figures, see Patrick McGeehan, "In New York City, Jobs Comes Back Without Wall Street," *New York Times*, February 15, 2015; also Greg David, "A Year of Change in Store for NYC Businesses," *Crain's*, December 11, 2016. For projected reduction in poverty, see "CEO Poverty Measure 2005–2014," *Annual Report from the Office of the Mayor*, April 2016, p. 15.

6. Josh Dawsey and Mara Gay, "Tardiness Reputation Dogs Mayor Bill de Blasio," *Wall Street Journal*, November 11, 2015.

7. Eric Alterman, *Inequality and One City: Bill de Blasio and the New York Experiment, Year One*, The Nation Co. LP (Kindle Locations 558–66).

8. See Ginger Adams Otis, "Central Park Horse Carriage Company Seeks to Rein in Animal Rights Activists' 'Taunts and Insults' via Legal

Action," *New York Daily News*, December 9, 2016; also Amber Jamieson, "Sleepy de Blasio Doesn't Work Most Early Mornings," *New York Post*, March 29, 2015.

9. Cara Buckley, "As Landlord of Brooklyn Duplex, de Blasio Gets High Approval Rating," *New York Times*, October 28, 2013.

10. John Nichols and Robert McChesney, *Dollarocracy: How the Money and Media Election Complex Is Destroying America* (New York: Nation Books, 2013), pp. 100–11.

11. Graham Rayman, "Patrolmen's Benevolent Association Launches Second TV Ad Pressuring de Blasio to Back Higher NYPD Salaries," *New York Daily News*, May 31, 2016.

12. Ben Chapman, "Groups Spend More Than $13 Million to Push Education Reforms," *New York Daily News*, June 10, 2015. See also Families for Excellent Schools, IRS Form 990, "Return of Organization Exempt from Income Tax, 2014," p. 8. Accessed at: http://www.guidestar.org /FinDocuments/2015/452/870/2015-452870970-0c566ad5-9.pdf.

13. See Diane Ravitch, "The Charter School Mistake," *Los Angeles Times*, October 2, 2013.

14. Some examples include: "Students at PS 123 in Harlem Are Pushed Aside for Charter School Expansion," *New York Daily News*, June 3, 2009; "Harlem Success Academy Expands Further into P.S. 123 in Harlem," July 2, 2009; "Eva Moskowitz Has Special Access to Schools Chancellor Klein—and Support Others Can Only Dream Of," February 24, 2010; "Irate Parents, Teachers Say Brooklyn Public Schools Received Meager Improvements as Charter School in Same Building Enjoyed Big Makeover," April 18, 2013; "Success Academy School Chain Comes Under Fire as Parents Fight 'Zero Tolerance' Disciplinary Policy," August 28, 2013; "Success Academy Parent's Secret Tapes Reveal Attempt to Push out Special Needs Student," August 30, 2013; "Success Charter Network Schools Formally Accused of Violating Rights of Disabled Students," January 20, 2016. Beth Fertig, "SUNY Probes Discipline Policies at Success Schools," WNYC, January 20, 2016; Jillian Jorgensen, "Eva Moskowitz Defends Success Academy Charter Chain from Critics," *New York Observer*, January 22, 2016.

15. Moskowitz's group received $5 million in 2013 from the Eli Broad Foundation, several million dollars over the years from the conservative Walton Family Foundation, and $35 million from wealthy hedge fund executives at its tenth-anniversary celebration in 2016, including a single donation of $25 million from hedge fund pioneer Julian Robertson. See "Broad Foundation Awards $5 Million to Success Academy Charter Schools to Expand in New York Following CMO's Top Performance on State Exams," August 26, 2013. Accessed at: http://broadfoundation.org /broad-foundation-awards-5-million-to-success-academy-charter

-schools. See also Carl Campanile, "Charter School Network Lands $25M Donation from Hedge Fund," *New York Post*, April 12, 2016; also Juan Gonzalez, "Local Charter Schools like Harlem Success Is Big Business as Millions Are Poured into Marketing," *New York Daily News*, October 1, 2010.

16. Elizabeth Harris, "New York City Will Provide Free Space for a Dozen Charter Schools," *New York Times*, December 23, 2014.

17. Simon Van Zuylen-Wood, "The Uber Lobbyist Who Wants to Take Down Bill de Blasio," *New York Magazine*, August 21, 2016.

18. For Tusk's initial role, see Nelson Schwartz and Ron Nixon, "Privatizing the Prize," *New York Times*, October 14, 2007. For Northstar's performance, see "Lottery's Scratch-off Payouts Got Little State Oversight," *Chicago Tribune*, December 30, 2016; and "Rauner Fires Illinois Lottery Private Manager Northstar Lottery Group," *Chicago Tribune*, January 16, 2017.

19. "Bill de Blasio's Speech to the Labour Conference: Full Text," *New Statesman*, September 24, 2014. Accessed at: http://www.newstatesman.com/politics/2014/09/bill-de-blasios-speech-labour-conference-full-text.

20. Laura Nahmias, "De Blasio Group Cancels Planned Iowa Presidential Forum," *Politico*, November 10, 2015. Accessed at: http://www.politico.com/states/new-york/city-hall/story/2015/11/de-blasio-group-cancels-planned-iowa-presidential-forum-027787.

21. "MIA Mayor de Blasio Has Blown 33 Weekdays on Personal Travel," *New York Post*, November 2, 2015.

22. "New York's Mayor, but Bermuda Shares Custody," *New York Times*, April 26, 2010.

23. Michael Barbaro, "Blizzard Mystery Solved? Air Bloomberg Was Seen in Bermuda," *New York Times*, January 11, 2011.

24. Charles V. Bagli, "New York Secures the Most Affordable Housing Units in 27 Years," *New York Times*, January 11, 2017.

25. Brendan Cheney, "De Blasio Housing Plan Shapes up as Historic-Scale Tradeoff," *Politico*, July 27, 2016. See also Juan Gonzalez, "Growing Citywide Revolt Against Bill de Blasio's Affordable Housing Plan," *New York Daily News*, November 24, 2015.

26. Author's interview with City Councilman Ydanis Rodriguez, January 22, 2017.

27. Author's interview with Ismene Speliotis, June 30, 2016.

28. Author's interview with Jonathan Westin, director of New York Communities for Change, November 11, 2016. For increased very-low income housing production, see Christian Brazil Bautista, "NYC Financed 21,963 Affordable Homes in 2016, Most in 27 Years," *Real Estate Weekly*, January 22, 2017.

29. Michael Goodwin, "De Blasio Has Somehow Made the Homeless Problem Worse," *New York Post*, August 30, 2016.

30. See Giselle Routhier, "Mayor Bloomberg's Revolving Door of Homelessness," *Safety Net*, Spring 2012. Accessed at: http://www .coalitionforthehomeless.org/mayor-bloombergs-revolving-door-of -homelessness. See also "A Homeless Epidemic in New York? Thousands Hit the Cold Streets to Find Out," *New York Times*, October 21, 2015; also author's interview with Human Resources Administration Commissioner Steven Banks, October 6, 2016.

31. Marc Santora, "Cuomo Vows to Defend Charter Schools, Setting up Another Battle with de Blasio," *New York Times*, March 4, 2014.

32. Juan Gonzalez, "Hedge Fund Executives Give 'til It Hurts to Politicians, Especially Cuomo, to Get More Charter Schools," *New York Daily News*, March 11, 2015.

33. Blake Zeff, "A Year after Cuomo-W.F.P. Bargain, Everyone's a Sucker," *Politico*, June 1, 2015.

34. Joe Anuta and Rosa Goldensohn, "Real Estate Execs Gave to de Blasio While Seeking Key Decisions from the City," *Crain's*, April 22, 2016.

35. William K. Rashbaum, "No Charges, but Harsh Criticism for de Blasio's Fund-Raising," *New York Times*, March 16, 2017.

Afterword

1. "Acting U.S. Attorney Joon H. Kim Statement on the Investigation into City Hall Fundraising," March 16, 2017. Accessed at: https://www .nytimes.com/interactive/2017/03/16/nyregion/city-hall-investigation -statement.html.

2. Manhattan District Attorney Cyrus Vance letter to Risa Sugarman, New York State Board of Elections, March 16, 2017. Accessed at: https:// www.nytimes.com/interactive/2017/03/16/nyregion/cyrus-vance-letter -de-blasio.html.

3. J. David Goodman and William Neuman, "Now Cleared, de Blasio Gets Out of His Own Way in Mayor's Race," *New York Times*, March 16, 2017.

4. Lewis Kamb and Jim Brunner, "Lawsuit Alleges Seattle Mayor Ed Murray Sexually Abused Trouble Teens in the 1980s," *Seattle Times*, April 6, 2017.

Index

About the Author

Juan González is one of this country's best-known Latino journalists. He was a staff columnist for New York's *Daily News* from 1987 to 2016 and has been a co-host since 1996 of *Democracy Now!* He is now a professor of journalism and media studies at Rutgers University, New Brunswick. He is the author of *Harvest of Empire*, *News for All the People*, and *Fallout* (The New Press). Born in Ponce, Puerto Rico, he was raised in New York City, where he currently lives.

Celebrating 25 Years of Independent Publishing

Thank you for reading this book published by The New Press. The New Press is a nonprofit, public interest publisher celebrating its twenty-fifth anniversary in 2017. New Press books and authors play a crucial role in sparking conversations about the key political and social issues of our day.

We hope you enjoyed this book and that you will stay in touch with The New Press. Here are a few ways to stay up to date with our books, events, and the issues we cover:

- Sign up at www.thenewpress.com/subscribe to receive updates on New Press authors and issues and to be notified about local events
- Like us on Facebook: www.facebook.com/newpress books
- Follow us on Twitter: www.twitter.com/thenewpress

Please consider buying New Press books for yourself; for friends and family; or to donate to schools, libraries, community centers, prison libraries, and other organizations involved with the issues our authors write about.

The New Press is a 501(c)(3) nonprofit organization. You can also support our work with a tax-deductible gift by visiting www.thenewpress.com/donate.